Piece
by
Peace

I Have Been Both

Broken and Blessed

BRENDA CAIN

PIECE BY PEACE
I Have Been Both Broken and Blessed

Copyright © 2025 **Brenda Cain**

ISBN (Paperback): 979-8-89672-236-6
ISBN (Hardback): 979-8-89672-238-0
ISBN (Ebook): 979-8-89672-237-3

PROMINENT
B O O K S
EDGE

5830 E 2nd St, Ste 7000 #9983
Casper, WY 82609
USA

I dedicate this book to every hurt soul out there. God is waiting for you to let him heal you completely. I am so thankful for my wonderful husband and beautiful daughter. I am also thankful for the wonderful people in my life. I am thankful and blessed to have a Christian mother who has been broken and blessed herself. Thank you, Mom, for always reminding me to turn to God in my times of need. To my family and friends, I love you all.

Contents

If you choose to read this book and go on this journey with me, I hope you will see not just my brokenness but healing as well. This is a true story of heartache, pain, loss, death, courage, goodness, dark places, and bright lights. God is good, my friend, and healing is a process. Join me, and hopefully, you will find some healing yourself. Some of the best things come out of broken places. *Piece by Peace* healing can happen. I hope this book is that for you.

Let the Journey Begin

You know, life seems to be this incredibly difficult yet amazing journey with several ebbs and flows. It has rocky paths, mountain peaks, and, at times, very deep valleys we all know too well. Over the years, along the rocky path, I have learned to read God's word, to soak it in, and let it wash all over me. The scriptures that stand out to me are key. I try to write them down and store them up in my memory bank so I can recall them in the deep valleys of my life. God helps me recall them when I need them most. They are like little reminders—nudges if you will—to let God take the lead in my life. He will guide me to a smoother path if I pay attention and stay close to him. I do my best on a daily basis to wake up and start my day talking to God, reading a daily devotional and some scripture. This helps me remember who is in control so I can ease my worries, relax, and let God lead. Take it from someone who has had many bumps on this road called life. I know for me I was born with a very strong will. I was, and still am, at times very stubborn. I had a direction in my mind. I had it all figured out. I would set my own path in this life, and I would make it happen. The problem with that is, my life is not my own. God made me and designed me according to his will, not my own. I was put here on this earth by God himself for his purpose, not mine. We all are for that matter. It just takes some of us longer to realize that than others. And for me, well, let's just say it took some time.

I now know, at fifty years of age (see, I told you it took a long time), that God's will and purpose for my life is all that matters. As you begin to read this book, I hope you will get a window into my really human nature and are able to see all of God's work in my life that has brought me to where I am today, sitting at my kitchen table on a rainy Thursday morning writing to you in hopes that my journey can enhance yours. Many times over the past twenty years I have sat down to write this book. However, I thought, *Do I have enough to say? Would people want to read it? I'm just an average woman with an average life.* Well, the older I get and the more people I meet, I realize maybe God has brought me through so many fires so I can share my journey and help others. That is why I am writing this book today. You see, I know I am at my best when I am helping others. If we're not paying attention and really listening for God's voice, we can miss out on the purpose God has for us. It can take a long time to get to know one's self, and that process is still ongoing today. God has taught me some valuable lessons, and unfortunately at times, I have learned them the hard way. I don't have all the answers, but I know who does. God does. If we are listening for his voice, in his word daily, and living for him, he will show us our smoother path. The road will have bumps for sure, but he will help us to navigate them.

Before we go any further, let me just say, I have prayed that the words in this book will be just as God wants me to write them and as he wants you to hear them. I have come to learn that many words are spoken. However, probably less than half of them are ever really heard. It's amazing to me when I have a conversation with someone and I recap with them what they heard, most of the time they miss some of the parts I wanted them to hear the most. We tend to interpret what others are saying instead of really listening. It's our human nature. As we begin this journey, I hope you can find your favorite reading spot with your favorite blanket. Maybe pour a cup of coffee, tea, or hot chocolate (whatever makes you warm all over) and curl up. Know with God's help, I have shared my heart with you—all the broken parts and the blessed ones too.

Any good book I have ever read has been written through life experience, and mine is as well. I hope when you finish this book, you will feel God's love, power, and grace. Even in the worst storms of life, he is right there with us. We need only to tap into his great love. This book will take you on a journey of heartache, pain, adversity, and even death. It will also show you how a broken woman got back up to help others and to share her true story of healing through Jesus Christ, our Lord and Savior.

While sipping my morning tea and praying for God to show me his purpose for my life, I heard God's voice. Now I have to tell you I am a mother, wife, sister, friend; and I keep plenty busy with housework and school activities (never mind the honey-do lists). God spoke to me, and my ears were open. His voice literally ringing loudly inside my head, he said, "Tell them! Tell them how broken you were and how very blessed you are today. Others are hurting, and they need to hear your story." This rainy day in January, while having a come-to-Jesus meeting with myself, God spoke to me. I literally got chills over my whole body, and the hair on the back of my neck stood up straight. In that moment, I got so excited about my life and God's vision for it. I can honestly tell you God has his perfect timing, and even though we can't see it, he knows when you're ready to fulfill his plans for your life. For me, to sum things up, I have been in some very dark places in my life where I have been so broken, torn up, worn-out, scared, angry, bitter, and just downright sad. In those times, life was a struggle. Some very dear Christian friends of mine would say to you, "Brenda has been through a lot and has quite a story." A pastor might say (and I mean said) to you, "Brenda, has been refined by God—molded, shaped and melted into the person God designed her to be."

Here, yes, now sitting at my kitchen table full of God's love for me, feeling like I have learned so much and yet still hungry for more, God spoke to me. He wanted me to use my pain to help others. So, basically, it took me fifty years to shape up and listen. I'm laughing as I write the last statement, but it is very true. So before we begin and get too deep into my life journey, I want you to know it is never too late. If you are or ever have been where I have been, there is hope, a light at the end of the very long tunnel. God is that light. *Second Corinthians 5:17* says, "*Anyone who belongs to Christ has become a new person. The old life is gone and a new life has begun.*" My hope and prayer for you is that you find God in everything you do and that you learn to listen for his voice and completely follow him. Hopefully, a lot quicker than I did.

Ricky: Faithful and Strong

Allll along my life's journey, I have watched others try to go it alone
without God, and they fail miserably.

Psalm 105:4 says, "*Look to the Lord our God and his strength,
seek his face always*." I have to remind myself on a daily basis, today
and every day, for the rest of my life to be present in the everyday
moments of this life—all of them, even the painful ones, especially the
painful ones. I don't want to miss a single thing this life has for me. In
Proverbs 3:5–6, it says, "*Lean on, trust in and be confident in the Lord
God with all your heart and mind and do not rely on your own insight or
understanding. In all your ways know, recognize and acknowledge him
and he will direct and make straight and plain your paths*." So you see,
staying in the moment daily with God and accepting things as they
are, knowing I'm completely forgiven and God loves me right where
I am in all my happiness or in my sadness and pain, I can learn and
grow in my walk. I can share him in new circumstances that come
my way in the future, but I can't change the past. So many of us live
in the past we forget the here and now.

Well, I'm now composed, and my eyes are dry, so I am venturing
out on a hospital journey. Bear with me as I try to share this journey
with you. Before I share more with you, you will need to understand
that I am giving you bits and pieces of my hospital journey at a
time because if I do that, I can actually continue. You know, when
something is so hard to get through that twenty years later you can't
even write it on a piece of paper without crying that it's really rough.

We're in Detroit Children's hospital. The year is 1995. I met
many broken people during that time. When you basically live in
a hospital for 8.5 months, you see so much pain and grief. You see
many situations, especially when most of your time is spent in an

intensive care unit, or ICU. Just walking down the halls in the unit, you could feel people's heavy burdens. *So* many different families, so many different situations. There were days, as I look back, I know God was carrying me because I was so scared and hurt and broken that my feet wouldn't move. They literally wouldn't move. Even now, twenty years later, hospitals for any reason are hard for me.

Before I share stories or hospital situations, I need to stop and tell you that, through many tears, Bible studies, and a whole lot of prayer, I have come to realize that regretting the things I could have done or wish I had done differently is a waste of energy. During my 8.5 month hospital experience, one amazing young man in particular stood out to me. His mother did as well. I so enjoyed his room being right next to my son's room. Only a large glass window separated us. Sometimes the shades would be pulled. On those days, I knew things were extra hard. The reason I knew this is I lived this. Some days, you could let the world in and you even welcomed them, and other days you needed to literally shut them out. You couldn't even look at another human being or hear any of their problems because yours were so heavy. You just couldn't handle anymore. If I did hear anymore, I felt I would literally crack or split wide open at the seams. The days the shades were closed, I spent as much time praying for them as I did my own son. In such close quarters and in such painful circumstances, people easily got close very quickly. We needed each other. Strangers became quick friends. Sharing your pain with someone in pain themselves somehow made it easier. We weren't alone. Someone else knew how we felt. The world outside the hospital would go on as normal. People hustling to work, angry with each other, frustrated at someone's driving, or impatient and frustrated with their own lives or maybe their own family or their children or others. Some literally hating each other. While in the hospital, people were hanging on by a thread, needing each other. Their loved ones very ill, or even dying. They would say anything or do anything just to keep them there for one more day, one more hour, or even one more minute. Time is precious and priceless especially in situations like these. In desperate, painful situations, sweating the small stuff doesn't even enter in the picture. The big stuff is so hard, so raw, so real that the small stuff means nothing, literally nothing at all.

When I first met Ricky, the young man in the room next door to my son, I thought, *Wow, this is an amazing, wonderful, God-fearing young man whose only desire in life is to help others, whose passion was to become a youth pastor and bring other kids to know Christ. How could someone so close to God and wanting to do his will be so sick?* Tell me, does that make any sense to you? It sure didn't to me. I couldn't comprehend it. It just wasn't possible. Why, God? You could use him. Surely, you will keep him here on this earth for many years to come. You see, Ricky had leukemia. His mother had shared with me his entire story. She was truly a faithful woman of God and very strong. So many wise words of wisdom she shared with her son and with me. She had always wanted children and just couldn't conceive. I knew way too much on that subject with my own journey in this life. I too had the same situation happen to me before my son Cody. She and her husband tried and tried to conceive a child to no avail. They prayed about it and gave the situation to God. After a while, God laid it on their hearts to adopt two beautiful children, both of them girls. Their life was full and rich. They were so blessed. I remember her telling me how happy and content they were. They had a great family. God was so good to them, she would say. After many years went by and the girls were older, she found out one day, out of nowhere, she was pregnant. You see, she was told she couldn't have children of her own, so this was truly a gift from God. God gave her a beautiful blond-haired, blue-eyed little boy. They named him Ricky. Completely blessed beyond measure, their life overflowed with love, and their house was full of blessings. They were strong in their faith, and their little boy was growing up to be an amazing young man.

One day Ricky came home early from school. He was feeling sick, like all kids sometimes do. Anyone who has children knows all children at one time or another have come home from school not feeling well. Ricky had a fever and flu-like symptoms. No problem, Mom to the rescue. Cold cloths, medicine, soup, fluids, and a warm blanket. He would be fine. She had loved him through many of colds, as all moms do, and she would love him through this one.

This cold or flu, however, hung on and on. So off to the doctor they went. Surely, it's an infection, and an antibiotic will take care of him. Two prescriptions later, the doctors decided something else must be going on. Ricky just wasn't getting better. At this point, he was tired of being sick. He was a bit weak, and Mom was worn right out as well.

His doctors said, "Let's dig deeper. Let's run some blood work, a few extra tests than normal."

His mother agreed, of course. She thought, *Let's get the right medicine so my boy can get back to sports, school, church—you know, life*.

Blood was drawn, tests were run, and the results were in. Off to the doctor she and Ricky went, only to find life that day changed dramatically forever.

Without hesitation, the doctor said, "I'm so sorry, Ricky, you have leukemia."

His mother remembers thinking, *What? Are you serious? This gift from God, my son, has leukemia?*

I could feel her pain as she told me their story.

She said, "I've only had him for fifteen years. I can't lose him yet."

I knew her pain as my son was lying in the hospital bed next door. I remember thinking, *Will I even get one Christmas with him?* She had fifteen Christmases, and it wasn't enough. It could never be enough. We aren't supposed to outlive our children. That's not how this life is supposed to work.

She thought Ricky is a strong boy; he could fight this. And fight they did. The doctors and them went at the leukemia full force. All medications onboard. They were in for the fight of their life. In the hospital, out of the hospital. The drugs are working; they aren't working. The ups and the downs.

By now, a year had passed. Ricky is now sixteen and eager to be normal. He wanted his friends; he wanted to drive. He so badly wanted to play hockey again. His mother said he was a good hockey player. He wanted his life back. Who could blame him?

He would get angry at times. I remember that so well. It was then that his mother would say, "Look at that poor baby in the room next to you. He may not stand a chance. He hasn't experienced anything in life yet."

Yes, that was my Cody, my baby. So ill, so small, and so fragile.

She would say to her son, "God gave you sixteen years. When you feel sorry for yourself, pray for him."

See, I told you she was one strong woman.

Days, many days, went by. Weeks, actually. Ricky got worse; and my son, Cody, wasn't much better. We had lots of time to get to know each other. Every shift change, trying to pray and lift each other up. This was extremely difficult and painful. She was farther along in her faith and spoke of God openly and often. That helped me so much. I wish still today I could see her. I wish I could wrap my arms around her and we could have a good cry. I can still smell her perfume and hair spray. I wish I could tell her what an impact she and her son had had on me. His life wasn't in vain. I had been so blessed by them.

Ricky was worsening. The leukemia was overtaking his body. I watched him wince in pain. I watched his tears flow. The whys were written all over his face. His mother was beside herself, doing anything to ease his pain. I remember one day him raising his voice and wanting the boots they had on his feet taken off. The boots were used to keep his feet from turning out in case he could walk again. He told his mom he wouldn't be here long and he didn't need them. She had them taken off and then left the room in tears. I followed and talked to her while her tears flowed. Ricky's time on this earth was coming to an end, and I think we all knew that. Make a Wish foundation was called in, and Ricky had his opportunity. You see, he loved hockey and would watch it on TV every chance he had. He also had a favorite player, Sergei Federov of the Detroit Red Wings. His wish was easy for him. He wanted to meet Sergei and shake his hand, and of course, he wondered if Sergei knew God. You see, sick and dying, Ricky still wanted to bring people to Jesus.

He told his mom, "Just think if he's a Christian. Someday he will be in heaven with me." Ricky had obviously accepted his fate. See, I told you, an amazing young man. His wish was granted. Sergei would visit him in the hospital. Later, I found out that this was Sergei's first hospital visit of this nature. He was humble and nervous. I was there the night he visited. You see, I was there all the time. My son was there. Where else would I be? The shade was drawn for privacy, but this time, for something good. Ricky was so anxious and happy to be meeting him. I remember the joy on his face earlier in the day. He was a bit nervous too, I think. His mom was so happy for him. Joy, now that's something that room had not seen for a long time. A last request before dying. Can there be joy in the face of death? There was for that young man that night. I prayed it would be all he hoped for and be one of the best nights of his life. His family was all there. You see, most of the time it was us moms. Dads at work, kids in school or college. Not tonight, they all got to witness his last wish.

Later, they told me Sergei told him he would try to score a goal for him in the upcoming game. That kept him excited. He told him he would put up his hand, and Ricky would know that goal was just for him. It sure didn't take much to make him happy. I can still picture his smile. Even with his dark, sunken eyes, thin hair, and gray skin, his smile shown bright. His face was beaming.

In a couple days the Red Wings would play, and the whole family was in his room again with him watching the game. Sergei gave him a hockey jersey, and his frail body was dwarfed in the red-and-white jersey. What a picture that left imprinted on my mind. Sitting on his bed, jersey on, Dad and son with Mom right next to him in a chair, sisters standing by his head. What a beautiful family. I forgot to tell you Ricky looked just like his mom, only taller. The game was played, and Sergei scored not just one goal but three goals, a hat trick, and each time raising his hand for Ricky. He played the game of his life while Ricky watched intently the whole time. Wow, what an ending. They won. Ricky was so happy. I knew God helped Sergei play so well just for Ricky. Thank you, God, for that special gift just for him.

Shortly after that game, only a few days had passed when Ricky went downhill fast. He and his family knew it was only a matter of days or hours. I think his mother literally prayed without ceasing. Not for God to save him at this point, but for God to take him home, to ease the pain. That is hard to do. I can tell you that from experience as well. When you get to that point as a parent the pain is so great that you think you might literally die yourself. There is nothing worse than watching your child suffer and being able to do nothing to make it stop. It's only by the grace of God anyone survives that.

Whether you are a believer or not, I'm telling you it's in our toughest times God carries us. When we can't even walk or when you literally can't even breathe, he takes over. My friend, if you don't have God, you need him. Struggles of different shapes and sizes will come along in life. From small tidbits to huge boulders, and without God, I don't see how people survive. Even with God, when the boulders come, things seem almost impossible.

By the grace of God, Ricky died quietly and peacefully with his family by his side. Straight into heaven right into God's hands where he exchanged his Red Wings for angel wings although I'm sure he is still wearing the jersey. No more pain or suffering ever again for Ricky. That, my friend, is comforting. Being a witness to so much pain, that brings me comfort. His family on the other hand, much grieving needed to be done. I knew one thing: they had God, so they would be okay. It would take a lot of time, tears, and pain to get through this. How long it took each of them? No one knows but God. Grieving is such a long process, but it's completely necessary to get it all out, or the pain will eat you alive. Trust me, I know.

Good News

The good news is that God says in *2 Corinthians 12:9*, "*My grace is sufficient for you, for my power is made perfect in your weakness.*" Without God, we are all powerless especially in overwhelming tragedy in our lives. In *2 Corinthians 4:7*, it says, "*We are like jars of clay, we crack under pressure, we experience brokenness and sometimes we fail completely.*" It also says there are benefits to weakness. Twenty years later, in all my failures and brokenness, I can finally say there are benefits to weakness. Can I get an Amen? We can grow stronger in our faith. We can grow closer to God. When we need him so much, it's then we can feel his closeness. God longs for us to completely lean on him, to trust him, and to fall into his arms and grieve, if that's what it takes. There are benefits to weakness and brokenness. It just may take you some serious grieving and time spent with God to see them. When you finally come out on the other side of all that pain, God will still be there holding you in his arms. The trials in this world that we may have to endure, some of them may be insurmountable, and some of them may be less, but everyone will experience weakness or brokenness at some time in their life's journey. We can hold our heads up because God's grace is the strongest when we are weak! If we dive into that for a moment and really think this through, when we are weak, we give in, we crack or bend. We may do things we never ever thought possible before. Thank God for his unfailing grace and forgiveness. All we have to do is ask.

I remember distinctly having an all-out screaming match with God. Oh yes, I was telling him what for. At the top of my lungs no less, in my house, alone one day while my son was lying in a hospital bed very sick and I couldn't be there because I was sick with a cold. You see, I couldn't chance giving it to him. His immune system was just too weak. I was one angry mama. It's bad enough my son is this sick, why me? I need every second with him. At any point, I could lose him. I let God have it for all my anger, pain, and suffering. You see, I am completely human. I am a sinner, and by no means did I have it all together. While in the hospital, the nurses and the doctors at times would hang on to my words because I knew my son so well. If his breathing changed or his skin was off color or any one little thing, I could read it. I would tell them he needs an x-ray of his chest, and they would look at him and say, "Really?" His heart rate is good, and his oxygen is okay, but they had gotten to know me, and they knew without a doubt not to question me. So they would take the x-ray, and sure enough, his lungs were not looking so good. I studied my child like my own life depended on it. Actually, it did. I thought surely if God took him to heaven, he would have to take me too because I would surely die without him. You see, on that particular day, while yelling at God so loudly the windows should have cracked, using choice words I should never ever repeat, he knew my pain and he gave me his unfailing grace and forgiveness. Many times I needed his grace during my hospital journey. I begged for his healing hand on my son and on my heart, but I also let him have it when I thought he had failed me. Thank goodness for his grace in my weakness. Remember whatever you are going through or have gone through in the past, whether you realize it or not, God's great power was, or is, right now present in your weakness. I can tell you this much, I would never be writing this book today without going through all I have experienced. God can use your pain if we let him. Don't be like me, I fought God for twenty years on writing this book; and every few years I would sit down, start writing, and the pain was just too great. I couldn't—or should I say, wouldn't—write. I always put it away and ignored the voice inside my head that said, "Brenda, you can help others. Tell them about me and your journey." That scared me. Who me? I don't think so. You must be talking to someone besides me. If we open up our hearts, minds, and bodies to God's plan, anything can happen. I'm just sorry it took me so long to obey him and finally write.

I love *Isaiah 40:29*. It says,

> *He (God) gives strength to the weary and increases power in the weak. Even the young grow weary, stumble and fall. But those who hope in the Lord will receive renewed strength. They will soar on wings like eagles. They will run and not grow weary, they will walk and not be faint.*

If that verse doesn't speak to the weary, I don't know what does. There may be times in our lives where we've had enough, we feel like giving up. I sure did. When we do, remember God will give you strength if you ask him to. If you've had too much and you're broken into tiny pieces, I get you completely. If you're depressed, sad, alone, grieving, maybe addicted to something, whatever your situation, hold on tight and lean in. God already knows your pain. He already knows your situation. He's got you. You just have to let him. *Luke 12:7* says that *"even the very hairs of your head are numbered."* God knows your situation inside and out. He is the giver and receiver of grace. He heals all in his way, not ours.

Listen to me, you can't fall so far that God can't catch you. Please know that. Pain is of this world, but if we're a believer of Jesus Christ, he paid for our pain on the cross, and one day this cruel world will be no more. We will be in heaven with God himself. No pain or suffering. No tears or sorrows. Think of it. Our pain on this earth is temporary. I can do temporary! Thank God for temporary. You see, Ricky's family has to temporarily live without him here on earth. I'm not saying that's easy. I know firsthand it's not. They can't touch him or hear his voice or see him, but they can be rest assured that his pain is no longer and they will see him again someday. They will live forever with him in heaven, never ever having to be away from him again. Now that's not temporary. I can grab on to that, that's forever. You see Ricky is in heaven soaring on wings like eagles, running and not growing weary. His mama knows that, and as a mama, having our children pain free is a must. So temporary means she is without him here on earth but his pain is no more, and one day she will hold her son again, as I will. As my grandpa King used to say, what a glorious day that will be. Remember if or when your situation seems hopeless, put your hope in God. Things of this world are temporary, but he is eternal. *Second Corinthians 4:18* says, "*So we fix our eyes not on what is seen but what is unseen for what is seen is temporary but what is unseen is eternal.*"

We are guaranteed a protection plan straight from God that is bought and paid for by his only son. There seems to be a son theme here. If we pray and ask Jesus into our heart and life and live according to God's word and study the Bible, we have eternal life in heaven. It's that simple. Thank you, God. In *Philippians 4:13*, it says, "*I can do all things through Christ who strengthens me.*" Try to recite this one, and keep it locked in your memory bank so you can pull it out whenever you need it for reminders. In fact, when you're reading your Bible, try to memorize a few verses you can recall easily to help you on life's journey. One little tidbit for you: remember at times when you might be down, God can use your situation in the future like he is using mine right now to help you. Everything in our life has purpose, and that right there is a benefit to our weakness. Also, think about this: some of the great Christian people in this world are just people like you and me, being used by God to fulfill his purpose in their lives. Their strength comes from deep roots that are planted firmly in God. (I can do all things through Christ who strengthens me). They're not using their power. They're strictly relying on God's power and following his lead. That is what I am doing while writing this book. God wants us to be completely dependent on him for all our needs. I know, I know, it will take some serious growth and lots of faith to get there; but you can do it. Remember, your willpower can only take you so far, even if it is like mine. We can't run our life on our own strength and energy. We have limits. Good news: God doesn't. Tap into his power. Take life one day at a time with God. Start every morning with him. Let God worry about tomorrow— you can't change it anyway. Trust me, I've tried.

Sweet Little William

Getting back to my hospital journey, I certainly can't forget a little boy named William, a baby so tiny and fragile, like my sweet little Cody man. I use to call my precious son my little man. I would tell him, "Stay strong, little man. Mama loves you so much." Speaking of William's mama, she had an ironclad will. I mean, a strong one. I have been told more than one time in my life that I have a strong will, but William's mama, all I can say is, "You better look out, don't get in her way when it came to her precious baby." Who could blame her? That was her flesh and blood we're talking about. She may have honestly been the only other woman, besides me, in the hospital that didn't care what the odds were or what the doctors said. William was going to be fine, and she would be taking him home one day soon. She was a strong Christian woman, and she told me, "He will survive if it kills me." Now I know that. I felt that with my own son. I understand that completely right down to my core. The only person that was going to tell me Cody's fight was over was God, and even then, I might not listen. She and I really connected on that level. We understood each other completely. Sweet little fragile William and my son were in the same critical care room for a while. I would watch her with the doctors and nurses and think, *I get that woman*. I really get her. You see, she completely studies her son and would argue with them at times if she thought they were wrong. She would let them know. I didn't argue so much with the doctors, but if there was a point to be made, I made it, and I also made it a point for them to get to know me. Both of us, however, let everyone know we were here with our sons and would be from here on out. They weren't just another baby; they were our babies.

One thing I will say, no one knows your children or family like you do. You are their voice when they don't or can't have one. You should pay close attention to what they like, whether or not they are comfortable. Look at their face or body movements. Trust me, even with a baby, you can tell. Don't ever think when a loved one is in the hospital that they don't need you there. They do. Don't get me wrong, doctors and nurses are great. My sister-in-law is a nurse. Nurses and doctors are angels in my opinion. The care and nurturing my son received was amazing. Now some are better than others. I've come to learn they have bad days too. They're human. Have patience and grace for them as well. However, when your loved one is lying there in the hospital room and you're upset, that is very hard to do. That's why you need God's grace. I got very close to two of my son's nurses: Sharon and Stephany. When your son or loved one is as fragile as my son was, keeping the same nurses with him was imperative, if at all possible. They each worked twelve-hour shifts, one during the day and one at night. I remember thinking when he had to have a different nurse so that they could have a day off, *Oh God, please help them care for him.* I was nervous for them, for me, and for my son. You see, if he became too upset, his heart rate would soar, and that wasn't good. William was the same fragile way, except his issue wasn't his heart. He had intestinal trouble. They did the same for him when they could. They tried to have the same nurses work with him. However, he wasn't quite as fragile as Cody. The nurses getting to know their patients, especially when they're babies and they can't tell you what they need, is so very important. They could work with and study them as well daily. If they were really good, like Stephany and Sharon, they figured out what position they could lay him in so he could breathe easier or rest. They could love on them and meet their needs without upsetting things too much. I learned so much from them. As good as they were, they would always save Cody's bath for me. He just wanted Mama to do it, they would say. He would cry, fuss, and carry on to the point that his heart rate would go through the roof. His face would get red, and they would give up. They would say, "Wait for Mama, she will do it."

Cody and I had so much fun with his baths. He would smile and coo. They were in awe because they tried so hard to please him and give him his bath and just couldn't. I would sing to him and kiss his feet (mommy secrets). I would keep him covered and warm where I wasn't washing, do one part at a time, be gentle, make sure the water is warm but not too warm, and don't ever forget to sing. I would sing "When You Are a Soldier" by Steven Curtis Chapman. It's an older song. If you don't know that song, one part of the song says,

> When you are a soldier, I will be your shield, I will go with you into the battlefield. And when your strength is almost gone, I'll carry you until you're strong. I will be your shield, because I know how it feels when you are a soldier.

God's son knows what it's like to be put through the ringer. And so did my son. Jesus was a warrior, and so were Cody and William. They certainly had been brought into this world and immediately put straight into battle. Being born with so many struggles and suffering so much pain, they both knew how to fight from day one. William's mom and I would say these two boys are warriors for God and they don't even know it. You see, we would at times be in the same room on our knees, by our children's beds praying and praying and praying some more. Others would see that, and I hope it resonated with many. A few said so.

One of Cody's nurses would tell me of her wild and adventurous days off getting drunk, etc. I would say something like, "Well, thank God he got you through that and got you back to us safe and sound." She looked confused, but she smiled and thanked me for looking forward to her return. After some time passed, I could see changes in her. She loved us and wanted so badly to help Cody thrive. He was still there fighting against all odds, and so was William.

I remember William's mama had other children at home missing her. She was so torn. She told me at times her children would cry themselves to sleep wanting her home. Some days her mother would come for a few hours. Like my mother did on the day I was home sick yelling at God. My mother remembers that day telling Cody, "I'm your grandma," while stroking his hair and rubbing his hand. She prayed for my son and for her baby, me. So did William's grandmother. She was a Christian as well, as my mother was. There were days all four of us were there, and you could walk into the room and feel God's presence. How could others not notice? These sweet babies were touching so many. They were like soldiers for God. I remember William's parents had some difficulties. It is hard on families going through something this painful. The fathers get completely worn-out as well. Trying to go to work to support their family financially, trying to make sure things at home are okay, doing their best to support their wives, all the while their baby was barely hanging on. Men have this thing us women weren't born with. They have to take a problem, look it over good, assess it completely, and then plan their attack to fix it. If men can't fix a situation, at times, they are beside themselves; and as you have read, they can't fix this. It is completely out of their control. That will handicap them for sure in their approach to handle this type of situation. That will send their stress level soaring. While praying for my son, I had to add my husband to the list. This was almost killing him. He could literally feel my pain and see Cody's pain, but he could do nothing but pray himself. He did however add humor in impossible situations. That was helpful for all of us. He would take in air from Cody's balloons and sing Michael Jackson songs like "Beat It." The nurses would laugh, and they would say to me, "How does he do that?" I mean, inject humor like that. He would say it's a gift. I think it kept him from literally breaking. I was very lucky my husband put his head down and pushed through, working, taking care of the home, taking care of me, and coming to the hospital daily right after work. He would spend precious time with his son and then drive us home very late, if I went home, and rise very early the next day, only to do it all over again. He would have to make me leave at night sometimes if Cody was doing okay just to go home and shower or rest a little. I didn't want to, but he knew I would literally break in two. I would get home and call the hospital immediately into Cody's room and talk to his night nurse, Sharon. She would promise to call if there were any changes, and I would usually cry myself to sleep with my arms and legs wrapped tightly around my boxer, Briecin. You see, before Cody, she was my only baby. She was an awesome dog, very sensitive. The phone would be right by my head. I would also wake up in the middle of the night and check in at the nurses' station as I didn't want to wake Cody. I just couldn't stand being away from him.

William's mother had to have someone there all night (his dad, mom, or grandma), and it was wearing on them for sure. I certainly did not leave every night, and man, many nights were spent at the Ronald McDonald House right there at the hospital. Thank God for the Ronald McDonald House and the people helping out there. Knowing I was so close, I could get a little more sleep. The one thing people tend not think about is, while going through all of this hardship, it is also financially draining. The expenses add up quickly and that adds a lot of pressure to the situation. The Ronald McDonald House lets you stay at a much cheaper rate than a hotel and sometimes volunteers bring in food for the families staying there. It was a godsend for us. They had a hallway phone hooked up straight to the hospital operator that gave me comfort, and trust me, I used it. William's mom slept in the waiting room, or his room, as finances were really tight.

My church pastor's wife asked me what more could we have done to help. Well, I never really helped her on that subject, and I should have. She even gave me a paper she made so I could fill it out so they could do an even better job in the future. I've always felt bad about that because I didn't do it. One thing I would put on that list is to take up an offering. It's one thing to be in the hospital for a short time and another to be there for months. The occasional visit just doesn't hold up. People are good for the first week or maybe two, but their lives go on while yours seems to be caught up in this tornado that won't settle down. Taking up an offering would help, because then the hurting can use it where they most need it. Taking financial pressure off is a big help to those in the heart of the storm. Our pastor and his wife were of great comfort to us during our hospital journey. They were there multiple times. Their support and prayers helped us for sure. William's parents had pastoral help as well. Thank God for faithful pastors and their wives. William's hospital journey was shorter than my son's. We ended up on different paths, in different rooms. You see, William improved; and Cody, well, not so much. At times I would see her in the hallway or in the cafeteria, and she would say, "We are going home soon. I just know it."

Now let me tell you that William did finally go home, but there were many challenges up the road ahead. His eyesight was impaired, his intestines would need further surgery in the future, and eating was an issue and may always be. However, he went home, and his mom beamed with excitement. Unfortunately, the last I heard from William's family was from the grandmother several months later. She told me he was hanging tough, but Mom and Dad were not. This had rocked their world, financially, physically, and privately. Their marriage had suffered, and they were split up. You see, William's mama had worked, as I did, before he was born. She could not work during the hospital journey, and she sure couldn't work after he was home. William needed too much care, and only she was trained enough to handle it. She also had to move her sleeping into William's room. She slept with him every night so she could feel him and hear him breathe. This had taken her away from her husband and their private time. I knew she would be right there in his room, she couldn't drop the ball after all they had been through. She would never forgive herself. Her husband just didn't understand that because that pressure had always been on her while he was working and taking care of the other children. I know this pressure—it's huge. There were no nurses there to pick up the slack, only her. She had to care for him, and care for him she did. She had her son home, and now her husband was gone. Life as she knew it would never be the same. You see, when trauma (physically and financially) wears you out, you at times do break. See, William's daddy broke. He was a really good man who tried hard on his own strength and will. He just couldn't sustain on his own. William's mama had a lot of faith in God, but I remember her saying that her husband didn't. He was not a Christian. She shared with me that this worried her. He would get so angry at the whole situation. He would say, "If your God is so great, why is he letting this happen?" He blamed God for sure.

Listen, people, if there is one thing I have learned, we do not have God's wisdom. His ways are above ours. We may not be able to make sense of everything, and that's okay. That is where faith comes in. We have to have faith that whatever this world throws our way, he is there to catch us. We may never know why some things happen, and unfortunately, we have to accept that. This is so hard to do even when we do believe in God. Some things just don't make sense. Look back at Ricky. We can see God used Ricky to enlarge his kingdom and to spread his word even through his awful ordeal. He used him in me, and with all I have been through, he is using me right now. He used William and his mama too. I just wish his daddy could have relied on God's strength instead of relying on his own. Maybe they would still be together as a family today, and maybe they still are. I wish he had God and that he believed in him. I truly think God, through William's situation, was right there trying to reach him. Too bad he missed it. God wants to ease our pain. He doesn't cause the pain we suffer, but he can ease it. Look what he did for us. He sent his only son to live among us, to perform miracles so we could see his power, and then allowed him to be beaten and broken for us to cover our sins. Now that's love. As a mama, I was trying to save my son, and I sure wouldn't allow anyone to lay a hand on him let alone beat and kill him. That's how much God loves us. There is no pain or suffering God's own precious son, Jesus, can't understand. God let that happen to his son in a human body so that we could know he completely understands our pain. He knows our suffering. With nails pounded into his hands and feet, thorns jammed into his head, and beaten beyond belief, his only son died on a wooden cross for the whole world to see. He gets it, people. I promise you, he gets your pain.

Remember pain and suffering are temporary and of this world. As *2 Corinthians says, "Our suffering is temporary and is producing for us an eternal glory that is far greater than we can imagine."* Temporary is key. Heaven, that's forever, and it's suffering and pain free. In my short fifty years spent on this earth, I have had some serious suffering.

I had a friend ask me, "I wonder why some people have a lot of suffering and some only have a little?" I really wish I knew the answer because I would have said, "I'll take the little line. Please sign me up right there." Unfortunately, that's not how it works. I sure wish it did. I bet some of you fellow sufferers do as well.

Home Will Never Be the Same

My suffering and brokenness started at a pretty young age. So did my mothers and my siblings. I have one brother and three sisters. There were five kids and two adults that made our one-bathroom-with-no-shower small house very tight for sure. Waiting in line to use the bathroom certainly wasn't new to me. As a little kid, you don't care how big your house is, at least, I didn't. You just care that you have each other. There was lots of love to be had for all. We lived way out in the country, on a small gravel road called Prentice Bay with not much traffic to speak of. So when my dad or mom would say jokingly go play in the traffic that was a hint for us to go play outside. It was tight, and they probably needed space. As an adult, I understand that now. As I look back on my own life, there are things I would certainly change, but that is not my decision or within my power to do so. Looking backward and longing to change our past is human and of this world. We all have done it if we are being honest, and at times, it can be very painful. We can't change our past, only our future. I would like to journey back into my past here with you just for a bit, just to give you some insight on where I came from and a little more about me personally.

I grew up in a small town in Northern Michigan called Pickford. Growing up in a small town had it pros and cons for sure; but for me, as a child, mostly pros. In a small town, most everyone knows everyone. There is a comfort in that. Also, growing up there, you were kept an eye on, if you know what I mean. People knew you and your family, so most business wasn't very private. Life for me was great. I had no complaints. I had friends, family, animals, food, and clothes. Who could need more?

Unfortunately, for me and my family, life got serious very quickly at the ripe young age of twelve. You see, we lived outside of our small town in an even smaller place called Stalwart, Michigan. In Pickford, where I attended school, there was at least a gas station, restaurant, and one flashing yellow light marking the town to slow down. In Stalwart, there was one small country store with penny candy (along with a post office). That's it. Oh, how I loved to go there. We would get a quarter or sometimes only a dime or nickel, but that was just fine with me. I was getting penny candy, so I was getting five, ten, or twenty-five pieces. That worked for me. We didn't have much, but from a child's eyes, we had everything. Love, lots of love, and let's not forget each other and our animals. You see, to this day, I am a huge animal lover. For me, still today, if you have God, family, food, friends, a roof over your head, and animals, you have it all. No matter how big or small or how rich or poor you are, you are blessed beyond measure.

Let's get back to age twelve. It's then my whole world would change, and I would experience brokenness for the first time. At that point, I wasn't able to see all the blessings that were in my life. I was a kid. My whole world was about to change, and to a twelve-year-old kid, it hit me like a hurricane. This is where my brokenness began. Unbeknownst to me, my father had become ill. At the ripe young age of twenty, my father had become a brittle diabetic, but he was also a rugged tough man. He had survived his own father dying at age five and working on farms from about that age. We have a picture of him with his twin brother driving a milk delivery wagon at age five. Today, at least for me, I can't even imagine that. He survived the front lines of the Korean War and so much more that life threw at him. He had bone issues. That I was aware of. He had only the use of two fingers on his right hand; the others were curled with pins in them. But he still trained horses with those two fingers. He had sustained a bad injury on his job to his back. You can see he was one strong man. In my childish eyes, nothing would stop my dad. He just kept going through all of his adversity. Nothing was going to happen to my dad that he couldn't handle, or at least that was what I thought. Well, something was very wrong for sure.

One night they gathered us kids together, sat us down, and told us we were selling our house. We would be moving to Pickford, closer to school, stores, etc. My mind started racing. There better be land for our horses and a spot for Lucky, our dog. There I go again. As long as the animals are coming, I'm good. Let's roll. I will do whatever we need to do with no trouble from me. Just take our animals. Well, you can probably already see where this is heading. Sorry, kids, the horses can't come. What about our Sunday afternoon rides through sand ridge to the little Stalwart country store? It's bad enough that we have to move. My dad loved those horses and our land; he can't be serious. I remember thinking as that twelve-year-old little girl, *Over my dead body*. Well, as a twelve-year-old kid, you are limited on the choices in your life. I guess that's why as kids, we all long to be adults so we can make choices for ourselves. I was so angry and so very confused. You see, my dad looked fine to me. He seemed no different. What's going on?

Well, time passed, and that's exactly what happened. We sold our house, and the day came for a great family friend of ours to come take two of the horses that weren't already gone. One of them being Buttercup, our Shetland pony. I loved him so much. This appeared to be the worst day of my entire twelve-year-old life. I was told by my dad to stand and block the opening to a very large field that could take hours to catch the horses if they got through into the field. I had my arms stretched out wide and wasn't afraid. Dad knew that. You see, Buttercup had a knack for running full throttle straight at you and planting his feet at the last second if you didn't move. We had played this game many times while getting the horses ready for our rides. I knew the drill: don't move no matter what. I always obeyed my dad. He had a cowboy boot that would remind you to do so if you had trouble remembering.

This was the big day. Our family friend had a four-hour drive back home ahead of him. There were to be no mistakes or messing around. Okay, I got it. Only my heart was so broken. I was crushed. Not Buttercup. This wasn't fair. Please, God, don't let this happen.

You see, I had God even then. My mother would get ready, feed, and dress five children, then take them all to church by herself every

Sunday. I was blessed with my mother for sure. We were in Sunday school and church. So I knew God, or so I thought I did. I've got it. I will just act scared, and when Buttercup comes at me full force, I will move at the very last second. Maybe then he can stay home, and he can run and run, and they might give up, and we can keep him. Oh, the mind and thoughts of a child. That's exactly what I did. Bad move, my dad was angry, and I met Mr. Cowboy boot.

"Get in the house," he said. "You're in so much trouble."

I remember thinking for the first time in my life, *I don't care if I'm in trouble. You can't do this.* And out of my mouth came, "I hate you."

I don't know if he heard me because I said it walking away, but I know I did not get in any further trouble that day. They had to chase Buttercup for a very long time, and I watched out the small window of our home crying hysterically, saying to myself, "Run, Butttercup, run." And run he did. But he finally tired and gave in. In my twelve-year-old head, I knew he didn't want to leave and was just as confused as I was. He was going to a great home, but that wasn't the point. It wasn't our home. I will miss you, Scutterbutt. That was his nickname. Well, the horses are gone, and hate had made a home in my heart. Do your worst, world. Let's move. My walls were up. I don't care now.

Moving day neared, and the news came that we couldn't take Lucky either. For a serious animal lover, this was just too much. The tears flowed, and the begging began. Luckily, for Lucky and I, Dad caved, and Lucky stayed with us. It helped that the house we were moving to had a doghouse and outdoor penned area for him. My mom didn't like dogs in the house. Today, I have three dogs all in the house and at times sleeping in my bed, or should I say most of the time.

The move came and went. The house was much larger, so we got our own bedrooms. That was nice, though at times I missed sleeping with my sister and the talks we would have.

We adjusted to life in town the best we could. Dad's health was slowly going downhill. I still didn't know exactly what was wrong, but I knew it must be bad. Unbeknownst to me, my father's doctor told him he was dying, thus the move.

Over the course of the next two years, hospital visits and mini strokes and weakness fell on my father. Sadness filled our once happy home. My mom recalls it was a few days after Christmas (the goal was to get through Christmas) and my mom kept my brother home from school. Taking care of dad at home had become too hard. He was weak. They took him to the hospital that day. Before they left in the car, my mother told me that, with tears in his eyes, he said goodbye. She said she thinks he knew he wouldn't be back. Such a strong man, yet so frail. The past year had taken its toll. He was having more trouble walking now. My mom thought maybe they could help him build up his strength so he could come home. Unfortunately, that never happened. My father passed away in a veterans' hospital alone. We couldn't afford a regular hospital close to home. So he was a few hours away. I was the last one to see him there alive. My sister, Cathy, had taken me to see him and got really sick; so it was just me and dad. I was a fourteen-year-old girl walking down the long hospital hall to see her daddy. How I missed him being home. Nothing was the same. I fed him strawberries and apples and put some extra fruit in his nightstand before I left. With a large hug and an "I love you," I had to leave my father in that place. It was heart-wrenching. I just didn't understand why. Soon, though, he would come home. I just knew it. Well, needless to say, my father didn't come home. He slipped into a diabetic coma and never came out and never came home. I hope to this day I see my dad again in heaven. The hospital chaplain told my mom, not too long before my dad slipped into the coma, that he had asked him if he wanted to give his life to the Lord and he said yes. So he prayed with him. God's timing. As my grandpa King would say, "What a day, glorious day that will be."

The day came, the funeral and the tears and heavy sorrow that comes over you like a crashing wave. I still can't explain the pain today. My mother was in her room, alone, tearful, without her husband. And she had kids to still raise. Insurmountable and overwhelming comes to mind. If you ask her today, she will tell you, "I don't know what I would have done without my kids."

I slept with her for a long time. We would talk, and falling asleep seemed easier, calmer, and less sad. We always said our prayers every night as I was growing up. Mom made sure of that. So as you can see, we had an uphill battle to climb out of the pit of sadness, but we always had each other and God. That I'm so thankful for. You see my mom was raised in a Christian home, an amazing home, full of love and completely Christ centered. There was a sign on the wall that said, "As for me and my house, we will serve the Lord." My mom was given a firm foundation rooted in God, and she was going to need it. So were we. Now I'm sure many of you have seen a sign like this, but to see the words lived out in action was nothing short of incredible. My grandparents, Anna and Harold King, were a living example of Christ's love. From being in church whenever the doors were open to being there even when they weren't if help was needed. My grandfather was the church treasurer. I'm sure for the church, that was a no-brainer. He was one of the most honest and humble people I have ever met.

My mother said all the while she was growing up she never heard him even raise his voice. If you were around him today, you would feel God's love come through him. I remember as a kid my grandmother would cook a great meal, never forgetting dessert, which I loved, of course. Then, after dinner, she would play the organ; and sometimes my grandfather would play as well. He could only play by ear. He couldn't read music. Still today I can't understand how someone can do that, but for my grandfather, it was probably heaven's sound coming right through him. Evening would come, and Grandpa would get his Bible out. We would gather around in the living room and listen to him read. Oh, how I wish I could experience that today as an adult. As a kid, at times, I was antsy, as all kids are. But I still loved it. I have his Bible today. It's so worn, and I can still smell the soap he used and can see the dirt marks from his fingers where he turned the pages. How I love his Bible. When he was done reading, we would all recite the Lord's prayer: "Our Father who art in heaven, hallowed be thy name…" Oh yes, I knew that by heart at a young age. We all did.

My father, who wasn't raised in a Christian home and only went to church with us on special occasions, would listen quietly, never saying anything. He was always respectful of my grandparents. I think he enjoyed the family life and a father figure in my grandfather. His father died when he was only five years old. Childhood was much different for my mother than my father. You know my grandfather never criticized my father for not going to church, for smoking, or anything for that matter.

Breakfast the next morning, yum. "The most important meal of the day," my grandparents would say, but no eating before we ask God to bless this food and to thank him for all we have.

My mom, as you can see, had deep family Christian roots. You know how you see those families that have long legacies or traditions they carry on. You know deep roots they treasure and want to live out. Her roots have served her well in life and, of course, me too. My mom says when she lost her father, who was her rock, she remembers distinctly when God became her Heavenly Father. She had to rely on him when her father was no longer here on this earth. Don't get me wrong, she loved God before this, but her relationship deepened as her need grew.

It's interesting how close we get to God when we really need him. In those broken places where no one else is or can go with you. She lost her father at a much older age than I, but I doubt if the pain is any less. The more trials I go through, the closer I become to God and without my father as well. He is definitely my Heavenly Father. I completely understand my mother in this area for sure. My grandfather died at age 92 and my grandmother at age 101. My mother told me the only job outside of their home that my grandmother had was cleaning a house. And my grandfather said the vacuum was too heavy for her, so he would go and do that. You see what I mean, the man was a treasure and my grandmother was as well.

After my father's death, we learned many new things. First of all, our own deep family roots came in handy. We have always worked together on things, and this was going to be no different. We needed each other. I remember one night my mom telling my then sixteen-year-old brother, "You're the man of our house now. The basement is flooding. Well, okay, what do we do about that?" My brother especially had to grow up fast and learn quickly because you see, we had no money, so calling someone to fix it wasn't our first thought. We needed to fix it. Oh, Dad, we could really use you right now. This was just one of many things we had to handle. I tried to help as I have never minded getting wet or dirty especially when helping family. We waited awhile, but we had to sell that house. We just couldn't afford it. We, of course, had our first Christmas without Dad in that house. Talk about hard. My mom couldn't bring herself to get a tree, so my sister and brother got it. The Christmas cookies were still baked, and Christmas music played, but the reality that Dad wouldn't be there hit hard on all of us.

I remember at the young age of fourteen, I went to work washing dishes at the local restaurant, the Village Inn. I needed to help out, and money was a good start. That Christmas I bought my mom a good leather pair of winter boots. She needed them, and I was so happy and proud to be able to do that. She wore those boots for several years. One of the memories my mom shares:

A teacher at our school told her, "Good luck raising those teenagers. You're going to need it." That did not help or make my mom very happy. You see, what he didn't know is our father, Merle, was very strict and taught us respect and how we should behave and carry ourselves. That was part of our deep roots. If you ask my mom today, she would tell you she didn't have too much trouble. If she did have to discipline us, we took it and did what we were told. No questions asked. Her mother, my grandmother, told her, "Boy, you were lucky, Merle was strict and taught those kids to respect you." Life was hard, but we worked together and got through it.

One of my fondest memories after my father died was church camp at Covenant Hills. It was about four hours from our house, and my mom went there when she was young. They had teen camp and family camp. Oh, how I loved this place. There was a large tent where we would have nightly camp worship services. You could feel God there. It was amazing. I had so much fun at teen camp that I wanted to go to family camp. So my grandparents paid for a family cabin to stay in. So much fun. My grandparents would do anything to help us. This treasured camp is where I ended up meeting my now husband at fifteen years old, and we're still together. My grandparents really liked him. I always wished he could have met my dad.

This year, November 7, we will be thirty years married. It only seems like yesterday I walked into the dining hall of the camp where I saw a young, handsome boy playing piano and singing to Barry Manilow music. He was playing *Lay Me Down*. Every morning early, I would knock on his cabin window by his bunk and wake him so he could play piano for me. Still today I love when he plays and sings. My mother was smart to take me to camp. Not only did I meet my husband, a faithful man of God, but my roots in God grew deeper. *Colossians 2:7* says, "*Let your roots grow deep down into him. Let your lives be built on him. Then your faith will grow strong in the truth you were taught and you will overflow with thankfulness.*" That couldn't be more true today. My roots in God are deep and continue to grow. Thank you, Mom, Grandpa, and Grandma. Miss you, Dad.

Brenda's Family

Childhood Church

Childhood Home

Grandpa and Grandma King

Sister and Brother with Lucky

Buttercup and I in our older years

The Years: How They Fly By

I grew up, graduated high school, and left my little hometown and my family to journey out on my own adventures. It wasn't easy, but God was with me. My husband and I have been happily married now for a while. He finished his degree in computer science and had a good job. Thank God. I was also working with troubled teens. My job was rewarding for me. I really loved it. It was very stressful at times as these young teens were angry and at times would be brought in with shackles and handcuffs on. This would be their life for now. Their world got very small and structured, which they didn't like at all. Some looked at these kids as unruly, undisciplined, menaces to society. Always causing trouble, trying to steal, hurt others; and some in gangs. Most were really rough around the edges. Not wanting to be touched or told what to do was first on their agenda. Of course, they were told the rules right away, and if they refused, they had to put on a yellow shirt as to show other workers who was going to be a problem. Also, if they had on a yellow shirt, they had to scrub toilets, wash dishes, clean—you know, work until they decided to follow the rules. Some complied, and some didn't. At times, those who didn't had to be restrained as they would fight, throw things, and act out. I think mostly to show other teens they were in charge and strong. They never wanted to show weakness. I learned after a while each situation and child were different. Some had no daddies; some had no mamas. Some had only gangs to protect them. Some stole because they had to survive, or they thought so. Some girls we had would sell their bodies for money, drugs, or just for protection out on the streets. I didn't know much about the city streets as you know by the way I grew up, but I got a quick lesson.

In working with these kids, I did what I was trained to do. My boss asked me one day, "Why do you give so many chances to these kids before you put them in restriction, a yellow shirt?"

It took me a minute to respond, but the long and the short of it is, I felt deep down these kids had good in them somewhere and I was giving them a chance to let it out. My grandpa would call this grace. Some kids really appreciated someone believing in them, telling them they're good, that they can change and do better. Some kids wouldn't show it even if they did like it. However, my approach was being noticed. A good friend of mine got me the job, and he was always fair to those kids and as kind as he could be. There had to be a balance, because as workers there, we also couldn't show fear or weakness, or they would find it and use it to their advantage.

As time went on and I tried harder in every way I could to reach these kids, I noticed it was working quite well for the most part. One thing I would do is separate a kid who was acting out and take him where he could express feelings without everyone watching. At times, those feelings were anger at the situation, at their families, or even at me. In anger situations, I would let them punch pillows and scream into them. Hey, it would make me feel better. Any way possible for them to have an outlet.

Time passed, and my tactics were noticed. I was asked to work with the kids in a different way: taking them to court, placing them in foster homes, and getting them into school—basically, transitioning back into somewhat normal life again. Some went back home. I loved this even more. They were so pleased with my work, they offered to pay for my schooling so I could become a social worker. I really felt I had found my calling in life. School it was. I got enrolled and was working. Loving life. My marriage was going great. Life is good, so good until…

The Accident

It was 6:30 a.m., and I was on my way to work as usual. Only today was anything but usual. It was May, and I had awoken to a snowstorm. In May? It was a bit of a shock, but I was up and ready early as usual, so I had lots of time and would take it slow going to work. Coffee in hand, driving slowly. I was experienced driving in snow as I grew up in northern Michigan. I had not really a care in the world and thinking how blessed I was. How beautiful the snow was on the trees and the sun glistening off it. I remember it well, being so happy. I had a good job, a great husband, a nice place to live, family, pets. Who could ask for more?

Heading into a large curve, I see this car losing control and coming at me. It was coming into my lane straight at me. I had no time; it all happened so fast. I swerved my car to the right, trying to go in the ditch, saying, "Oh, God." That's all I had time for. Well, there was the loudest sound I have ever heard in my entire life. *Wham!* When I woke up, I remember patting my body on both sides to see if I was truly alive. I thought, *I must be dead.* Looking right at me was a young girl crying, saying, "Help me." Help her? Help me. She had hit me head on, but mostly in my driver's side door. Direct impact to me. When I got my wits about me, I realized we were sitting on a curve. It's icy, and someone could slam into us easily. I knew I needed to get out of the car. Pain was racing down my left arm like I had never felt before. My head was pounding, and there was metal in my left leg. Okay, God, help me. I have to get out of this car. With his strength, I climbed out my back side window as I was in my back seat and climbed over her car hood to help her, all the while saying, "God, help me." I helped her out of the car all the while repeating, "God, help me." If she didn't know God, she probably thought I was crazy, and if she did, she was probably thankful.

I got her out of her car, and we started walking to a nearby house. All I could think was, *I need to call my husband.* You see, my car was new. My first new car ever, and I was in shock, thinking, *My poor car,* when I should have been thinking, *Poor me.* Who cares about the car? Looking back, as we were walking, I thought, *Why didn't I get in the ditch? How did she hit me?* Then I realized there was a guardrail because the ditch was so steep, and she had pinned me against it. Now I get it. I couldn't get out of her way. The pain was really setting in now. We reached a nearby house finally, and I started banging on the door. A woman came to the door in her robe. I now look back and think how scary that must have been for her. Two girls standing outside banging on her door and one being really bloody—that one is me. I didn't realize it at the time, but I had hit my face on the steering wheel on impact, besides other things. I told her I needed her phone; and before she could help me, I saw it on the wall, walked in, and called my husband. I told him my new car was smashed, just ruined. He told me he would be right there. The lady took the phone, explained, and called the ambulance. My husband remembers walking in the house and seeing rescue workers trying to help me, but I wouldn't let them touch me. You see, I was in shock. I didn't know anyone, and old habits die hard. After my dad died, it was rough. We had no insurance, and my brother broke his ankle while playing football. It was bad. He was so strong. He said, "No ambulance. We can't afford it." We took him to the hospital, and he was in so much pain. I wasn't going with them. I wasn't thinking clearly. I had insurance. It was no problem, and they were only trying to help me.

I remember clearly hearing my husband's voice saying, "Brenda, let them help you, babe."

Oh, a familiar voice. You're here, okay, I know you. Go ahead and help me. My husband is here, and he will make sure I'm okay.

Well, on the ride to the hospital, I heard them calling in to let them know I was on the way and, in their opinion, in rough shape. I hear compound fracture in left arm, broken pelvis, blow to the face among other things. The fear set in. Oh God, help me, please. My roots were deep, and I knew where I needed to go for help. Well, my clothes were cut off me for x-rays and a visual. Thank God my pelvis was only bruised badly. My face would heal, but my arm was not good.

This is where another form of brokenness began. It wasn't just emotional; it was physical. Fear and anger again to deal with. Why me, Lord? I remember having to go to the bathroom and looking in the mirror for the first time at the hospital. I was shocked. Would my face ever look the same again? My lips were huge. It actually made me physically sick. I also remember lying on a hospital bed with a nurse trying to get an IV and a doctor working on my broken arm, cleaning my open flesh with a syringe of iodine. I told my husband I was going to be sick and threw up in a small banana-shaped container they gave him. He was thinking, *This isn't big enough.*

I told the doctor, "You are really hurting me. Can't I have pain medication?"

He said, "How will you ever have a baby someday?"

Wow, this guy is really lacking in the compassion department.

Actually, I pulled my good arm from the nurse and told him I still had one good arm, of course, with a doubled-up fist. I'm pretty sure I had had enough, at my max, if you will. A college buddy and friend of ours came to pick us up and take us home as my husband had left his car and went in the ambulance with me. I was in a lot of pain but was happy to be alive. Little did I know there were many obstacles yet to come.

That night was a very long one. The next day we went to my regular doctor. I was still in so much pain but in the neck area. Unfortunately, whiplash had gone untreated. I didn't know, but my neck should have been stabilized and action should have been taken for correct healing. Of course, I was young, and the insurance paid for my car. I would be okay, so I signed off on everything. Big mistake. I ended up in so much neck pain and from doctor to doctor. Some suggested fusion; some, injections, which I had. We killed the nerves in my neck, only to grow back in a year. Long story short, I still live with neck pain today. Also, osteoarthritis and problems with my wrists, ankles, knees, jaw, etc. With the problems came other changes. I was in too much pain, and I couldn't continue my job that I loved so much. That was a grieved loss for me, and it saddens me still today.

No social-work degree, no working with the kids, on top of living in daily pain. Oh, God, what is happening here? What is the lesson? Losing my father, our animals. Now this. Come on, what did I do to deserve this? By the way, the girl who hit me, she was okay, just a badly sprained ankle. The front of her car slamming into mine protected her. Fair? Not really, not even close. As I sit here today, fifty-three years old, wrist hurting as I write, wearing a brace and in neck pain, I could easily go back to that angry, dark place again. I promise you, friend, it's not worth it. Life, just when you think you have it all worked out, can throw you a wicked curveball like it did that snowy day in May all those years ago.

One doctor told me, "A lot of this will be a mental game. Learning to accept the pain and to live with it." I thought that day he's the crazy one. After all the doctors and pain medicines, today I see an amazing chiropractor, who has helped me tremendously. There are many good days. No pain medicine, yoga stretching, natural pain relief, and, of course, no working out of the house, only in house and rest on the bad days. God has been good to me.

In *Ephesians 4:31–32*, it says, "*Let all bitterness, wrath, anger, clamor or slander be put away from you. Along with all malice, be kind to one another, forgiving one another as Christ forgave you.*" It took me awhile, but I forgave the young girl for hitting me. I forgave the doctor for missing my neck trauma. I forgave the insurance company for being in a big hurry to settle my case and, most of all, myself and my own body that I felt let me down. Bitterness and anger will eat you alive from the inside out. Trust me, I know. My days are certainly different than I thought they would be when I started out my adult life, but they are still priceless and are beautiful, adventurous gifts from God. Here's a quote that I read often and wrote down for myself. Maybe you would like it too.

> Today is an incredible, unrepeatable gift from God. Let's embrace the journey, no matter the treacherous path.

We can't get today back, so whatever the outcome, be present and embrace it. Let God guide you and remain close to him.

My Sweet Star

The age for me was thirty and the year was 1994. We were in Davison, Michigan. I was blessed to live in the country on six acres with my handsome husband in our first home. We were so proud to own our first home. We had moved back from Rochester, New York, where my accident happened, and my husband had graduated college. It was good to be back closer to family. We missed all of them. I was working for Dr. Penwell at the time. He was an amazing man and well ahead of his time, medically speaking. He treated me for chiropractic care, natural vitamin care, and neck injections. I was feeling better than I had felt in a long time.

On our small six-acre farm, we had horses. Two at the moment to be exact. Their names were Boutique and Chantilly Lace. They were Tennessee walkers, and I loved them. When I would look out our back kitchen window, you could see our barn with the white wooden fence. Horses were so tightly linked to my father and my family. My plan was never to be without them. They're a lot of work, people say, but to me, they were great joy and wonderful memories. I bought my very own first horse in Rochester, New York, before I was married. I bought him from a wonderful Christian, a tiny woman who bred, raised, and showed Tennessee walkers. I met her through a friend, and we became very quick friends. I would help her in the barn with the horses, whatever she needed. The horses needed exercise, so once she knew me and that I could ride, she let me ride her very beautiful, very expensive babies. I was blessed so much by her and learned so very much. I had my own apartment then and a pretty good job. I asked her one day if it would ever be possible to buy one of her babies she bred. I could never afford one of the palominos, though I would have loved to. She asked me how I would pay for it and where would I keep it. She already knew my love for them, and I was already working for free just to be around them. I told her I could make payments and that maybe she would let me board the horse there. I remember her smile that day.

She said, "You remind me so much of myself. How can I say no?"

She had a pregnant mare at the time named Boutique. I used to ride her. She was anything but flashy, and her gait wasn't smooth. Lord knows I didn't care. She said that as long as it's not a flashy baby (i.e., palomino), she would give me a good deal. I could pay payments, and of course, I could board it there. She didn't take on many boarders, though she had plenty of room. She liked her barn clean, peaceful, and only hers, if you know what I mean. That was her happy place she had wanted all of her life, and she worked hard at keeping up. She had some of the most beautiful horses. How I loved spending time there. It had become my happy place too.

The day had come I was so anxiously waiting for. It was a little interesting, and at times, we had laughed at the situation. You see, Boutique was having her baby. She was hoping for a flashy baby, and I was silently hoping for plain. We had discussed if I couldn't buy this one, there would be more, and of course, that was fine. It had to be. The call came in. Boutique had her baby. I waited. He's handsome and has sort of a star on his brown forehead. I was trying not to jump up and down, and she was smiling. I could tell through her voice.

"He's yours if you want him. We can work out the details. Come see him when you can."

"How about now? I'm on my way."

So small, so handsome, and mine. Pinch me. Next, the name. I've got it—Star. His full papered name is Images Star Boutique. His mama, Boutique, is a sweet girl; and his daddy, Images Gold Dust, is a very flashy palomino with the most beautiful mane and tail. My dad bred one of our mares when I was young from his palomino, and he was beautiful. His name was Sir L Bronco, or Bronc for short. My very own baby to raise. I had watched my dad with his crippled hands train Bronc. I was ready for the challenge. Star and I became best friends. Every day after work, straight to the barn I would go. How I loved him.

Mary Ann, the owner of the farm, said one day, "Look at him following you around almost like a dog."

She was right. He wouldn't let me out of his sight when I was there. His mama loved me too. Some horses can go through a bit of a nasty stage when their babies were born. Not Boutique. She was sweet as ever. I still have a picture of Star following me in the pasture wearing a baseball hat of my husband's. He would do anything I asked him to even if he was scared. I took him on his first trail ride at only two years of age. For those who don't know horses, that's young for all he did: the horse trailer, hills, woods, and even through water. What a smooth, safe, trusting, easygoing boy. I was so proud of him.

Other riders noticed and said, "Wow, he trusts you."

I said, "Oh yes, I trust him too."

The time had come, as I said earlier, to move back home to Michigan. We missed family, and it was time to plant our married roots, as people say. We came home and stayed with my husband's parents to look for a home. My husband had a job lined up, and I would find one. House hunting would be in the near future, and as for my Star, he would stay with a dear family friend for a while until we could get settled. I could visit him there and ride there. It was all settled. We borrowed a truck and trailer. It was bittersweet for me. I wanted to be with family, but I would miss the farm and Mary Ann and her beautiful horses. The move went smoothly. Star loaded in the trailer, we said our tearful goodbyes and made the long trip.

Star was nervous, but he trusted me. I stayed with him for a couple days. We took a ride, and he was fine. The cool thing is this family friend might as well be blood family. When I was real young, we lived just down the road from them. I consider them family and have known them my whole life. In fact, they were the ones who our pony Buttercup and Bronc went to. Buttercup was still alive. It was neat to see him. Things felt right. Star was okay, and we needed to go back and move the rest of our belongings. My one request before leaving was not to put him in a pasture by a large open field they had. The fence wasn't great, and if a combine or hay bailer came by, I didn't want Star to get scared, with everything being so new.

We made the trip back to Rochester. We weren't back at our townhouse long and the phone rang. It was our family friend, and he sounded very upset, tearful.

What's wrong? He's a very strong man. What happened? Did someone get hurt in their family?

Out of his mouth came, "I'm so sorry."

Sorry about what? He wouldn't hurt me for anything.

"Star is dead. I put him in that pasture, and a hay bailer came by, and he must have reared up, got caught in the fence, and he broke his neck."

I screamed, started crying and literally dropped to the floor. I dropped the phone and balled. My husband grabbed the phone and tried to figure out what was wrong. He had to hang up. I was sobbing uncontrollably.

"What have I done? What have I done?" I just kept yelling. I cried so much I almost vomited and couldn't catch my breath.

Once I calmed a little, I told my husband to call back. We have to go now. I have to say goodbye. I have to see him. I can't process this. My husband called back. He was so sorry. He had tried to do the right thing. He already buried him on the farm. I've known this man my whole life, and he's always tried to do the right thing.

"I buried him," he told my husband. "She couldn't see him like that."

He was torn up too. He never dreamed this would happen. The thing is, I had called it. That was my one request. He thought I was too worried and nothing would happen and Star would enjoy some grass. He's gone, buried. No, no, no. That was a very long night and a very long week or two. He tried. He offered me the pick of his horses. I could take any one I wanted. He was a good man. Today, he's still a good man, and we're close, but that was hard to forgive and move on from. It was also very hard to process my life without Star. I didn't want—or should I say, wouldn't take—one of his horses he loved. That's not the right thing to do in life. Forgiveness, that's the right thing to do. It takes time. For me it takes prayer and quiet time with God. We all make mistakes in this life. Some are bigger, more impactful than others. Some are easy to get over, and some take serious time. In *Ephesians 4:32*, highlighted in my grandfather's Bible I love so much, it says, *"Be kind to one another, tender hearted, forgiving one another as God forgives you."* In *Matthew 6:15*, it says, *"If we do not forgive others neither will our father in heaven forgive us."* In *Luke 6:37*, it also says, *"Do not judge or condemn other people."* *Colossians 3:13* says, *"Bear with one another, if one has a complaint against another overlook the offense. Forgive as the Lord God forgives you."*

Complaint, oh, I had a complaint. When you get down to difficult situations like this in life really, honestly, we need to follow God's word and lean on his strength to make it through, to handle ourselves in the right manner, to follow in God's footsteps as not to sever relationships. Here again, I can thank God for my grandparents' examples I was able to witness. Living examples here on earth for our eyes to see. My mother's living examples. I've witnessed her turning her cheek several times. It takes trials, prayer, practice, patience, spending time in God's word; but it can be done. I did it. I missed my Star. I had that deep longing ache in my heart for so long. Time and prayer are great healers, never ever forgetting, but the deep pain lessens. I still miss my Star today. I can't lie, and though it's been many years now, I sometimes drift off into the what-might-have-beens. The long trail rides, hugs—all of the love. I sure hope he's in heaven so some-day we can meet again.

As I said earlier we bought a house with six acres and the barn and white fence. When I told Mary Ann what happened, she was devastated for me. She saw firsthand the love, the time spent, the training. She received every payment I worked so hard for. He was not cheap, and it took me some time to pay him off. He was worth every penny. She was amazing. She offered to breed Boutique again, except this time she would only charge me the stud fee at a discounted rate, and I could have this baby. She was so generous. She knew I was crushed. She wanted to help ease my pain. She bred Boutique; she didn't get pregnant. She bred her again. No luck. Third time is the charm, right? No luck. She felt so bad for me. She gave me

Star's mama, Boutique, in hopes that this would help me feel closer to him. She was also getting older and obviously couldn't have any more babies. I accepted. She also offered me a two-year-old female, beautiful horse with a full white blaze down her whole face and a light mane and tail for a very reasonable price. My husband and I discussed it. He was hesitant, but me, I was a bit desperate. This felt like a gift to me. The agreement was made. This way, Craig and I could both ride, and I would have my sweet Boutique. I had good memories with her. We rode in a few parades and a couple horse shows; and she was, most of all, Star's mama. We again borrowed a truck and trailer. We brought them home to our new home. That was a good day for me. Bittersweet for sure. No Star, but no empty barn either.

Star

Ah, Pregnancy

By this time, I was feeling the baby nudge. We had been wanting one and hoping to get pregnant but nothing. We were considering IVF. It was an option but an expensive one. The doctor told us to set up an appointment for my husband, which he wasn't thrilled about, but prayer was constant for me, and I wanted to be a mama. While waiting for his appointment to come, one day at work, I was feeling a little sick to my stomach and a friend and coworker said, "Maybe you're pregnant." Yeah right, that's funny. She finally talked me into taking a test, and to my shock and surprise, I was pregnant. No way. I called my husband right away, and he was as shocked as I was. So thankful and so excited I can't even explain and glad he could cancel his doctor appointment.

Here we go, now were really getting started. My pain is less these days, and all I had on my wish list was being a mother. Thank you, God. You have heard my persistent prayers and answered them. I can't really put into words my deep, unexplainable joy. To be thirty years old and have gone through such pain already, thinking maybe the one thing I want more than anything just isn't in the cards for me. It was a relief to see that it was. When I got married, I planned to be done having children by age thirty. Three of them to be exact. You see, we all do this in life. We have our perfect plan or dream if you will. I wanted to be a young mother, a fun mother able to do anything my children could dream up. The crazier, the better. Today, if you asked someone close to me, someone who really knows me, they would tell you I love to four-wheel ride, boat ride, Jet Ski, etc. If you asked me to jump out of a plane, I would say, "When and where?" I'm there. The only thing is, I'm limited after my accident. The doctors say no diving in a pool, let alone skydiving. Aw, life plans just don't always turn out the way we want them to. It's okay, I'm doing better now. I can adapt. We will still have adventures. I can still be a fun mom even though I'm thirty and just starting, not finished with three children.

Morning sickness, now that's not fun, and I was experiencing plenty of it. Public restrooms were not my friend. I have a very sensitive nose, and still do to this day, so they were no place for me. Carrying a bucket in the car on the way to work was my new normal. My daily thoughts were, *This pregnancy thing it's not for the weak*. I was ready though. Bring on the challenges. I was stronger physically now, definitely stronger in my faith now and thought that I can handle whatever is thrown at me. I want to experience all of it. I want the whole mom journey. After all, I've been waiting so long and praying so hard for this. There is scripture on God refining us like silver, us being put through the fire like gold. It's in *Proverbs 17:3*. With my car accident, losing my father, losing Star, and all the challenges it brings, I figured I've been put through my refining process. That, that part should be done. My hope was that I was coming out on the other side of refinement. So I was ready for joy—real joy. Picking out baby names, colors, a boy or girl, the nursery, baby proofing the house, all of the above. Here's the thing I've learned today. We can be refined, fine-tuned, if you will, put through many fires, some that we could never anticipate or even dream up.

In *1 James 1:2–8*, it tells us *"to count it all joy when fiery trials come, knowing that the testing of our faith will make us complete, lacking nothing so we can truly know God."* I have to be honest what I am about to share with you was anything but joyful. There were joyful precious moments mixed in with all the raw, open painful wounds that scarred my heart like nothing ever could. Today all these years later, I can finally tell you I am much closer to God. I lean into God when fiery trials come, and they do still come. I'm much quicker to turn to him and rely on him, really listen to his voice. You see, when I was young and my dad died, I found out at such a young age emotional pain. I knew God but not intimately like I do today. My car accident taught me physical pain. The kind of pain that almost takes away the person you are. Just way too much that you can't keep going without God, or at least I couldn't. The pain I'm about to share with you was heart pain like no other and had me wishing I could take the physical pain from the situation. I had learned how to handle physical pain myself, but to see it and not be able to do anything about it was unbearable.

Back to my joyful, newly pregnant self. It's good to be able to reflect on that innocent, joyful time. Life was good, exciting, and full of anticipation. I was twelve weeks along now. As they say, past the scary stage. It's time for my ultrasound doctor's visit. I was, needless to say, so anxious to see our baby. Just to get a glimpse of who is growing inside me. This miracle baby we had waited too long for. My heart was overflowing. I loved my doctor, his nurses, and the office staff. I knew this was the place for us. I had all the warm and fuzzies. It wasn't like this at first. When I found out I was pregnant, I was determined to have a female doctor. She could truly understand what a woman's body goes through. I made an appointment with a highly recommended doctor. I left that appointment so frustrated and a bit misunderstood and frankly mistreated. My perspective had been shaken. Life has a way of doing that. Some doctors and people in this life lack empathy. I've been through enough, and empathy was number one on my list. Back to the drawing board. I'm not going back there. If there is anything I've learned in this life, a good demeanor, compassion, and bedside manner are key to a good doctor, not just knowledge. But don't get me wrong, knowledge is important too. At work the next day, I was given a doctor's name. He was a man, but kind, compassionate, and caring. Okay, okay, I will give him a try. I will get past my idea of only women can truly understand.

Back to the ultrasound. Well, you see, life has this way of bustin' your image bubble. The ultrasound showed us our precious baby. It also showed what they call a hygroma, a sack of fluid on his neck. What is that? The doctor assured me sometimes they absorb and go away, not to worry too much as that's not good for the baby. When someone tells you not to worry, our human instinct is to worry, right? I tried to keep my head down; work; take care of myself, my home, and my pets. Keep my focus off worry.

With the hygroma lingering, I would be having more frequent doctor visits and ultrasounds. A couple weeks went by and another doctor visit and ultrasound. Thank God the hygroma hasn't grown. That's a good sign, I'm told. Okay, I will carry on. I can do this. I will do all the right things for my body and my baby. I'm strong. My body won't let me down, not now. I willed my body and my baby well. The problem with that, though it sounds good, is we can't do that. Oh, how I wish we could.

Two more weeks passed. Time again for another visit. We've got this, only we didn't. The hygroma had grown in size. What could that possible mean? Well, nothing good, I'm afraid. The doctor looked very concerned. It's time now to get more information. No need to panic, but... (oh, how I hate the "but...") We scheduled an amniocentesis. It was explained to me what that entailed because this is the first time I had heard in detail what this meant. A very large needle will be inserted into my stomach into the amniotic sac that holds my child and keeps them safe. Aw no, I'm not onboard with this. Sometimes in life we're faced with decisions, hard decisions. We discussed it. Our doctor was confident with this procedure and had had a lot of success with it. Okay, I'm convinced. We need information to help my baby. I'm the vessel, so let's do this. The definition of this word, *amniocentesis*, is scary all by itself without the actual process of it. It's a medical procedure used in prenatal diagnosis of chromosomal abnormalities and fetal infections. It will also determine the sex of our sweet baby. Let's get to the bottom of the problem so we can fix this. I went into fix mode. Time for the procedure. I thought I was ready. I don't exactly know how to prepare for such a procedure. Strength, keep fear in control, be steady. Your baby needs you. We got through the procedure. I have great compassion for other mothers having to do this. It wasn't fun, and it was scary waiting for the results. I felt like they would never come.

The results are in. The words over the phone rang through my ears loud and clear.

"It's okay, you have a healthy baby girl. The hygroma should go down eventually."

Music to my ears. A healthy girl. Time to spread the good news. Let the joy, pregnancy glow everyone talks about, shine on me. A healthy baby girl, now this I can do. This is the dream and the family I always wanted. We're on our way. As broken up as you were, body, I knew you wouldn't let me down.

Time to celebrate. My good friend and neighbor who lived right next door was throwing me a baby shower. This is what being pregnant was supposed to be like. Bring on the pretty baby things. I can't wait. Paddington Bear was the theme. I loved me some Paddington Bear. Yes, he has red and blue bright colors, but I'm good with that. He's a cute bear. The shower was a success. Family and friends came, and we had such fun. From a homemade quilt from my sister to sweet pink pretties to a homemade photo album from my sweet neighbor. Yes, laughter, games, food, and punch were had. All is right with my world. Onward and upward. Time to show my husband all the goodies we had for our sweet girl, and of course, the nursery was soon to come. Happiness surrounded our home like a big, bright light. Now this is the picture bubble I want to visualize and keep at the front of my mind. Work and daily life marched on. My belly was growing quite a bit now. A little bigger than I expected, but okay. I will control my food urges, can't get too big. I have to come out on the other side of this and someday fit back into my regular clothes. I'm sure all women think this.

Another doctor visit and ultrasound. We still want to keep a close eye on her and the hygroma still lurking on her neck. I remember thinking, *Okay, today, God, it will surely be smaller or hopefully gone, right? You're hearing me right, God?* I have this all planned out in my mind, and I really need it to go accordingly.

Excited to see everyone at the doctor's office including my doctor. Smiles all around. Everyone so happy for us. You see, at the time I didn't think that they were, day in a day out, seeing all the good, bad, and even the really bad. So good news was to be celebrated as it should be. I love this day. This is a good day. Time for the ultrasound. Let's see this sweet girl. I felt lucky at the time to have extra ultrasounds that others didn't usually receive. This gave me a window into the growth of our sweet girl.

The Bubble Busted

With much excitement, we began the ultrasound. The mood of the room shifted in an instant. What is going on? The hygroma has grown substantially. How can this be? This can't be. My doctor got very serious and took a closer look. He was looking intently for his eyes to tell him what was wrong, so was I. You want to talk about happiness and excitement coming to a complete halt. This can't be right. Something is wrong, very wrong. What to do now?

I kept telling myself, "Don't panic, don't panic, stay calm, just breathe, your little girl needs you."

With the whole room quiet and all the air in there, how is it I'm having a hard time getting any? Oh God, how bad is this? What is coming next? I thought the worst was behind me. Oh, dear Jesus, help me walk out of here. Hold my hand, I can't move. This is too real. Craig's not here. I feel so alone.

In a shaking voice, tears streaming down my face, I asked the doctor, "What now?"

In a soft voice, he said, "Nothing at this moment. I need to consult some of my colleagues. Someone with more experience with this than I have. We will get some answers. You go home and rest. Try not to worry. You don't want to stress your baby."

Seriously, try not to stress? So many emotions, feelings. What to do with them? Where to store them? Lock them away. The doctor's words ringing in my ears. "Don't stress the baby." I won't hurt our sweet girl. Body, don't fail me now. I will not be the cause of any undue trauma on my child. Deep breath, dry it up. Rubbing my belly, taking deep breaths, I headed home.

The conversation with Craig was shock all over again. Remember, stay calm. No stress on the baby. It was the same with anyone we decided to tell. Our world was very small and fragile right now. We kept a small circle. It's best. We're trying to process this ourselves.

Life kept moving around us. Work, pets, food, etc. The thing is, I felt like I was moving, breathing, working; but it was like I was watching myself from a stunned place in slow motion. Almost like I was watching this happen to someone else instead of me. It's like a movie that keeps playing over and over in your head that you can't stop, mostly because you hope to see a different picture or outcome. It just never came. The visual bubble I spoke about earlier just keeps moving, but the trouble is, I can't find one good image or thought to stop it on.

I was unable to sleep, on pins and needles as they say, anxiously waiting a call from the doctor's office. To be honest, patience has never been my thing. This isn't helping at all. Finally, the call came in.

Again, I hear, "I'm so sorry, but we just need more information. A closer look at what's going on, Brenda. We can't see enough from a regular ultrasound. We need a specialist for this, and they will help us determine what's going on."

"Okay, let's do it," I said. "But I don't want to wait. Please do it quickly. We need to fix this."

My mind kept going into fix mode. I guess that helped me keep it together. I'm kind of a fixer. Tell me what it is, I will try to fix it. With this, I definitely wanted and needed all the information I could get. Let's do this. Let's fix this. Appointment was set only a few days away. Sleep, rest, breathe, eat right, and don't take any medicine for my headache. Don't do anything to hurt my little girl's chances to be healthy and happy. I had to control the controllable, as my husband says. So many things were spinning out of my control. I needed to hold fast to all I could do: talking to our sweet girl, rubbing my belly to relax her, and me singing to her. Anything to make all of this go away; to change the picture, the image, the outcome.

So many things on this life's journey are out of our control. I know that. I've lived that. We're learning that painful lesson again here and now.

Appointment day. Quiet ride to the hospital where the test was being done. Reality was just too real. Numb to my core, off we go. Let's do this, sweet girly. We've got this. The ultrasound is starting, and everyone keeps asking me if I'm okay.

"No, I'm not okay," a loud voice shouts in my head. "Stop asking me." But out of my mouth comes, "Yes, I'm good."

Why do we do that in life? People ask us if we're okay, and we say, "Oh yes, we're fine," while the whole time our voice inside us is screaming, "No." Maybe it's a gift God gives us: strength. You see, if I come unglued here and sob like I need to, they can't do their job. So I tell myself, "Hold it together. You can do this." Strength comes from within, my friend, and I've learned it's from God, whether we know it or believe it or not. *Isaiah 40:29* says, "*The Lord gives power to the faint and to those who have no might he increases their strength.*" It's not from ourselves though. I keep telling myself I had this. I didn't at all. God had me, and it was his strength carrying me.

Pictures of my little girl, the hygroma. What's wrong? Tell me right now. Fix it, please. I thought this would be over quickly. How long can it possibly take? Well, a long time. Over two hours. Uncomfortable, to say the least. Doctors in and out of the room. More coming in, another expert. Please, someone, with all your schooling and training, know what this is. I thought it would never end. It finally did. I could get dressed, and someone would be with me shortly to explain.

They did explain. They explained so much, too much for me to process quickly. This would take me some time. Hold on, let me take a breath. Okay, go ahead.

First, a deep calm voice from the doctor said the child inside of me is a boy.

A boy, what? The amnio said a healthy girl. Where's my little girl? I had a shower, all the cute things. This can't be. I can't hear this. Wait, we have a boy? Okay, so the hygroma is on his neck. Too much too soon. I can't process. Wait, okay, what is this hygroma?

"Well, ma'am, he also has club feet, which can be fixed." Okay, fix it. I can hear that loud and clear. Let's do that.

He explained he was probably missing some pieces of a chromosome. They would need more information. They could also see he had a heart defect as well. The hygroma is our sign of the things wrong.

Okay, okay, okay, a heart defect? That's serious. No, no, no...I can't fix this. Can they? Can anyone? Can it be fixed in the womb?

At this point, they sent us two floors up to a genetic counselor so they could speak with us.

That was not only an eye-opener, but a confusing and frustrating discussion. The counselor said many things, and we were trying to grasp them all. We hung on to every word. Our child's life was in this discussion. If I had it to do all over again, I would have asked if this counselor knew the God I know. If he believed, what kind of man he was, his credentials. This is important and powerful stuff. I should have known more about him before I let him speak to us. I wanted medical information, not his personal opinion. However, in that meeting, I got both. We got both. I learned more that day than the words he had to say, and it was a mouthful, that's for sure. He said that the child you are carrying may have ambiguous genitalia. What does that mean? Well, we learned, and many people today face this. This is where a child is born with both female and male parts. He thought maybe this was why we received a female reading from our amnio or maybe they got some of my skin cells when they drew out the fluid. Maybe even possibly there could have been a lab mix-up. They finally determined we had twins. They had drawn out of the female sac with the amnio, and we had lost her. We did not have a healthy baby girl. We, in his mind, had a defective baby boy. You heard me, he was not right! Excuse me, are you talking about our sweet child? He was cruel, to say the least. He explained how we would live in a hospital, if he lived at all. He also explained how awful this would be for our son. He pressed and pressed until I lost it. He thought we should abort our beautiful child. He made us feel like if we didn't, we were somehow choosing to have him be born so we could allow him to be tortured. That was it. My husband got very angry. He asked me what I wanted. I said I want my baby however God has him and for however long he allows us to have him. He told the counselor that day in no uncertain terms that if he didn't stop, and he asked him several times, he would literally punch him. That's not the right reaction, but it was just too much. Enough was enough. Looking back, I can sure see what side of the fence that guy stood on. Somehow mere men could decide the life and death of our child. I don't think so. God is the giver and taker of life, not people.

We were asked to come back to the hospital the next day. More information was needed. Really, more? What now? Our body is an amazing creation by God himself. We can endure much more than we think we can. Trust me, I was finding that out. Tomorrow would give us more answers. Okay. Again, let's do this. We need all the information we can get especially at this point.

The drive home was quieter than on the way there. How can this be? I know every child is a gift, a miracle. Until something goes very wrong, we don't really think about that. We take for granted those statements until we're living them. Some in our society are literally throwing children away, abusing them, aborting them. How can this be? Here we are trying desperately to hang on to ours. None of this is fair or can make any sense. Fear, anguish, anger—they are already trying to set up home in my body. What are we going to do? What is going to happen? How bad is tomorrow going to be? Worse than today? I feel trapped, and there's nowhere to run. So many thoughts racing through my mind.

We made it home, both emotionally and physically exhausted. We needed advice and support. We made phone calls, informing our families. Every conversation, the shock in their voice, the loud sadness coming through the phone. We needed them to tell us everything was going to be okay. However, the news we were sharing was anything but okay, so how could they possibly do that? It wasn't okay. Nothing was okay. Another sleepless night, lying still in the loud silence, all the while holding and rubbing my belly, somehow trying to comfort my now son, not daughter. I guess in hopes to comfort them, I mean him, and to comfort me. Like somehow he was still safe and warm inside of me. So he was still okay.

The next day proved to be more grueling than the last. This time they would do a cordocentesis. Another medical term I never thought I would have to learn or experience. This is where a specialist will take another large needle and put it into my stomach, but this time into the umbilical cord to be able to draw blood directly from the cord. This was to give us all the answers we needed. The room was set, and it was time. The nurse on my right, the doctor on my left, and my husband holding my feet, per my request. I just wanted his touch. Tensions were running very high. As the nurse nervously tried to get an IV in my arm, she hit an artery. Blood shot all over the wall beside me. To say the least, the doctor wasn't happy. He told her to go get a competent nurse in there right now. He and my husband tried to comfort me. This needle would be ultrasound guided. Another form of ultrasound. Another nurse arrived, and she was calm, reassuring, and got her job done quickly. The other nurse left shaken. I felt a little sorry for her. The doctor was a very large man with a deep, stable, strong voice.

After giving me something to relax, not put me out (oh, how I wish they had), he proceeded to begin. I did not realize, I should have, that he would have to take stabs at the cord, if you will. He would get the cord in sight and try to poke it. After a couple attempts that felt like he was going to put the needle through me, I hear him say, "Someone get Dad juice and a chair." Yes, my foot holder and comfort was passing out. I guess watching me get jabbed with this large needle had gotten to him. Who could blame him? I thought, *I wish I could pass out.* There is no way out of this for me, my body, or our child. At the moment of that thought, out of the mouth of this doctor came music. Beautiful music. He started singing, "Sweet Baby James" by James Taylor. The whole room calmed down, and it brought an ease to the situation. My husband was doing better. The nurse was comforting with her bright smile and soft touch on my arm as the doctor's beautiful God-given voice filled the room. We finished the procedure. He finally got the cord, and we were done. That was a day I never ever wanted to repeat ever in my entire life. Now we wait for the results. We needed answers, and now hopefully, we were going to get them.

The Waiting

During this waiting period, many people had many different opinions, and they were sharing them. Some supportive; some telling awful hospital stories as if to be saying, "Maybe you should abort." Even going so far as to say, "The counselor might be right." Like it would be kinder to end our son's life now. I remember calling my mom in tears, asking her what I should do. Like I didn't know better, God is the giver and taker of life, and no one should make that choice except him. I make no bones about that. I just wanted to hear her say that. You see, it was hard for her. Not because she didn't know the right thing to say, but because she would have to say that to her baby, and she knew I had a lot of pain left to endure.

She hesitated and said, "Honey, you have to make that decision."

I dried up my tears and said, "What would Grandpa King say?"

She paused, and in tears, she said, "God is the only giver and taker of life."

I thanked her and knew that night that the long, painful journey was only beginning for us and our son.

The next day I drove to work in a literal fog, not in the air but in my body. Trying to block out the pain and move forward. Only my body seemed extra heavy, pulled down by the weight of it all. I remember making it almost all the way through the day when a coworker decided she wanted to corner me and ask me if I was crazy, that if she were me, she would abort and start over, like my son was trash and I should get rid of him. This sent me into a bit of a tizzy, as they say. Tears, anger, the stupidity of her. Listen, if you know someone struggling, don't lead with your own thoughts and what you would do. Please go to God first and lead with what he would do. Lead with love, compassion, support, and kindness, and for Pete's sake, if you can't, put a sock in it. You don't know what's right for that person, only God does. My close friends will tell you, "Brenda says it like it is," and this is just me being me. My close friend, Debbie, would say, "I need a Brenda in my life to speak for me." It may not always be good, but at this point, trust me, it is. If you've lived it, you know.

On my ride home from work that day, the tears were flowing so hard I could hardly see to drive. I was angry now, very angry. My emotions were flowing out of me, and I was unable to stop them. I was sobbing, hitting the steering wheel, and yelling at everyone and anyone when all of a sudden, I felt this big, warm, all-encompassing hug wrap itself all around my body. It's like time stopped. I couldn't believe what I was feeling and experiencing. A voice in my head said, "I've got you, Brenda. You are going to be okay. I am here with you." You have to understand, no one was in the car with me. I was literally experiencing the hands of God, and I wish I could have you feel how that felt. So warm, strong, loving. I never wanted it to stop. In fact, I have to tell you I don't really remember the roads or turns or how I even drove home. I would have to say that "Jesus took the wheel," as the Carrie Underwood's song says.

When my husband got home that night, I told him, "No more, no more opinions. I don't want to talk to anyone who doesn't support us or agree with our decisions." I needed him to handle all of that. I was going to handle carrying our son and keeping him safe as long as God let me. Craig did just that. He handled friends, family, coworkers, anyone that needed handling while I handled being a mama. I did what I was told to do and prayed continually. This was not the picture bubble I had in mind, but this was my reality, and I was going to see it through to the end.

The results were in. Our son was missing a hairline piece of his twenty-second chromosome. A hairline piece had done this? Are you kidding me? This is a cruel joke, right? No, this is no joke. This is our reality. Our very own personal nightmare. How can this be? Now you know what I mean when I say every child is a miracle from God. Every perfect little hand, eye, toe is made perfectly by God himself. Why wasn't our baby?

The days passed like they were going by in slow motion. As if they went around in one large circle, every time leading back to the same painful spot. This is not a road I want to be on. However, some roads just have to be travelled to reach our destination. This would be no different. Though bumpy, at the very least with boulders that seemed impossible to move and no happy ending in sight. No beautiful mountaintop in the distance. Oh, how I wish there was. Answers, we now had a lot of them. Now too many and none of them easy to hear, simple to process, or fixable, so it seemed. We knew our son, our sweet boy, has club feet, a heart defect, and was missing a hairline piece of his twenty-second chromosome. What else? With the decision we made to carry on, come what may! We were on our journey, on our way, one way or another. That didn't mean we were somehow different people or the journey was changed or rearranged. The doctors, however, their journey would be much different. There was no easy out for any of us. We all were on this road together. It was time to play defense, to gather a team of doctors, specialists in their field, the best we could get to try to have the best outcome possible. To give our now little boy the best chance possible for life outside of my shaken, tired, broken body. To breathe the air we breathe, to experience human touch, to see Christmas lights especially for the first time.

Life, so precious, and yet so many of us take it for granted. Our straight feet, our mobile legs, our pumping heart, our priceless eyes to see. So many moving parts that all work together in harmony—until they don't. So many chromosomes to line up perfectly. She looks like her mama; he has his daddy's eyes. You know, all the miracles we take for granted. I know I'm not the only hurting soul in this amazing, somewhat broken world. Trust me, as my journey went on, I met way too many of them. If you have your own uniquely different version, tailored just to you and your family, my heart goes out to you. The picture bubble in my head, you know the one, the perfect one that makes you happy all over—we all have them. Whether it's a perfect summer day, a Thanksgiving dinner, Christmas morning, or so many more. Too many to say. Those precious moments we want to keep, lock in a vault, never to move on from. Those pictures need to be stored up in our fabulous mind to be brought up on the days that get so hard. You need to be transported to another time and place. Those are gifts from God to help us get through the pictures that are just way too painful to see. If your unique situation or pain is too real, too raw, you daydream a little, like I did, to take yourself somewhere your body cannot, to some happy memory to cling to, to get you through, I get you. That is a small miracle in itself and just one of the tools we have inside of us that God gives us, to store up, to draw from. That picture we focus on like the drawings on my son's walls. They are part of the big puzzle that gets us through the really rough times. I'm grateful for all my precious memories. I'm always saying this went too fast or I wish I could freeze time, if only for a while. To stay in the beautiful frame I'm capturing in my mind. To stay there where all is good and all is well with not only me and my soul but all the others I love as well. *Psalm 46:1–3* says,

> *God is our refuge and strength, a very present help in trouble. Therefore, we will not fear, though the earth be removed and though the mountains be carried into the sea, though the waters roar and the mountains shake, there your hand will guide me still.*

Well, I have to tell you, I was afraid. We are all mere human flesh and bone, and this was a lot, to say the least. The one thing I witnessed in the months to come was every time I had it really bad, someone else in the hospital had it worse. My eyes were wide open, but seeing anything good amongst so much pain and heartache was difficult. You had to be looking for it, searching for it. But it was there all around me. Still today, I tell myself to look for the good. A simple hug from even a stranger helped. Love is one thing you will see a lot of in an ICU if you're looking for it. Try not to only see your pain if you possibly can. Try to capture the entire picture. There is so much more to the content than we're usually seeing. When you invite God into your situation, no matter the outcome, there will be light in the darkness somewhere waiting for you to see it. Nighttime in the hospital has darkness for sure, not only by less light but people tend to be sicker, have a harder time. It was always a relief to see daylight come. I did a lot of praying in the hospital all the time but extra at night time for sure.

My sister-in-law came to the hospital to visit one evening. The night nurse was on, Sharon. She loved my son and worked tirelessly to keep him well. I was happy when she was there. She was a good nurse and knew my son well. There was a lot of comfort in that. Cody was asleep and resting so comfortably. I did not want to disturb him. My sister-in-law wanted to hold him. His nurse gave me the look. She didn't want to move him either. Rest, good rest, meant healing; and he never got much peace. Anyone who's been in a hospital knows that all too well. We didn't move him. I said no. I just cannot wake him. I've always felt bad about that. I wish I had.

Going back, it was time for another doctor appointment. Now the mood there was always uneasy. We did a lot of ultrasounds to keep an eye on the hygroma. Because our son was missing a piece of his twenty-second chromosome, my body was trying to protect him. I was getting bigger and bigger. So uncomfortable. I asked the doctor why. He said I had polyhydramnia. It is extra fluid, a lot of it. When our babies have problems, at times the body will do this. Great, I'm glad my body is trying to protect him, but how big and uncomfortable am I going to be? Protection for my baby, I can grab on to that. Okay, protection. I like that. Unfortunately, for more protection, I had to stop working and be put on bed rest.

"The last thing we needed," the doctor said, "is for him to come early. We need his lungs to be fully developed for him to have a fighting chance."

No pressure there. Rest is what I did. I had an amazing dog, a boxer named Briecin. She was named after our two dachshunds, Briena and Cinnamon. I missed them so much, but she filled their big shoes. She was everything you could want in a dog and more. We would joke and say she was almost human. She really was. She was my comfort on really hard days, so many hard days. The love we had for each other was from God for sure. My husband would let her out before he left for work, and she would lay by my side, touching me.

She always had to be touching me. She never moved unless I did. She never ate unless I did as if to say, "I'm in this with you. You're not alone, Mom." She was so much comfort to me, and God knew I needed it. I still miss her today. She was truly amazing.

Time was passing, and Christmas was near. My husband had to do all the extra things I always loved to do while I watched, resting, instructing. My poor husband. I'm so picky about the Christmas tree, too picky. Patiently, he worked hard to please me. Christmas has such a strong link to my family and my father whom I've missed so much for so long. Christmas is always special and a bit emotional every year.

Decorating all done, the tree and its light brought me so much comfort and many beautiful picture bubble memories to recall. It helped to pass the stressful time as it whisked me back to happier times. Again, so grateful for God's gifts of all the memories our brains can hold. For me, sadness had tried to creep in for weeks now. A time for happiness, decorating, shopping, gatherings with friends and family, really all my happy things; and I couldn't do any of them. I bounced between anxiety to anger, from anger to sadness, from sadness to feeling a bit sorry for myself. The why me's kept me on edge for sure. When this went on for a bit, a phone call from a friend, flowers from my husband, and long chats with my mom would remind me of all my blessings and the good that was still in my life. I had to remember that even though this seemed to go on forever, things were always changing. Our son was still safe inside me, and we were still in this fight.

Christmas was over, back to normal life. If you could call what I was living through normal. It was my normal: my son and husband are normal at this point. The status quo meant our son's lungs were still developing. We all still had a chance at being a family, whatever that would look like. Only God knew that. Looking back, I remember my husband telling the doctors and genetic specialist at the hospital that awful day, "You might want to figure out what to do to save our son because we were not taking his life." He was my rock, my steady voice when I was too tearful to use my own. He had a job to do as well as I did, several jobs. He had to hold it all together, work, figure out finances, especially since I couldn't work anymore. That took a serious hit to our budget for sure. He had to keep it together emotionally, take care of me, our animals, and so much more. Not only did we have our dog but our horses as well. To say the least, he was tired, scared, and worn himself. I'm sure you can imagine. Remember, men in general have this inherent need to fix things. His was on overdrive. It's during times like these that we all need God's strength, including him. I prayed a lot for God to give him strength, and he did.

It's three days after Christmas now, December 28. I was so restless. You see, what I haven't shared with you yet is the doctors also told me to pay real close attention to my body and my baby. I mean, laser focus, if anything changed in the way I was feeling, if our son's movements changed at all, like less movements. They were worried about my excessive fluid and his heart. At this point in the pregnancy, we had five weeks to go, and we needed every bit of them. They warned me over and over of signs to watch for and reminded me to rest. Stress wasn't good for me or my baby. Really?

We had already had a couple of close calls, some cramping. Then a couple weeks earlier the cramping turned into contractions. This could be deadly, they warned me, for our son, that is. My husband rushed me to the hospital per doctor's orders. He met us there. I was put on a medicine called Pitocin. Let's just say it can have some side effects. The contractions stopped, thank God. On the car ride home, I remember telling my husband to stop the car. I felt claustrophobic, like I couldn't get air. I had to get out, walk around, and he reminded me to take deep breaths. After I settled down, we were able to go home. Needless to say, I don't want to do that ever again.

Worst Best Day of My Life

Back to December 28. I woke up restless as I was saying. I told my husband I have to get out of this house. I'm going crazy. Not literally, but it felt like it at times. So we decided to go to the mall and look around. That's right, the mall. Of course, in a wheelchair for me. I decided to shower, put on the only maternity outfit that would still fit me at the time, and out the door to the mall we would go. I needed to see life still moving. That not everything had stood still like I felt my life had. I wanted to see the decorations before they were all taken down. I had noticed our son hadn't moved quite as much during the night as he usually did. He liked to kick my ribs a lot. I thought I will shower, eat, move around; and he will go back to his normal bruising of my ribs. Needless to say, he didn't. His movement was basically nonexistent. I rubbed my belly, moved it around. I moved around more than normal. Is this one of those warning signs? My mind started racing. No, no, no, not yet. We still have five weeks left. Not yet, son. You are not ready. What about your lungs, your heart, everything, and so much more? Stress was coming on strong.

At this point, my husband and I decided it was time to get our doctor involved. This was his call. He's the doctor. He has the knowledge and the schooling. This is up to him, less pressure on us. We needed that right now.

No doubt in his mind or any hesitation. "You need to come to the hospital. I will meet you there. His heart could be failing."

His heart? No, God, we need his heart to have any fighting chance at all. No trip to the mall. To the hospital we went. This was the beginning of the worst and best day of my life.

We arrived at the hospital, the emergency exit, of course. Could this be an emergency? Could our son's heart be failing? Could my body be failing me? Did I do something? So many thoughts were racing through my mind at this point. Everything, honestly, felt like an out-of-body experience, like I was right there in the center of chaos, fear, and so much unknown. Everything was so loud at the hospital and moving so fast, but it felt like slow motion. I really think my mind was trying to catch up with my reality because everything in me was trying to slow down that strong will I have. It was literally trying to will all of this out of existence.

We got in a room quickly, and our doctor was already there. He knew this could be go time. He was a good man, caring and compassionate, and he was there to do his job to the best of his abilities. A lot of discussion was had. I did my best to be in tune with my son and my situation. I was the vessel. God had chosen me and our boy. Together, today we're going to face this, come what may.

Our doctor said, "Okay, let's do an ultrasound, just to take a look."

Okay, deal. Let's just take a look. Look we did, however, we could not see any movement at all no matter how we tried or the position of the ultrasound wand. Nothing, no movement. There was so much stillness in that room. All of us breathing shallow, making no sounds, as if that would somehow help. Okay, this is serious. I could tell by the doctor's face. Some decisions had to be made.

He said, "We can't really tell if his heart is failing, but no movement isn't good, especially as active as he has been."

At this point, I'd give anything for those powerful rib kicks. I remember so clearly, like it was yesterday. It was a Wednesday, the year 1994. You see, it was right between Christmas and New Year's Eve. Many doctors had taken this time off to be with their families. Who could blame them? Our doctor said he wished we could have another amnio to determine the stage of his lung growth, how developed he was. Okay, another big needle, another test? I was almost in robot mode.

"If we didn't have the amnio," he explained, "we would have to decide with the information we had, which was not much."

We decided to try to get the amnio, which was a challenge itself. There was no way we were making any decisions without as much information as possible. After much to do, if you know what I mean, remember no one is eager to be called in while taking vacation time, amnio, it is. Some things moved so fast while others seemed to move in slow motion. Check, amnio done. Every time my husband and I got a moment alone, it was a relief for me. I could shed a tear. We could comfort each other, the best we could in our situation. We knew God was there with us. We just didn't know what the rest of this already traumatic day would entail. Every time a nurse or doctor would come in our room, you could feel their pressure as well. Say the right things; do the right things. Can we get you anything, a warm blanket? They were kind, just a bit void on how to help. It's understandable; after all, they are only human, and this is an uncomfortable situation at best.

Results were in. Well, his lungs are developed to the five-week early stage.

"Okay, but it's still a judgment call," the doctor said.

A judgment call? Who is going to make that?

"We were," the doctor said. "If we leave him in the womb, he can grow, and with his challenges, he needs that. However, if we leave him, his heart could fail, and he could die. We do a C-section today." There was never a plan for a normal delivery. His heart couldn't take that. We knew that already. Then again, it is five weeks early. He may not make it. "Again, with all of his challenges, we just don't know. Take some time to decide. I can't and won't make that call for you. This is your call."

"Hold it, wait a minute. You want us to decide?"

"I will give you some time alone and will be back."

"Oh, no, you won't." Here's feisty Brenda. "Not happening. We're not doctors. We're not deciding this. We already have to go through this trauma, and you want us to make the call? If he dies today or dies in my stomach later, we have to live with that forever. No, we won't make this call. You will. I'm sorry, but you are the doctor, and we want the best fighting chance for our son."

With a sober-looking face, he took a deep breath and said, "Okay, I understand. Let me consult with the specialist, and I will be back."

My thoughts were, *You do your best, and we'll do our best. Our son will do his best, and God will have to handle the rest.*

When he left, the room was quiet, tearful; and reality was a little too real. Would our son live or die today, in the future, or not at all? What would he suffer if he did live? Too much to process. I needed an escape from this difficult reality, if only for a moment. I closed my eyes and pictured the Christmas lights, snuggling with my sweet Briecin, memories with our families, the nursery we so happily prepared. This calmed my heart a bit.

I prayed, "Dear God, help me be strong. Give me your strength. Mine is fading quickly. Help me, help us, help our son, help the doctors and the nurses. This is bigger than all of us combined."

After a while, the doctor came back in the room.

"Okay, guys, this is what we think."

I think it helped him to have more opinions than just his own. No one wanted to make the wrong decision.

He proceeded, "Our thoughts are, if we leave him alone, we're not doing anything to help him. Out here, in the world, we can help him have a fighting chance. We think we should do a C-section today and not wait any longer."

Okay, we can agree with that. It's not just me, my body, and my son. We're not in this alone. Specialists, doctors, technology, machines. Let's do this. Let's meet our son today and help him fight. Things moved faster once a decision was made. Our team of specialists would have to get there, and the operating room ready and me prepared. I went into fight mode myself. The doctors were worried once they all spoke that the lack of movement had gone on too long and it was time to move. Plans were in the works. People rushing in and out of the room, the noises, smells, the activity. Phone calls were made to our families. We needed support, and we got it. We called our parents, and they made the other calls. I remember talking to my mom only for a minute after my husband explained the situation to her.

I said, "Mom," with tears flooding my face.

She said, "I know, I know, hon. I'm so sorry. I'll be right there. I'm on my way."

That's all that needed to be said. I needed my mom, and I needed her right now.

She said, "You can do this. Everything is going to be okay."

That jolted me back into fight mode.

"You're right, I can do this. I have to do this."

It's amazing how things change when you become a parent. The strength God gives you when you need it. If you told me I was going to go through this in my life, I would have told you no, I'm not. I will make sure of it. No kids for me. Unfortunately, that's not how life works for any of us. I believe that's why God made it this way. We only know the moment, not the future.

Matthew 6:34 says, "*Therefore, do not worry about tomorrow, tomorrow will worry about itself. Each day has enough trouble of its own.*" And today had enough trouble to deal with on its own.

The doctor came in. They were almost ready. It won't be long. "Are you okay?"

"Am I okay? No." I couldn't hold back the tears.

He said, "Today you can refuse anything you don't want. You have choices and some control."

For some reason, that made me feel better. I guess because there was so much out of my control.

First of my many choices.

With a tender voice and holding my hand (I think to let me know we were in this together), he said, "You've been through so much. I think you should let us put you completely under sedation. I think it is best for you and your body. You have already been through too much stress today."

Just at that moment I looked up at my strong, brave husband and asked can he at least be there. You see, being put out would be much easier for me. I already had an IV. I could just get medicine through it, and when I woke, one way or another our son would be here. They had already told us he could come out blue. They didn't want us to see that. I could tell.

The doctor said, "No, he can't. He's not allowed in the operating room while you are out."

I could see the slightly tearful, sad look in his eyes.

"So neither of us will see our son born?"

"No, you won't."

My husband said, "Do what is best for you, Brenda. It is okay."

I thought a minute, as I was so tired, and said, "Well, one of us has to see our son come into the world. Can you handle seeing him, even if he's blue?"

"Of course," my husband said, "I can. If you can do all of this, I can and I will."

I knew he wanted to be there.

I asked the doctor, "What other option do we have?"

"We can inject medicine into your spine to numb your lower body, and you would still be awake."

He reminded me what he thought would be best for me, and I said no.

"My husband wants to be there. I will take one more needle."

I had to get prepared. Nurses were prepping me, and others were preparing the room. I remember the nurse telling me they were putting a catheter in, and I looked at her and said, "No. I don't want one. The doctor said I could refuse whatever I want."

"Well, not this one, sorry."

I wasn't thinking clearly as you can't have surgery without it. I wasn't happy as it was the only thing I said no to. I was getting a little feisty at this point. Since I wasn't being put out, I would be awake for this too. Sitting on a table bent over, don't move, a large needle was inserted into my spine. That was not fun. As a child, I was so terrified of needles, and now look at me today. Adulthood, not fun. I once broke a school nurse's glasses over a shot in the arm. Poor thing, and she was always so sweet. So much preparation. I was not happy, but it needed to be done.

The sterile surgical room. Nurses and doctors in masks and gowns. Their hands washed and ready to go. They put a curtain up so I couldn't see. That's probably a good idea. No one wants to watch themselves get surgery. A nurse at my head, and two nurses with suctions in their hands to try and capture some of the fluid at my feet. My doctor, specialists, I don't remember how many. This was getting real, real fast.

I asked the nurse at my head, "Where is my husband?"

She nervously said, "It's okay, I will go see."

For me, this wasn't happening without him. I went through all this; he was going to be there.

For me, I had a limited view. Lying on my back, curtain drawn, numb from the waist down. The nurse brought my husband in quickly. At least it seemed to me.

He said, "What's wrong? Are you okay?"

I told you, the nurse was nervous, and I think she wanted him there now. She wanted to do her job but wanted him for me. She was not a comforter, I would say. Some people in this life are great at comforting others or saying the right things. One exchange, calmly in my eyes, "Do you know where my husband is?" seemed to invoke a bit of panic for her. Poor thing. This was no place any of us wanted to be that day.

The doctor said, "Okay, it's time, Brenda. We are ready to begin."

I responded, "Okay."

It was life or death here.

He said, "Everyone, ready, all set."

This was all hands and specialists on deck. Sharp, alert, all ready to do their job to their very best of their ability. I'm sure not exactly like this, but we've all been in different situations in life where your senses were heightened. You knew you had to perform at a high level or things weren't going to go well. This was a very heightened situation.

Here we go. All of a sudden, I hear a splash. All that fluid that was making me so miserable yet protecting my son went all over the floor, everywhere. The two nurses with suctions didn't stand a chance. Everyone remained calm, not a sound or movement. They needed to all do their part to get my son out of my body as smoothly and quickly as possible. They told us time was critical. I didn't feel pain but lots of tugging and pressure. It felt strange and scary. All of a sudden, I hear this cry.

Dear God, that's amazing. He must not be blue. I started saying, "Is he okay? What's he look like? Can I see him?"

My husband was trying to watch the doctors, to see our son and talk to me. Poor guy, this was so hard on him too. Before I could see him, they whisked him away. That's not good.

I told myself, "They're doing their job, be calm." I started praying.

The doctor was still working on me. So it was the specialist and nurses at my feet who whisked him away. I told myself that he has a heart defect, club feet, he's five weeks early, and he is going to need all the help he can get. People in the room, the doctor, the nurse, my husband kept asking if I was okay. It was very nice, no offense, but I don't care about me.

I thought, *Is my son okay?* He was out in the world now. It was up to the doctors and nurses and God. But mostly God, as the doctors and nurses wouldn't have any of their talents or gifts without him. None of us would. The doctor had stitched me up, and they were taking me to a room. All I wanted to do is see my son. Everyone to this point had been kind and professional. They all had such empathy for me, my husband, and our son—until now.

I was in a room. My mom and husband were with me. His parents were in the waiting room. I should say this all took place at Hurley Hospital in Flint, Michigan. I had an older nurse who was less than gentle and not empathetic in my opinion at all. As she was taking care of things, I asked to see my son. Then, in a while, I asked again. The pain medicine was wearing off, and I was asking when I could get pain medicine.

She was snappy and said, "When it gets here."

Okay, lady, you haven't been almost cut in half today. My mom and husband knew this was not going well. My mother had worked in a hospital for years as an aid. She, I'm sure, wanted to step in. After all, I am her child. Time went by, and still no pain medicine. She would finally call down to see where it is, wherever down is. I was getting angry with her and her lack of compassion. We asked once again if I could see my baby. My husband had seen him being born; I needed to see him.

The nurse finally said, "To see him, you will have to get in a wheelchair and be taken to him."

With no pain medicine onboard? I was really hurting by now. Yes, really that's the deal. I'm sure she thought, *That will shut her up.*

I said, "Then get the chair. What are you waiting for? Why are you still here?"

I was done with her nonsense. That is not how one should be as a nurse. I told my mom, "She is in the wrong profession." The lack of pain medicine, the rough way she yanked the catheter out, not seeing my child, waiting and waiting for even a drink felt almost like punishment.

In came the wheelchair. I was determined to see my son. The doctor had already told me a team from Detroit Children's hospital was on their way to pick him up and take him there.

I told my husband that I have to see him. What if he dies on the way? I try to have an abundance of compassion for others still today. Until you've lived the journey someone is going through, walked in their shoes, please don't pretend to know what they are living through. You don't. You can't. You can only have compassion, kindness, love, and consideration for them.

The pain was unlike anything I've felt before in my life. Remember, I lived through a lot of pain with my car accident and still do today. This was different pain. A little like my arm the day of the accident but more. Crazy, I know. Getting from the bed to the wheelchair was excruciating. I was determined to see my son.

"I'm doing it," I told my husband. *It would take a Mack truck to stop me*, I thought.

I was in the wheelchair, and the nurse was rolling me out of the room. And, *smack*, she ran the wheelchair into the doorway. It was hard and felt on purpose. I told her to let go now, and my husband took the wheelchair. I was done with her. "Get a new nurse in here, Mom. She's done."

Another nurse showed us to our son. So small, so frail. So innocent. Born into this cruel reality. I wanted to instantly take his pain, his place. Dear Jesus, help him, help us. He had a full head of dark hair and beautiful blue eyes like his daddy. In an isolette, unable to hold him, to comfort him.

"Be strong, little man. Mama will be right behind you, and Daddy is going with you."

We couldn't stay long. More for the doctors and nurses to do before he leaves for Detroit Children's.

Back to the room. Medicine is finally here. Thank you, God. I wish it would have been here sooner, but I will take it. Please give it to me quickly. Another nurse came in.

"Let's give it to you through your IV before you try to get back in bed."

Aw, compassion and kindness. That is something that will never go unnoticed. Amazing. Thank you, God.

Back in the bed, pain less now. Physical pain less but certainly not emotional pain.

I thought, *At least I had seen my son*. He was still alive, and he was perfect to me. There was a fighting chance now. A long road ahead but a chance. The right call was made by the doctors. I'm sure they were relieved to hand over the baton as they say. Plans were made.

"Detroit Children's is here. He's ready to go," the nurse said. "Don't worry, ma'am, they will bring your son by the room so you can see him before they leave."

What? I was almost boiling over. I wanted that nurse punished, written up, fired. She is a terrible nurse.

My husband and his parents will go to Detroit Children's, and my mom would stay with me. I needed her at this point. I didn't want any nurse to touch me, compassionate or not. Anger had set in. I wanted to be with my son and husband. The new nurse was kind. She shut the door and left me alone with my mom. Smart move, I have to say. No more pokes, prods, catheters, cutting, needles, leave me alone. I referenced earlier this day being the best and worst day of my life up to that point. I'm sure you can see that. My son was here, still alive, fighting for his life; and then there's the rest of the day.

Thank God for Detroit Children's

I finally had some peace and quiet with my mom and with God. My husband finally called me.

"We made it. He's here. They are working on him, but his color is good. He's still fighting, just like you asked him to. Please try to rest. I'm here with him. I'm worried about you."

Of course, I said, "Don't worry about me, I'm okay."

He had enough to worry about. To be honest I was a little worried about me too. Thank goodness, I had my mom. It was a long night, to say the least. I just wanted to be with my son whatever it took. I did have a nice nurse that night. She mostly left us alone. That was the right choice.

Morning came, a new day with new challenges for me and for our son. As you can probably imagine all I wanted was to get out of the hospital and get to Detroit Children's. I told the nurse.

She said, "Oh, not today, it is much too soon."

You see my C-section was anything but normal. I was cut very wide, and she said, "The only way to keep you with enough pain relief is to keep you here with IV medication."

No, not happening.

"Please call my doctor. I need to speak with him."

She said, "Okay, I will. No problem."

She was probably thinking, *I will let him tell her no.*

We waited, and what seemed a long time, he finally came into my room.

He asked, "How are you?"

"Fine," I said. I was anything but fine. "I need to get out of here."

He looked at me and said, "I'm not going to stop you."

He knew all the details of my journey. He also knew my son was still alive and no one knew for sure how long that would be. He told me he would give me the strongest pain medicine he could, but he warned me, "It won't completely cover your pain."

I looked at him with tears and said, "Let's go. Please hurry up."

Again, arrangements were made. My husband's mother would stay with him. My mom would get a change of clothes, this she needed, and our neighbor was taking care of the animals at home. My husband's father was coming to get me and drive me to see my son.

The ride there was tough. We hit a couple bumps, and I thought, *Okay, this is going to be harder than I thought.* It was a fairly quiet ride. He told me he actually looks pretty good. Really, what can you say? The trip seemed to take forever when really it's only a little over an hour.

My husband came outside and got me in a wheelchair. Transitioning wasn't fun at all. He was gentle and did his best. I was finally going to be with my son. The nurses and doctors were all very nice, and he was in a quiet room in his small isolette.

By the way, we named him Cody Joseph Cain. His dad's initials were CC, and his would be no different. His middle name was named after my husband's uncle. He had heart trouble and had died after being in an emergency surgery for his heart. They couldn't stop the bleeding. No time to take him off his blood thinners. His middle name was Joseph. He was a wonderful man. It only seemed fitting to make our son's middle name Joseph too. They had a sign made with his full name on it on his isolette. It's amazing, the feelings rushing through my body. He's here, he's finally here. Aw, his poor little feet. They are not too bad. They said they can be fixed. His dark, full head of hair was thick. His blue eyes, he looks like his daddy. Would he know me? Would my touch soothe him now the way I tried to soothe him in the womb? Oh my gosh, what's next? We knew he needed heart surgery as soon as possible. I need to get to know everyone here. He is no ordinary baby, and I was his mama. Just mama at this point, no mama bear needed at this time.

They needed to feed him. He was small but was born five pounds and thirteen ounces, so that wasn't bad for five weeks early. His breathing was fast at times and shallow other times, so this was challenging. They assured me he was doing great. I tried feeding him, so did his dad. It was clear he knew us. He would settle down and look at us with those big beautiful eyes. I used to call him my little man. I told him not even a grown man should have to handle what he was going to have to go through and especially not as a baby. Little did I know, this was as calm as it was going to get for the next 8.5 months. The machines, the noises, the pokes, the watching his heart rate and oxygen. There's so much now, heart surgery. How bad is this going to get? I kept reminding myself he is here, we still have a fighting chance, and fight he did, and so did we. I would love to tell you heart surgery went great and we went home and lived happily ever after. Unfortunately, I cannot. Life is full of color. There is so much more. I wish things were black and white or cut and dry as they say, but they were not.

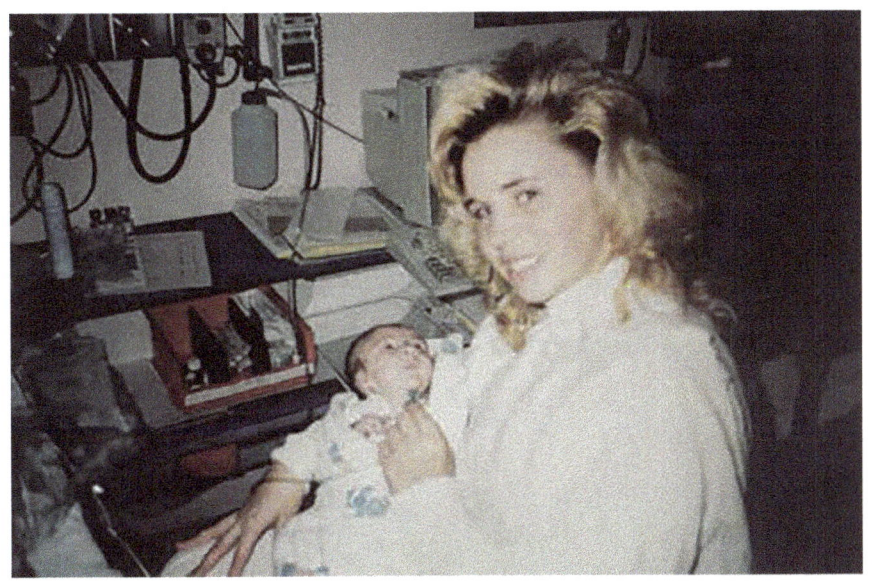

Brenda and Cody

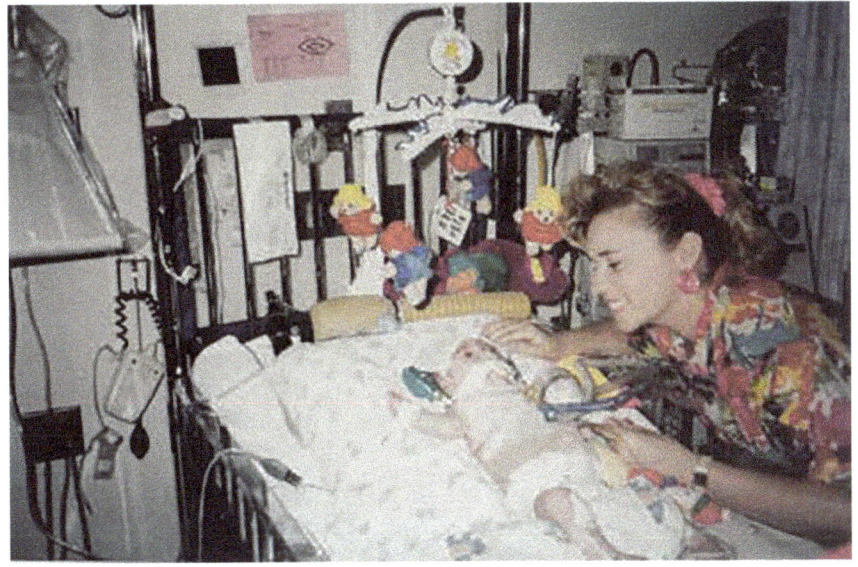

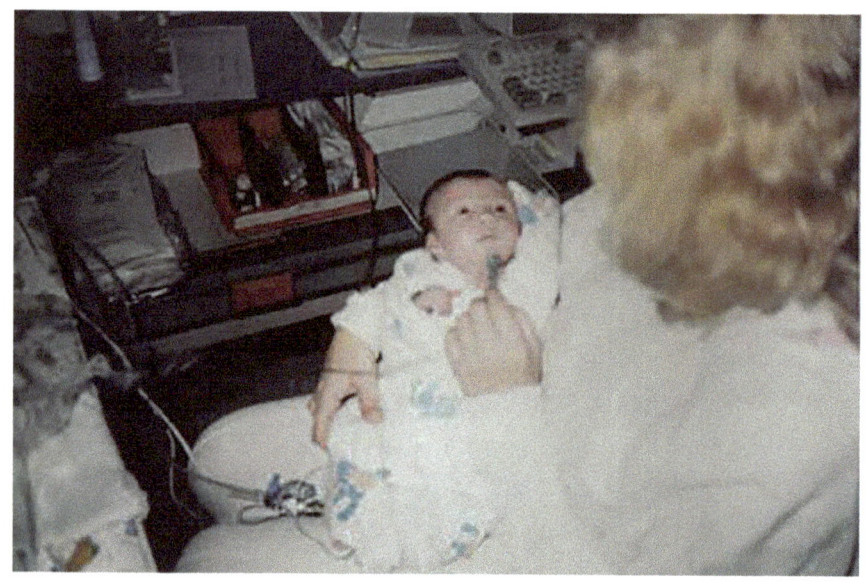

Heart Surgery

One thing we all knew we had to keep him healthy and as strong as he could be to face heart surgery. We were so careful with gloves, masks, gowns, etc. There was a nasty virus in the hospital, and a few children had it. It was called RSV. It stands for respiratory syncytial virus infection. He absolutely cannot get this. Some don't survive this virus alone, let alone a preemie with heart issues. Thinking back, I don't think I shared his actual diagnosis from the hairline piece of his twenty-second chromosome being missing. They called it DiGeorge syndrome. It was named after the doctor who discovered it. With DiGeorge syndrome, there could be a number of things: heart problems, club feet, immune disorder. I haven't gotten to that yet. Cody had a suppressed immune deficiency as well. So getting RSV could be easy for him to catch. With DiGeorge syndrome, we were told there can be so many different things that can come with it. They range from cleft palate, behavior problems, low calcium in blood, a number of things. They can have certain facial features, wideset or narrow eyes, low-set ears, a groove in the upper lip. Cody had none of these. Breathing problems, yes. We had that at least at this point. Speech issues, nasal sounding, poor muscle tone… you get the gist. Unfortunately, we had the big ones: heart defect, breathing, and immune deficiency. The rest we really didn't think so. His beautiful blue eyes were perfectly set. His cry was normal, not nasal sounding at all, and for a little guy, he would sure get his hands and arms involved when they were doing things he didn't like. He would kick his strong legs.

His nurses would say to me, "Mom, he sure isn't happy with me."

I could already see that.

His daddy would say, "He might look like me, but he has his mama's fight."

Even tiny, with some broken parts, he let everyone know he would have his say. If they messed with him too much at one time, they were going to know it.

As careful as we all were, well, let's face it, one of the nurses, aids, or doctors, in my opinion, must not have been. My husband and I were careful almost to the paranoid extent. With all the monitors and machines, Cody was watched carefully. We noticed his breathing had become more labored, and his heart rate was up quite a bit. When you are in a neonatal ICU with just our fragile little man and one other baby, when something was off, things moved quickly. Breathing treatments, more oxygen, blood test.

The doctor said, "We don't know how, and I'm so sorry, but your son has RSV."

This can't be. He's so small and frail, and we need heart surgery as soon as possible. At this point one of our worst fears had come to fruition. What do we do? Dear God, why? What now?

The doctor told us, "Now your son will be in for the fight of his life. In case you haven't noticed, he already is. We will have to see if he can survive this before we talk heart surgery. He can't go into heart surgery with RSV. He just can't. His heart and lungs just won't take it." Again, the doctor said, "I'm so sorry."

To be frank, that doesn't help us at all. I needed something to take away from the doctor. Something positive I could hold on to. I pushed the doctor to give me signs, good or bad. What do I look for? What is too high of a heart rate or too low of an oxygen level? Coloring, let's talk coloring. I told him give me everything straight. No sugarcoating it. If my son was in more of a fight for his life than he already had been, I need facts—cold, hard facts, all of them.

I told you, the doctors got to know me. I wasn't taking no or "we have this" for answers. I was focused, clear-minded, and hanging on to his every word. He knew that. He could see that.

Out of my mouth, when he said the nurses here will watch him close, be extra careful, and consult me if he changes at all, I responded, "Oh, will they? No offense, Doctor, but someone wasn't careful enough. Things needed to be tightened up here."

He assured me they would be, and I assured him I was going to see to it they were. Not with rudeness or anger, just with laser focus. This is the time I began to really study my son, the machines, the nurses too for that matter. Any changes in my son were critical and crucial. His life, or death, were hanging in the balance. Leaving him even to eat was a struggle. I wouldn't at all unless all those machine numbers were in the safe limit and even then only for a very short trip to the restroom or for a few bites of food I didn't even want. I was reminded more than once to take care of my own health. I had to eat to keep up my strength. My strength, who cares? Well, I knew I had to if I was going to continue this journey however short or long it was going to be.

Let's not forget here that it had only been three or four days since my C-section, where they literally cut me open from hip to hip. I was also in pain, but the laser focus wasn't on me. I told my husband when he was getting me up from bed after forcing me to lie down that I had been hurting now more than I was right after the surgery. I thought maybe this happens with healing. My husband being the smart, caring man he is would lay a folded sheet under me when I would lie down because getting up was so painful. He would lift the sheet on both sides of me to lift me. That was a blessing. The first time I tried to get up without it, I thought, *This is going to be so much harder than I imagined.* Thank goodness he thought of the sheet. He could see the pain all over my face, though I tried to keep most if it inside.

The pain right at the incision site was definitely getting worse, a lot worse. It appeared red and swollen a bit too. I decided to consult my doctor. He told me to take a warm bath with just water to see if it would soothe it at all. Unfortunately for me, that did not work. I consulted my doctor again. He wanted to see me ASAP. His office was over an hour from my son. I did not want to do that, but he insisted. He wanted me to come now. He mentioned a possible infection and that could be dangerous to my health. One step at a time. These days

I was dealing with things one step, one hour, one minute for that matter at a time.

Arriving at the doctor's office, I'm not sure how I looked, but the staff, though there was a full waiting room, took me right back and put me in a room. I had told my doctor the stress of the situation with my son and I wasn't going to be away from him long. They were kind and swift. He had communicated, and they were following through. His nurse said he will be right in after she took a look. He has a procedure scheduled, so he will have to be quick. He came right in and took a quick look. No infection. I didn't think so.

He said, "You are having an allergic reaction to the metal staples we closed your incision with. It's rare, but it does happen."

I had never had staples before. Stitches, yes, but no staples.

I said, "What now? Can you give me some medicine? I need to go. I need to be with my son."

Well, unfortunately not. Once again, why do things have to be so hard? Can one thing be easy? Of course not. In stressful situations in life like mine, all of your senses are heightened, and we definitely did not need any more issues. This had to be taken care of. No pill will fix this. I hadn't thought of an allergic reaction. I think of them as something that hives up or itches a lot. This area was red, swollen, and burned a lot. Almost like something very hot was in my skin. It had gotten to the very uncomfortable point, or I wouldn't have been there at all.

The doctor said, "These have to come out right away."

What? Seriously.

He said, "My nurse would be right in to take them out. I can't. I have a procedure. It will be fine, she can do it."

"Will it hurt?"

"It will hurt, I'm sorry about that."

I could feel his frustration and sadness for me and for our son. In came the nurse with this tray and tools.

"Lie back," she said. "I will do my best to get this done as quickly as I can."

Preparing yourself for something like this, how do you do that? No idea, honestly. The doctor had said there were stitches inside as well that would dissolve and they would use steri-strips. I would need to be extra careful, but things should heal, and I should be okay. The click sound the tool made when pulling them out one at a time wasn't bad, but the burning was like someone was sticking me with a hot knife. The nurse did just a few while I had tears streaming down my face.

I said, "This is cruel. It is really hurting me. Can I have something to numb me?"

She stepped out of the room and asked the doctor, but he was right in the middle of the scheduled procedure.

"Unfortunately not," she said. She pulled a couple more, and with tears in her eyes, she said, "I'm sorry, I can't do this."

Some were giving her trouble coming out, and she knew she was hurting me a lot. She left the room in tears.

Just a few minutes went by, and she came back in. She had gathered herself. Later, I found out the doctor told her he couldn't do it, that she had no choice and to go finish the job. She was calm, gathered, and a bit scared looking.

I told her, "I have to get back to my son. Yes, it hurts, but it has to be done. Please, just get it over with."

With that she knew I had gone into fight mode myself. I guess the look of determination, pain, and frustration did the trick. She pulled them a little harder and faster. Slow wasn't any kinder. I told her, "Let's go." Mama bear was coming out, and I wasn't planning on missing any more time with my son than absolutely necessary.

It was done. We both shed a lot of tears. She was with me through every visit and every ultrasound herself. She knew the reality I was living in—in more detail than most. When it was over, she gave me a big hug and told me how sorry she was. I met quite a few compassionate people on our hospital journey.

"Any paperwork?" I said. "Or can I just go?"

"Go, be with your son, I will keep you both in my prayers."

That stopped me. "Do you mean that?" I said. "I would really appreciate that."

Not many know what to say. That was the right thing that day, at least for me. The hug; the "I'm sorry, truly" tearfully; and the prayers. That's what we all need: comfort and prayer. And we need God.

Back to the hospital as quickly as possible. Things were somewhat stable when I left. Please, God, it has been a long day, let him be okay when I return. The evening was fairly quiet. He was holding strong against the virus. He had lost a few ounces, but they said it was to be expected fighting this. He didn't have much to lose at five pounds and thirteen ounces. We needed every ounce.

The next morning's light brought trouble. There always seems to be a calm right before a storm. This was going to be no different. At this point, he was still fighting, hanging on for dear life, but his heart appeared to be struggling more now. Everyone rushing around, doing all they could. They told us they were calling the heart surgeons as it was their call. They came fairly quickly. I remember being surprised. They definitely weren't in surgery at the moment. There were two pediatric heart surgeons at Detroit Children's at the time we were there: Dr. Hakimi and Dr. Walters. Dr. Hakimi was older. I don't know why that gave me comfort. I guess, in my mind, the more years the more surgeries. And experience in life is the greatest teacher no book can ever teach. Dr. Walters was experienced as well. They were both amazing men. Dr. Hakimi came and assessed our boy. We stayed to meet him for a bit and then stepped out to let him work, think, assess. Whatever he needed to do, to focus only on our son. We don't need him to be worried about us right now. I saw many times in the hospital where doctors were not only dealing with emergencies with patients but with family too. In my mind, as hard as it was, he needed to focus only on my son and fixing him. Discussions were had. He told us he would consult with his colleague and get back to us. Cody was still breathing, and his heart beating, though it was labored.

"Nothing surgery wise would happen at this very minute. We will be in touch with you very soon. This is not an ideal situation with this RSV to go into surgery."

We knew that. We were holding our breath about that at times without even knowing it.

Later that day, a nurse told us Dr. Walters wanted to meet with us. We met in his office with the door closed for privacy. He was a very gentle, soft-spoken man. Both were actually. He introduced himself, and we all sat down. He explained in great detail what was wrong with our son's heart and what needed to be done.

You see, our son had truncus arteriosus. It's a rare type of heart defect where a single blood vessel comes out of the right and left ventricles instead of two normal vessels being the pulmonary artery and aorta. On top of that, he had pulmonary atresia. This is a form of heart defect where the pulmonary valve does not form properly. Also, there can be a hole between the bottom two chambers of the heart called a ventricular defect. He explained our son had that as well.

I give you the names and terminology because I'm trying to help you see the clear picture. It was intimidating to say the least. He told us our son's heart was the size of a walnut. A walnut? Now there's a visual.

"That's so small," I said.

He finished explaining everything. He also told us we couldn't wait much longer regardless the RSV condition.

"What do you mean regardless?"

He was giving us the cold, hard facts.

"Your son's heart is failing. He's losing weight. He will die without the surgery. And to be perfectly honest, he could not make it through the surgery."

He told us it would be several hours long. He also told us he would be put on an ECHMO machine.

"What is that?"

It's a heart-and-lung bypass machine."

Okay, we're processing. We are not doctors, but we're listening, hanging on every word. After all the technical verbiage was over, we set a date. They wanted to set him up for the best success possible. It would be early morning, as it would take all day. Not tomorrow, but hopefully the next day.

"You should go home. Let family know. Gather your things, rest. If he survives this, it will be a long road to healing."

Okay, we understood, and we thanked him for trying to save our son's life.

As we prepared to leave, with the room finally quiet, I looked at him and said, "How do we do this? I don't know how to do this. This is my baby." I thought, *I want to take his pain, take his place. Please, God, pick me, not my son. I can take it. He's a baby.*

He looked at me for a minute. I'm sure he was thinking on his response.

"You know I'm going to share a personal story with you. I usually don't, but I just feel I should," he said. "I lost a son at almost two years of age. He was born with Down's syndrome. He had many problems over the two years he was in our life. I became a heart surgeon to save people, and I couldn't save my own son."

Finally, someone who literally does understand. Most people will say "I'm sorry" and "I understand" in situations, but he really did. This poor man had lost his son. I saw the pain in his eyes while telling us. He also told us before he starts every surgery he prays over his patients. He does? Thank you, God. I needed this. He also gave us a scripture I've hung on to: *Psalm 139:13–16* says,

> *God you created my innermost being, you knit me together in my mother's womb. I am fearfully and wonderfully made. My frame was not hidden from you. I was woven together. Your eyes saw my unformed body. All the days ordained for me were written in your book before I ever came to be.*

Only God knew how many days, months, or years our son had on this earth. He told us he would do his best, and God would be there with him. It's hard to explain. Nothing was different about our situation, yet everything was different. He's human just like you and me. No matter our training or title, our days, our life and death are not in our control. God himself is the giver and taker of life.

I felt a weight lifting. I can't control this or will this. What was meant to be will be.

We went back and talked to the nurses who were with our son and the neonatal doctor. We took Dr. Walters's advice. We went home. Our son was on twenty-four-hour watch, and they assured us they had him. We made our phone calls, gathered our things, and made plans for the animals, tried to rest, calling the hospital a few times. He was hanging in there.

The next day we went back to the hospital. We made arrangements to stay at the Ronald McDonald house for a while. Friends, the Ronald McDonald house is such a blessing to so many, and it was to us. If you get a chance to help out with your time or resources, it is much needed. It certainly was for us.

Day of surgery arrived. We had prayer over our now four-pound-and-thirteen-ounces little man. At this point, he had lost a whole pound and still had RSV. The struggle was real, raw, and unlike anything I can even explain. There was a small round door on his isolette we could open to touch him or talk to him. I touched his tiny hand and softly rubbed his arm. At times, he would hold my pinky finger lightly. Today, as I was asking him to be strong, as I did so many times, he squeezed my finger. I almost lost it. It was as if he was saying, "I hear you, Mom. I've got this." I know that was one of those gifts from God I speak about. I will never forget it.

Off to surgery they whisked him. The nurse said, "Mama, we have to go."

I wanted to fall on the floor in a heap and sob, but I didn't. My husband took my arm, and my feet were moving, a nurse showing us where we would wait. Our parents were there, and my sister and brother-in-law came as well. We were so thankful they did. Being alone would have made the hours move even slower, drag on more than they already were.

How doctors work on a human heart as small as a walnut, I have no idea. I say it's God's hands guiding them, working through them.

Months later, my husband and I gave the heart doctors a plaque for their office with their names and praying hands on it, saying, "Two perfect examples of God's work here on earth." In my eyes, they sure were.

The hours dragged on, 13.5 to be exact.

The doctors told us, "Don't worry if you don't see us for hours, at least ten. Worry if you see us too soon."

Together with family, we would remind each other, "Remember they said not to worry if it takes longer and worry if it doesn't. That means we're still working, and he's still fighting."

"Okay, I will try and be patient." But all the while, I was screaming inside at times. Tell me if my son is okay, even an update. It wouldn't have helped. Their hands were right there where they needed to be. I knew that.

Thirteen and a half hours later, Dr. Walters came out to get us so they could talk to us privately. They had a room next door. Our family waited.

They said, "Well, it was rough." They looked exhausted. They tried several times, but his chest wouldn't close.

"What does that mean?" I said.

They said it was left cracked open with sterile bandages over it. He has a tree of IVs in him. Eleven to be exact. Eleven IVs, oh dear God, and an open chest.

The doctors said, "He's still here."

I said, "What next?"

They said, "Time would tell. Hopefully, swelling will go down in a couple days, and we can go in and close it."

The scene was like a battlefield for our son. So swollen, so small. I did not leave his side. I had to be forced to eat and drink. Okay, but here in his room. I'm not leaving. I would sing softly in his ear and pray for him, begging him to fight.

"Mama can't lose you, little man."

I studied every sound, machine, anything I could. I noticed he was in pain, I could tell. I told the nurses. I didn't get a quick enough response, so I asked to see the doctor. I told him he is in pain.

He said, "He is on a lot of pain medication. I can't give him more."

I explained to him, "I take almost double for pain medicine, and he is my son. I'm telling you, it is not enough."

At this point, my son was shaking. He looked at me.

I said, "Trust me, he needs more. Will it hurt him?"

"No, it won't."

They gave him more, and it was some better, but he wasn't out of pain.

The doctor came back and looked at me. No words were spoken. He looked at my son, and he instructed the nurse to give him more. He added a different one. As we all know, some medicines work for us, and some don't. Finally, his little body wasn't shaking. He had a clear bandage on the top with bandages under it soaked in what appeared to be an iodine solution. There could be no infection. He would never survive that.

Two days passed. The doctors told us it was time. They needed to close his chest. If they waited much longer, they risked infection.

"Okay, this is it, little man," I told him. "They are going to help you. You fight, and Dad and I will be right here waiting for you."

The doctors told us, "If we are successful, it won't take too long."

We waited, but I was so anxious. I told my husband that it was taking too long. I paced in the waiting room, my anxiety growing.

Out came Dr. Hakimi. He said that it was not going well. I knew it. My whole body knew it. As he was trying to talk to us, over the loud speaker came, "Dr. Hakimi, to the OR stat." He got up and said, "I'm sorry," and literally ran.

Panic, for me, set in. Don't touch me. I didn't want to be touched or distracted as if my body was preparing for a blow.

Time passed, too much time. Over an hour and a half. My mind raced. Was this good news? Was our boy still here? I was praying without ceasing.

Finally, Dr. Walters came out to speak with us. You see, they were both working on our son. He took a deep breath, and with a worried look, he said, "His chest didn't close. When we almost finally had it, he went into cardiac arrest. We had to physically massage his heart for forty-five minutes before it started beating again."

Yes, their human hands inside my son's body, helping his heart to keep beating. They never gave up. It wasn't time for Cody to leave this earth, not yet.

Physically drained, he said, "His chest has to stay open for now. We're in shaky territory at best here. We will take this day by day."

The next few days were torture. They had so many IVs in him, and seeing him lying there so helpless, it will age you, my friend. At this point, it felt like days took months. Watching his pain and unable to do anything about it. They kept him sedated. It was best for him. I still held his little hand and sang to him and kissed his sweet head. The doctors told us they weren't sure if any damage had been done to his brain while he was down. With all he and we were dealing with, we hoped not. You see, he was small and not lacking problems, but he was alert before surgery. His eyes would follow you, the squeeze of his hand. He knew when we were there. We prayed he would still know us if he ever made it out of this disaster. That's what it felt like. So many things going wrong when we needed every one of them to go right so badly. At this point, they told us we were setting records. Our son's chest had been open too long, and as far as they know from past history, no one with their chest open this long had avoided infection.

The heart surgeons told us, "We absolutely can't wait any longer. We have to close his chest. Tomorrow is the day. We want you to know, if we can't close it, your son will die."

My reaction was quick. "What do you mean? You already tried several times. What makes you believe tomorrow will be any different? We waited this long, he is still here. What chance does he have?"

You get the idea. I needed hard facts. Only there weren't any to be given. The unknown, oh, how I hate the unknown, especially now, with our son's life hanging in the balance. It's here, right here. When I talk about it being too hard for us to humanly handle, it is way too much. If God didn't carry me, friend, I couldn't have moved. Freezing time is something I still say today. At times in life, we all wish we could freeze time. I sure did that day. My son was still alive and fighting. That meant there was still hope. Hope that our son had a future, any kind of future, and for however long, whatever that looked like. Say goodbye to my son tomorrow? I refuse. I am absolutely not ready. God, you brought him into this world. I haven't even been able to hold him. Not tomorrow. I needed more time. Time, that's something I've taken for granted more than once in my life. I think we all have.

Almost numb, we headed back to the Ronald McDonald house later that evening after spending precious time with our son. In a time like this, there are really no words left to say that we hadn't already said. We tried to get some sleep. Exhausted and knowing the heaviness morning's light would bring, I really tried to sleep. Just to shut my mind off if only for a while. Thank God I got a little bit of sleep. Not a lot. Waking in the night to call and check on our little man.

The one thing about dark times, light always comes in one form or another. The morning light had come. Both of our parents had come. Our pastor had come. All to bring love, light, and support. We needed that today more than ever. The heart doctors were ready to go. We tried not to say goodbye to our son, just "see you soon, little man." He got his mommy's fight speech. We had prayer. It was up to God now. I knew his doctors never began without prayer as well. I knew God was in that room. *John 1:5* says, "*The light shines in the darkness and the darkness has not overcome it. God is light and in him there is no darkness at all.*" Our family and our pastor and his wife were with us praying. They were helping not to let the darkness overcome us that day. When someone is struggling, be the light for them whenever you can. I knew if our son did not survive today, he would be with God, in his light. No more pain or suffering. That gave me comfort. However, I also knew I would be here on earth without him, and that would surely kill me.

Our son survived the closing of his chest that day. I think it was surprising to all of us. We had gotten our miracle. He wasn't out of the woods yet, not by a long shot, but his chest was closed. Our prayers were answered that day. You see, none of us knew what was going to happen that day. None of us except God. He knew Cody's time on earth wasn't over, not today. If nothing else he looked better. That large iodine patch was gone. The incision remained, scary but closed. Healing, he needed rest and healing. His numbers weren't great: heart rate, etc. But day after day he fought, and by the grace of God, he was still here. With having so many IVs already in his short life, his veins were used up, at least the usual avenues were. He kept blowing veins and needing new routes. Over the course of our hospital stay, they had to get creative with our son, and by creative, I meant almost cruel.

I remember one day they were having trouble with his IV again.

"Mom," they said, "I think you are going to want to step out of the room."

"Why?" I asked.

It wasn't shift change, and I have watched so many IV attempts: arms, legs, feet.

"Where are you putting this one?"

"I'm so sorry," they said. "We need to try this one in his head."

"His head? Isn't this becoming a bit much?"

"Yes," the nurse said. "But the next step is a central line, and that means another surgery. We are trying not to do that."

Okay, I see. "It's okay," I said. "He is much calmer when I'm here, correct?"

"Yes, ma'am, much calmer."

"Okay, then. I am staying. If my son has to go through this, the very least I can do is stay and comfort him."

She pushed. "But, ma'am, we have to shave the area. And the head can be a difficult spot to get an IV. This will make him very unhappy."

I told her, "I'm okay. Have you seen me even flinch or lose it?"

"No, ma'am."

"Okay, let's move on. I'm not going anywhere."

She said, "If you cry, it's understandable. We hate doing this ourselves, so we can't imagine how much you hate watching."

I said, "Can you imagine how much my son hates getting this? If he can do it, I can do it. Let's all do our best. Don't be nervous because I'm here. Just do your best."

While they were preparing, I prayed softly out loud for God to guide them, for Cody to be still, and for strength for us all.

She checked his little head for veins. He already didn't like it.

I whispered in his ear, "You've got this, little man." I started singing to him. I remembered how much it relaxed me and calmed the room when the doctor sang to me during my cordocentesis procedure. I think that's why I sang to him, especially in the really difficult times. I held his little crooked feet and rubbed his thin legs all the while singing.

No, we didn't get it on the first time or the second. The third time was a charm. He did very well through all the shavings and pokes.

The nurses said, "Thank you, this would have been so much worse for all of us without you."

I knew the presence of God was in that room that day. I could feel it. After all, it was his strength I was relying on.

When it was all over, the nurse said, "We will leave him alone for a while, he needs rest, and his heart rate needs to settle down."

Though it did not go as high as they thought it might. When it was all over, his heart rate was down, and he was asleep. I went to the restroom. I was alone that day, no family, no husband. I was alone many days. Many of us moms were. Thank God that restroom was empty. I didn't have to be strong for anyone else. I had a good cry that day. It was needed. I remembered my mother at the hospital with my dad while in his coma having a good cry. At times in life we all need a good, ugly cry, and I sure needed one that day. One brokenhearted mama.

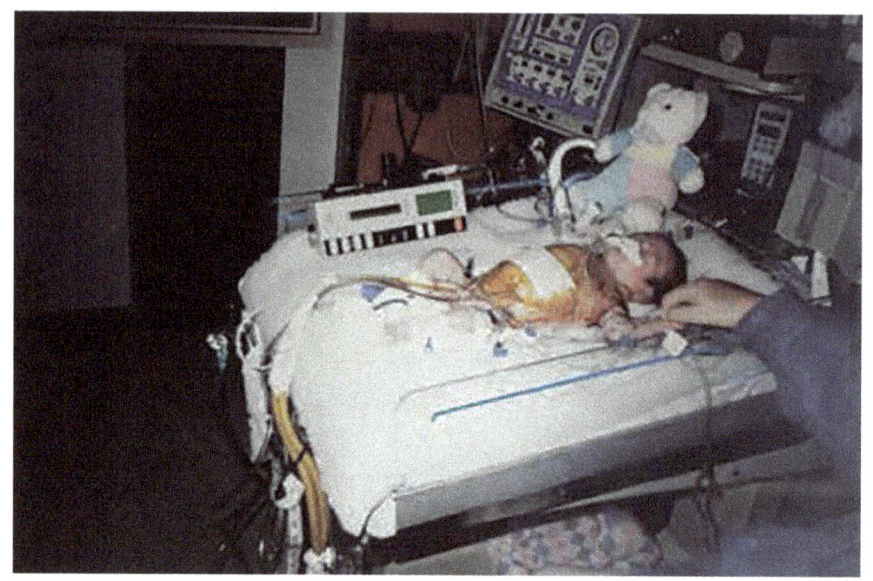

Cody "open chest" after heart surgery

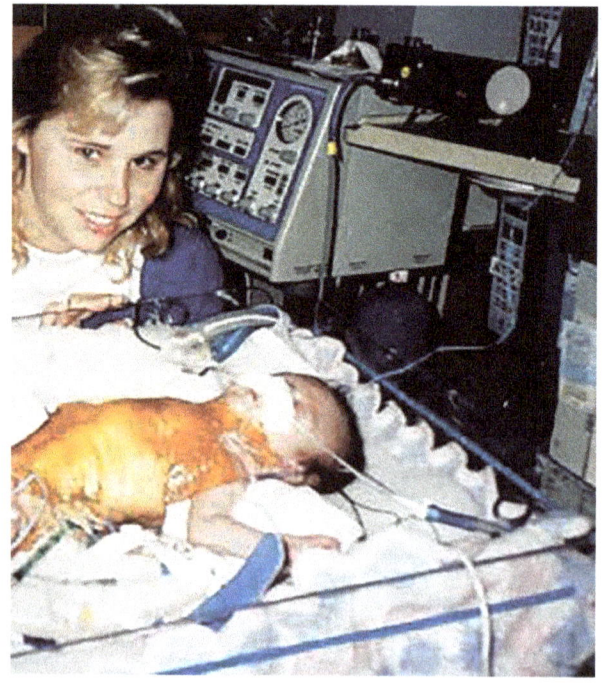

A Healthy Window

One day, while in the cafeteria getting something to drink during shift change, I met a wonderful woman with her little girl— blond hair, so cute, dressed to the nines, as they say. They were both happy. You could see her motherly love all over her face. I asked her why they were there at the hospital that day.

She said with a sad face, "My daughter needs heart surgery." She explained they needed to repair a hole in her heart. She told me they had scheduled it twice before, but her daughter kept getting a cold. They were there today to get a checkup and hopefully get it scheduled. They wanted to get it over with and get it behind them. I understood that more than she could ever know. Her daughter was almost a year old now, and the doctors told her it needed to be done soon. We chatted awhile. I told her my son had heart surgery and how much I loved the heart surgeons. She said they seemed really nice, that she liked them too. I did not tell her about my son's three-surgery open-chest nightmare. I didn't think she needed to hear that. Her daughter was born with Down's syndrome, like Dr. Walters' child that he lost. She didn't need to know that either. She needed to focus on the good. I knew that. There can be so much bad. She had almost a year at home with her little girl. Oh, how I envied her. I would love to have my little man at home with me, even if just for a while, or even one snuggling, normal day. She must have been able to see that I looked a little weary.

She said, "Are you okay? Is your son okay?"

I told her I was okay and my son was still here fighting. I thanked her for asking.

We seemed to have an instant connection.

I saw her about a week later in the cafeteria again, of all places. She was back for results of the test they had taken at the last appointment. They told her if everything looked good they would go ahead and schedule heart surgery ASAP. They had been looking for a healthy window for her daughter. They already felt like she was getting too big. It was time, they told her. We chatted awhile. It was nice. I was alone most days at the hospital. My husband had to work; my mom had to work. It was lonely at times. Thank God my husband would come for lunch almost every day. He says that was the only time he could get me to leave except for some much needed sleep. I did not have many visitors. My siblings were five hours away, and to tell you the truth, I'm sure people found it hard to visit. What do they say to me? I will tell you the truth here: visit your friends and/or loved ones. I know it's hard. I visited my father and my grandparents. Treat others as normal as possible. They are still the same person you knew before the situation they are in at the time. They like the same food, talk, and sound the same. Show up for them, even though it's hard for you. Imagine how hard it is for them. Say anything. Say sorry. Hug them. Stay awhile with them. If they need a good cry, let them use your shoulder. Don't disappear. If you can't visit, send cards. Just show up however you can. Send a gift card for food. See if they need help at their home or with their pets. I might be making a strong point here. I am intending to. I've been told in the past by more than one person they didn't know what to do, so they did nothing. Even the wrong thing, if that's what they were thinking, would still be showing they cared. This point was really sad to me and hurt more than they knew. My husband's grandparents told us they usually bought a bond for each of their great-grandchildren.

We thought, *Great. That's so nice.*

They said, "However, they didn't know if our son was going to make it or not, so they were waiting to see."

I loved his grandparents so much, and they meant no harm. This is one time, however, I would say, "Don't do this." Nothing is better in this case for sure, at least for me. They were good people and loved their family and God. They just at times said some things some of us wouldn't. They would never have wanted to hurt us.

I was in the waiting room again one day, the same waiting room I spoke about early on in the book, with the glass windows, and I saw the mother I had met in the cafeteria out in the hall. I went out and said hello. She let me know her daughter was in surgery as we were speaking. She was worried, stressed, and definitely anxious. She couldn't just sit in that small surgical waiting room. Oh, I knew the one. I sat there the first time for 13.5 hours. You can go stir crazy for sure. I asked her if she would like to sit and chat with me for a few minutes. She liked that idea. She went back to the surgical waiting room to let the volunteer at the desk know where she would be. There was always a volunteer at a desk to help you or update you. Nowadays, they have electronic boards so people can keep track of their loved ones. The aid would let her know when her daughter was in recovery. It would still be a while according to the doctor's estimate. We were having such a nice visit; however, it ended very abruptly. We were sitting facing the hallway so we could see the aid coming if needed, though she hadn't planned on staying long. Just to pass a little time and talk with another mama who knew what she was feeling and going through. I was so happy to do that for her, and as I said earlier, we had a quick connection. She had family in the other waiting room; however, she didn't need to be strong for me. She could be real, share her fear with me. It's nice when you meet someone who's been where you are; they can instantly relate.

Coming down the hall was Dr. Walters.

She said, "Why are you here and not in surgery?" She jumped up and rushed toward him.

I could see her through the glass, and now I could hear her yelling.

"No, no, this wasn't supposed to happen. We didn't have to do this today. What did you do? How could this happen? You were supposed to fix her heart."

Her body bent over in tears, blaming him, as if it were all his fault. He was trying so hard to explain, saying he was so sorry. In tears himself, trying to be strong. No doctor goes to school for all those years to lose a life, I'm sure. He was devastated as well. He didn't expect this to happen either.

I remember her hitting her doubled-up hands on his chest, saying, "Why, why?"

I knew I had to help him. Where was her family? I guess he had asked the volunteer over the phone where mom was.

I went out in the hall, looked into his eyes. He knew me well.

My son was still there under his care weeks after his heart surgery.

I told her, "Stop, stop, you don't want to do this."

"I'm so sorry." She grabbed me, hugging me. I'm literally almost holding her up. Sobbing, she kept asking, "Why?"

Dr. Walter and I locked eyes. I told him to please get her family. They were in the surgical waiting room. He hurried and did just that. Her husband and mother, crying themselves, all tried to console each other.

I backed away, watching their grief from a distance for a few moments. It made me want to get back to my son immediately. I thought, *How? How did this happen?* Her daughter's heart surgery was so much less invasive than my son's. Her daughter was gone. My son still here, still fighting, still having so many problems to overcome. Sometimes life just doesn't make sense to us here on earth.

Isaiah 55:9 says, "*As the heavens are higher than the earth, my ways are higher than your ways and my thoughts higher than your thoughts, sayeth the Lord.*" I could make no sense of this. Neither could she or Dr. Walters. Only God can see the future, the path her daughter had to endure. I know God is a merciful father. *Lamentations 3:22* says, "*The steadfast love of God never ceases, his mercies never come to an end.*" I know he had mercy on her little girl that day. I know she's in heaven with him. I actually did get to tell her mama that. I was sad because I never thought I would ever see her again.

A few days had passed, I was walking down the hall, like I did every day for weeks now, and there she was all dressed up with a beautiful bouquet of white roses, baby's breath, and greenery. It was beautiful. We spotted each other.

She said, "I'm so happy to see you. Would you like to get a cup of coffee and sit a minute?"

"Of course," I said.

I was happy to see her too. We headed to the cafeteria, our meeting place. She set the flowers down and wrapped her arms around me.

In tears, she said, "I don't know what I would have done without you that day. I feel so bad. I'm bringing flowers to Dr. Walters. I shouldn't have blamed him. He's an amazing man. I'm sure he did his very best."

I told her how sweet I thought that was and how much I thought he would appreciate that. I shared with her that he prayed over every patient before he started their surgery. Her eyes brightened.

I said, "He is a wonderful man." I also told her that her sweet baby girl was in heaven, free of pain.

She looked at me with a serious look. "You're sure of that?"

I said, "I am positive of that."

We exchanged another long hug. We chatted for a while and then parted ways that day, never to see each other again. I have never forgotten her or her sweet little girl. Sometimes special people enter our life if only for a short time, and they have such a big impact. That day I assured not only her, but myself that if my son did not make it, I knew where he would be. Her thread in my life was a short one but a bright one that's still vibrant in my memories today: sitting in that hospital talking about our children like we would always have them, hoping they would be with us until the day we die. Not knowing how much time we had with them.

Today, when I say I wish I had more time with someone or I wish our vacation didn't go so fast or I wish I could freeze time, I know time with loved ones is a clear focus for me because of the losses I've had in my life. I treasure my time with family and with friends. We just never know how much time we will have with them, and I'm going to make the most of it. I would definitely suggest you do the same. If some relationship needs mending, do all you can to fix it. Ask God for his help. Take time to speak with him and really listen to his words of wisdom. We all can have difficult, frustrating, and argumentative, you name it, people in our lives. I'm going to give you some scripture here I try my best to use in my life. I don't always get it right. None of us get it right all the time. That's what God's grace and forgiveness are for.

In *Proverbs 19:11*, it says, "*Good sense makes one slow to anger, and it's in their glory to overlook an offense.*" This takes practice. We are all human and do or say things sometimes we shouldn't. *Hebrews 12:14* says, "*To strive for peace with everyone.*" *Matthew 7:12* says, "*Whatever you wish others would do to you, also do to them.*" *Philippians 2:3* says, "*Do nothing from rivalry or conceit but in humility. Count others more significant than yourselves.*" This one can be hard as we usually come from our own thoughts and desires. *Romans 14:13* says, "*Let us not pass judgment on one another but rather decide never to put a stumbling block or hindrance in the way of another.*" And *1 Thessalonians 5:11* says, "*Encourage one another and build one another up.*"

It first takes knowing God and his word. Then it takes putting it into practice in our lives. God gives us clear instruction on how we are to live our lives and how to treat others along our journey. God intended me to be there at just the right time the day her sweet girl went to heaven. He knew the time and day her daughter would leave this earth and be with him. He knew the situation. He could see every thread. After all, he designed the tapestry. He knew what her reaction was going to be. She wasn't the type of person to place blame on the doctor or react with violent anger. He knew it would come as a shock to the doctor. He knew I was going to be there to intercede for him. He planned it that way. He knew they both would need me. He also knew when she had time to process, she would do her best to make it right, to apologize to him. That she did. In *Colossians 4:6*, it says, "*Let your speech always be gracious, seasoned with salt, so that you may know how you ought to answer each person.*" That difficult day, her speech was anything but gracious and seasoned with salt. Really, how could it be? She did her best to make it right. That's the important thing. Leaving the blame and anger with the doctor who did everything he could to save her little girl would be heartbreaking for him, I'm sure. Remember, I could see his face. I'm so thankful, for him, she came back, as hard as that had to be, and made it right, as right as she could make it.

In our lives, we need to watch our words carefully, as best we can. Words have so much power. *Proverbs 16:24* says, *"Gracious words are like a honeycomb, sweetness to the soul and health to the body."* *Proverbs 15:4* says, *"A gentle tongue is a tree of life."* I love these two scriptures. They speak of sweetness, gentleness, and health. We all need words to be spoken to us in this manner. How wonderful it is when they are. In *Proverbs 18:21*, the scripture tells us, *"Life and death are in the power of the tongue."* I believe that, friend. Do your best to be kind with your words, and when you just can't, go back and make it right.

Hope Enters In

Some days in the hospital were much longer than others. The heart surgeries were behind us now, for now. They told us, as he grew every few years, depending on how fast he grew, the arteries they placed in his heart would have to be changed out to a larger size. More surgery, how many? They weren't sure. Once he was full grown, he wouldn't need any more. Okay, I've got it.

I thought, *I can't focus on that. We still have to get through today.* He had survived three surgeries to get to where we are now. My focus has to stay right here in the now. It, however, did bring an extra weight, a heaviness that day. It made that particular day very long, though I did my best not to dwell on it. You see, our son could not breathe on his own without oxygen and, at times, a ventilator. He wasn't able to drink out of a bottle. He had been surviving on IVs. There was talk of putting in a feeding tube, which, of course, meant one more surgery. It's not that he couldn't eat, it just was hard for him with all the breathing issues he was having. His little club feet were an issue still, and the immune deficiency was always looming over us.

There were many days I sat in his cold, sterile hospital room with my frail little boy, at times almost lifeless, fighting to survive. Me there, willing him to survive, needing him to survive. Those days, my cup was so empty. It certainly did not runneth over. At times, my body was painfully numb and very worn. I'm present, praying, touching, singing to my sweet little man, trying to bring him all the love of a thousand years wrapped into this harsh, painful reality he had been born into. I am trying so desperately to give him something soothing, comforting, and warm for him to hold on to. Between all the doctors, nurses, machines, medicines, pokes, and breathing treatments, I watched my son, feeling a bit helpless some days, literally pleading with him to be strong and with God to heal him, to let me switch places with him, to take his pain if for just one poke or prod. I used to sing a song by Stephen Curtis Chapman called *When You Are a Soldier*. This song resonated with me. My son was definitely on a battlefield with nowhere to hide, unable to run, and I was right there with a front row seat, watching it happen.

Comfort can come in many different ways and through many things. The ICU is a place that needs to be sterile. It's a serious place where the struggle is real. So, you see, the normal, happy things we bring to brighten a room or bring joy and comfort such as flowers, balloons, stuffed animals were not allowed. If it could be cleaned to the sterile standard, it could come in. We did have a small starshaped music box and some hand-drawn pictures on the wall. Those pictures were priceless to me. Drawn or colored by children. Why a not perfectly done picture by a child brought such comfort. They warmed my heart so much. They took me to a picture in my mind. I dreamed of the possibility of coloring with my son, at home, with all the mess, papers, crayons, markers. Maybe homemade cookie crumbs and some spilled milk. I thought how much fun they had doing them and what a normal thing to do. A lot of us take this for granted. I know I did. The pictures took me to a hopeful place where I could visualize light and goodness. In that place, it reminded me of family, happier times beyond this sterile hospital room. Hope, it keeps us moving.

In *Psalm 71:5*, it says, *"For you, God, are my hope and my trust."* In *Hebrews 6:19*, it says, *"We have this as a sure and steadfast anchor of the soul. A hope that enters into the inner place behind the curtain."* *Psalm 119:114* says, *"You, God, are my hiding place and my shield. I hope in your word."*

There are many verses in the Bible that reference hope. I have a good friend from high school who lost her daughter at the young age of two. When we talked about her daughter, she says the thing is we always had hope. She is a bright light in this world and a faithful woman of God. See, she's been through the fire. She's been refined, tuned in, as I have; and to this day, she stays tuned in. We both do.

In the hopeful places, I could find some joy and some thankfulness. Thankful for this sterile room, the doctors, the nurses, the respiratory therapists. Thankful for anyone who was on our team trying to save our son. I was thankful for them, but my hope was clearly planted in God himself. I pressed on day after day with some images of light peering through the darkness. On some of the most difficult days, just a glance into the window of children drawing brought me straight back to hope, back to God. Thank you, God, for a small peek into the window of a child. *2 Corinthians 1:3–4* says,

> *Blessed be the God our father. The father of mercies and the God of all comfort, who comforts us in our affliction so that we may be able to comfort others in their affliction with the comfort we receive ourselves.*

The comfort I was able to give the mother who lost her only daughter that day in the hospital, I promise you, it was from God himself who was giving me comfort.

Our perspective in this life can change in the blink of an eye, so fast we can't recognize the change or feel it at the time. Just a glance at a child's drawing changed my whole thought process, which changed my mood and thoughts from sadness to softer, happier, hopeful times. Hope, that's something we can cling to. At times like mine, we have to. Hope is this precious gift God gives us to help us hang in there. To help us hold it together when we're so broken, so torn, frayed, if you will, that we're literally splitting at the seams. Hope is the light that entered my son's, at times, dark room. Hope keeps our feet moving when they feel so heavy we can't pick them up. Hope, my son was still lying in that sterile room. He was still here, still breathing, and me, still able to touch him and love on him. I was still able to sing to him and kiss his sweet little crooked feet. He liked when I did that. A little side note here. My husband has skilled feet. Well, really toes. He can pick things up with them and pinch really hard with them. He's always using his toes at times like I would use my hands. My husband always wants his feet rubbed, he loves it, where some people would think that tickles. My son seemed to be no different. Genetics. One day I walked into my son's room, and he had his oxygen tube (it was long) between his toes, squeezing it. I chuckled. Another talented toe person. He's just like his daddy. I shared with his nurse. She got a kick out of it.

Back to hope. It can be really hard to bring comfort to a hurting soul and painful body if you don't have hope. Our physical touch can bring warmth, tenderness, love, compassion. So much more than we can even put into words. All the nerves that run through our bodies, we can feel other's anxieties and/or emotions when we touch them. I didn't want my son to feel mine. Thank you, God, for the hope that you put in me.

In *Isaiah 41:10,* it says, *"Fear not for I am with you. I am your God. I will strengthen you. I will uphold you with my righteous right hand."* That's powerful, my friend. In *Psalm 34:18*, it says, *"God is near to the broken hearted and saves the crushed in spirit."* I certainly was in need of saving. In *Psalm 119*, it says, *"Oh God, you are my hiding place and my shield. I put my hope in you and in your word."* You see, if I was going to give my son hope, I had to have hope myself. I needed God to hold me up with his righteous hand and to shield my emotions from my son. I needed him to stay close to my broken heart and my crushed spirit.

Day one, the very first time I laid eyes on my son, my strength left me. The pregnancy and delivery had taken so much out of me. Seeing his tiny, heaving chest, struggling to breathe, made me feel a shortness of breath myself. My son had been born into this situation. He knew no different. I sure did, and I needed this to be different. When they whisked him away, I thought, *I'm done. I'm all out of strength*. I was tapped out, if you will. In *Habakkuk 3:17–19*, it says,

> *Though the fig tree does not bud and there are no grapes on the vine, though the olive crop fails and the fields produce no food. Though there are no sheep in the pen and no cattle in the stalls, I will still rejoice in the Lord. He is my strength. He makes my*

feet like the feet of a deer. He enables me to go on heights.

This scripture for me describes a very dark and bleak time. My situation, though very different, is similar. I was in physical and emotional pain. I didn't have an appetite, though I needed to eat. The sadness was heavy and very real. It was too much, way too much. It was there that God met my needs. It was there he carried the weight. He moved my feet. He took me on the heights I needed to go. Thank you, God, for the strength and hope you put in me that day and every day since. *Psalm 28:6* says, "*Praise be to God, he has heard my cries for his mercy. The Lord God is my strength and shield. My heart trusts him and he helps me.*" He will help you too. He helped me. I'm still standing today. Living proof, my friend.

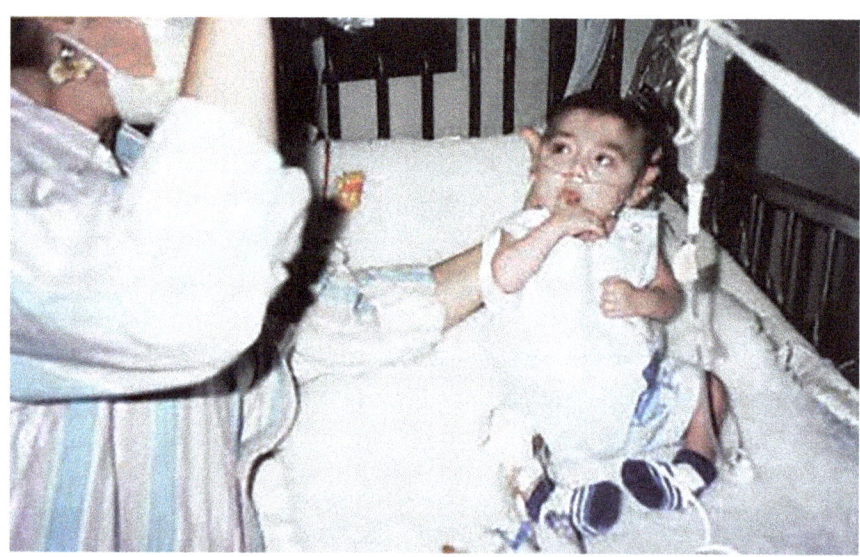

Mama hopeful—Cody's getting strong

Transition to Hurley

From Detroit Children's hospital to Hurley hospital in Flint. Our son was born in Hurley hospital. It was certainly closer to our home. Cody had been in Detroit Children's for months now, approximately four months. The drive, the gas, the overnights, with me not working, they were certainly taking their toll. Cody was still on several medications, still had a feeding tube in his stomach, and still had breathing treatments. Not as often, but they were still needed. So you see, at this point, the hospital was still needed. Closer to home would help so much. The hospital staff agreed. We were there to fix his heart. That had been done. The move was arranged. Cody would be taken by ambulance, and we followed. New doctors, new nurses, respiratory therapists. We've got this son. God has us. He's upholding us with his right hand, and I'm making sure of that every day, several times a day. Prayer was almost constant for me then. God was very present in my life these days, and I needed him to be. Cody had a very nice room. We met both of the doctors who would be caring for him: Dr. Zureikat and Dr. Nolan. It was there we also met Sharon and Stephany (the two nurses I mentioned earlier). All four of Cody's doctors and nurses hold such a special place in my heart still today. He had a few other doctors and nurses over the course of his life, when he was first born, the nurses in Detroit, etc. So many caring people. I, of course, am pointing out the four main doctors and the two nurses I really bonded with and who bonded with my son.

Everything was established now. We had a meeting with Dr. Nolan and Dr. Zureikat. They heard our concerns, and we felt they listened intently. They were very different personalities, both wonderful men. Dr. Nolan was a little more business, professional, if you will. He is very kind but more to the point. They're human just like you and me. We all have unique DNA designed by God himself. No two people will ever react the same. You definitely learn that in a hospital for that long of time. Dr. Zureikat was a people person. He gave an appropriate amount of human touch: a pat on your back, a hand on your shoulder. He, however, loved on my son. He would talk to him so sweetly and softly while examining him. Cody felt at ease with him. He would softly rub his little feet or hold his hand, rub his arm. All comforting things to my little man. It made all the necessary doctor visits easier for him. I was so thankful. They all got to know me and my husband very quickly. They knew we were active, loving, involved parents. They knew we knew our son very well and understood all the intricate details of his difficult life. I remember Dr. Nolan telling me, "We will take good care of him." He was thorough and good at his job. So was Dr. Zureikat. We were blessed to have them both.

I remember clearly one day walking back into my son's room. Well, I got to the doorway and stopped. There was Dr. Zureikat holding Cody's crooked feet and kissing them. He was telling him not to worry that he was going to be okay. Tears flooded my eyes, and it filled my heart up, overflowing with gratitude. When he saw me, he said, "I'm just giving our boy some love, Mama." When you are out of your son's room for only a short bathroom break and a drink and you come back to that, I have no words. I asked God to bless him abundantly that day. Only God can see what we do when no one is watching. You know who you really are at your core. That man was good down to his very bones. I don't think he could ever know what he did for me that day. I think Dr. Zureikat and I will see each other again someday in heaven.

I was praying over my son one day, and he walked in on me.

He said, "You go ahead, Mama. You are doing the right thing."

I had been surrounded by godly doctors, and that was no coincidence, my friend. I would so love to look him in the eye today and tell him how thankful I was for him and all the love and compassion he gave my son. Hopefully, you will see interwoven in this book all of the many threads, people who were placed in our life at just the right time. He was a beautiful thread in my tapestry. Dr. Nolan was too. It was a different kind of thread: strong, confident, and steady. I needed that too, friend. Oh, how I needed that. Sharon, Cody's night nurse, and Stephany, his day nurse, at Hurley were intricately daily, hourly woven threads. Smiles, day after long day; hugs for the bad days; and shared tears for the really bad days. They loved my son almost as much as if he were their own.

Being at Hurley was easier for sure. Our pets at home needed us. Our home needed us. Our lawn definitely needed us. My poor husband and our poor pets. My focus was still at the hospital. It had to be. I slept at home after leaving the hospital late at night. Not every day, only the good ones, and then it was like tearing myself away. At times, my husband had to force me to leave with Sharon, his nurse, saying, "I'm right here, I'm not leaving him alone. I know he's fragile. You have to sleep."

Sleep, that's something I had learned to live without much of. I, however, did get some sleep between the phone calls to the hospital making sure he was okay. I remember Sharon saying, "Please sleep. I will call you if he isn't okay, I promise." I trusted her, and I did my best to sleep. I just didn't want to be without my son. I'm sure you can understand that. My dog, Briecin, who I spoke of earlier in the book, loved me being at home. She slept in bed with me, snuggled as close as she possibly could. She could sense my pain and at times hear my cries. She would try to lick away my tears as if to say, "Please don't cry, Mom, I'm right here." I told you she was amazing, almost human.

When you are driving to and from the hospital day after day late at night and early in the morning, you are witness to God's handiwork. The beautiful sun rises, and all the night stars lit up the sky. There is a scripture that I love. It describes this so beautifully. I hope it is one you will remember and keep locked away to remind you of what an amazing God we have. It is in *Psalm 19:1 –2*. It says, "*The heavens declare the glory of God and the skies proclaim the work of his hands. Day after day they pour forth speech and night after night they display knowledge.*" It's absolutely true, friend. It was true for me.

God would speak to me through those beautiful mornings and star-filled nights.

The car ride was usually quiet and the mood heavy. It was a time when I needed to see God's handiwork and to feel his presence. I have a book at home that I have written scripture in through my devotionals over the past couple years. It's a 365-page book. I am now seventeen pages from filling this notebook. When I bought it, I thought this is a great idea for me, never thinking I would ever fill it. I refer to it all the time. There are famous human quotes at the bottom of each lined empty page. The quotes are interesting and meant to be read each day. The book is called *A Year of Inspiration*. I would add a scripture, personal to me and my situation at that given time. It has definitely inspired me and still does today. A lot of the scriptures in this book are rewritten from there. As I have grown in my faith, I read and reread it over and over again. In *Hebrews 11:1*, it says, "*Faith is the assurance of things we hope for, the proof of things we do not see and the conviction of their reality. Faith perceives real facts that are not revealed to the senses.*" I read and reread this verse. I want to grasp it and understand it. In *Job 37:16*, it says, "*Do you know how the clouds hang poised, perfectly balanced? Oh the wonder of God who has perfect knowledge.*" It also says in *Job 38:12*, "*Oh God, you have commanded the morning since your days began and caused the dawn to know its place.*" I love these scriptures. They give me such a clear, beautiful perspective. When people ask me about my faith, I tell them that faith gets you through. Faith is amazing and personal. It's key to your relationship with God. Our human minds want to make sense of it all, to understand every detail. I tell you, I can't make sense of my son being born with so many challenges. I can't make sense of losing my father at a young age. I can't make sense of my car accident. It clearly wasn't my fault. I can't make sense of so many things in my life. I can, however, see God's hands at work throughout my life. I feel his presence daily. I communicate openly with him, not just through prayer, but I talk with him about a lot of things. He has all my days ordained for me. When my days will be no more, I will join him in heaven. No more struggles. He alone knows when our struggle comes to an end. I am trying to give you an honest, clear look into my life and my relationship with God. You see, I am writing this book as God inspires me to do so. A scripture or a story, maybe a situation will jog a memory, and I will get the nudge from God to write once again. I am doing my best to be faithful to God and write what he is asking me to. I hope it helps you. It has certainly been challenging for me. But he knows that already.

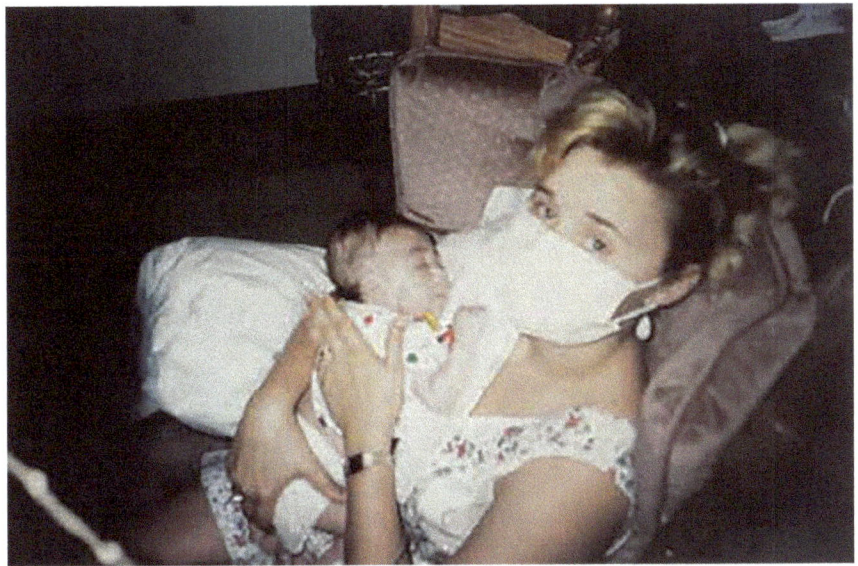

Brenda and Cody

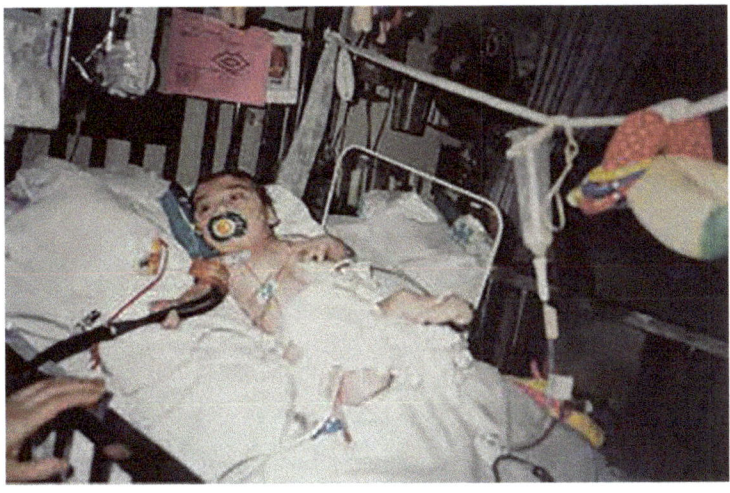

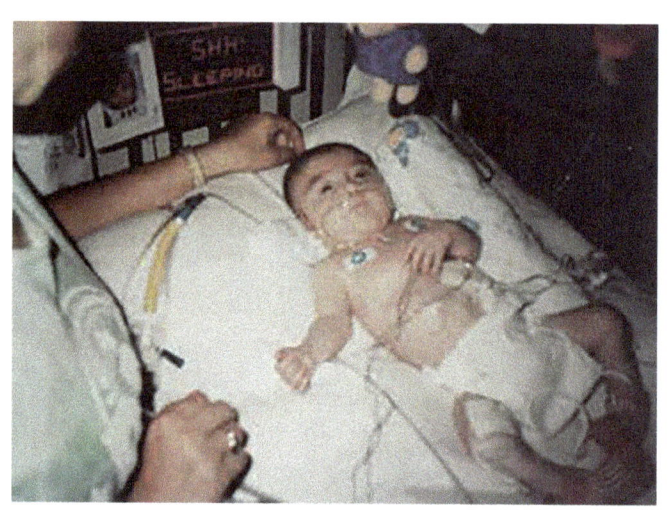

No Wiggle Room

Back to Flint, Michigan, and Hurley hospital. In *Psalm 56:8*, it says, "*Oh God, you have seen me tossing and turning through the night. You have collected all of my tears and preserved them in your bottle. You have recorded every one in your book.*" By this time my bottle had to be overflowing. Cody was hanging on, sometimes only by a thread. The doctors and nurses knew us pretty well by now. We talked pretty openly. There's no point in sugarcoating things. By now Cody's heart seemed to be strong. The thing we were most worried about was doing quite well surprisingly. His lungs, however, had been so compromised with the virus, heart surgery, and multiple times on and off the ventilator. Each time we are told we have to see what his blood gasses are—that is, how well his blood is oxygenated—it was a double-edged sword. The ventilator was keeping him alive yet hurting his lungs. Breathing and growing seemed to be the bigger issues now. When his breathing was doing better, off the ventilator and on a lower oxygen level, we would attempt to feed him more and try to push the food through his feeding tube a little faster. Just a little to see if he could handle it. It was set on a very slow drip. We found if we sped things up, his breathing changed. Things didn't go well. I studied him, laser focused, trying to figure out why. What now? The doctors determined he was refluxing into his already-compromised lungs. No feeding him any faster.

One evening I was at the hospital really late. Cody just wasn't right. All the machines were within safe limits; however, I knew something was wrong. I asked the nurse to have the doctor come in and check him. This particular night, Sharon was not working. I knew the nurse on shift. She had been with him a few times now. She didn't question me. The doctor came in fairly quickly.

He was younger, a resident. He looked him over. He said, "He's fine, ma'am."

I said, "He needs a chest x-ray. Order it, please, right away."

He looked at me strangely and said, "No, he doesn't need it."

Now he didn't know me or my son. It was the first time I met him. I pushed.

I told him, "You don't know me, I know my son. He needs an x-ray."

The nurse was now looking at me, a bit nervous.

He said no again.

I looked at her and asked her who was on call between Dr. Nolan and Dr. Zureikat.

"Dr. Zureikat," she said.

I said, "Please call him."

The resident said, "We do not call him at home unless it's an emergency. You are overreacting."

At this point, I told him that he wasn't needed and to please leave my son's room.

His demeanor was rude and condescending to me. I was focused, and he was wasting precious time.

I told the nurse, "Dr. Zureikat told me to call him at home if he was ever needed."

I walked around them both and went to the desk outside my son's room. The girl working the desk knew me well.

"What's wrong?" she asked.

I explained the situation. The resident, I think, was a bit shocked. She called right away.

She told him, "Mom's here with me, she wants a chest x-ray.

The resident told her no, it wasn't necessary."

He told her to order it right away. He also asked to speak to the resident. He told him not to ever question me. I knew my son. He also told him, "It's not a normal thing, but this mom, we don't question." He then talked to me. He explained what he told him. I thanked him and went right back to Cody. The resident tried to apologize. I wasn't mad; I just needed him to do his job. We needed the x-ray. This was nothing new to me with my son. This had happened several times over the course of the past few months. The x-ray was taken. Sure enough, his lungs didn't look good. He consulted with Dr. Zureikat. Medications were added. He was so frail, and things happened quickly when he got sick. There was no wiggle room. Dr. Zureikat had learned that, so had I. He ended up with an early stage of pneumonia. Catching it early helped. The doctors decided since Cody didn't move around or cough very deep that they would put him on a bed that slowly moved him side to side to disperse the fluid. Cody hated this. He was also back on the ventilator. At times like this, my focus kept me from noticing the world around me. I blocked things out, sounds, movement, and people. None of that mattered. The shades were closed. I had no space or energy for anything or anyone else. Cody was fighting the ventilator tube, trying to grab it and pull it out. He was angry. His heart rate was soaring way too high. The doctors decided to basically semiparalyze his body. They had given him a medication that we had to fight our insurance for that they had given him in Detroit Children's. It's called Versed. It will wipe out a bad experience, help you forget. He responded very well to it, and it was merciful for him. He needed it. He was only on the bed for a couple days. It seemed to be doing the job. Cody was improving; however, something needed to be done about his refluxing and soon. In consulting with Dr. Nolan and Dr. Zureikat, they decided he needed a procedure called a fundelplication. It's a procedure used to stop the reflux. Another surgery. Our poor little man. They explained it would give him what he needed to grow. He could keep food down. His immune system wasn't strong, and his lungs had so much scarring. His body wouldn't take much more. I can't tell you how many times I've been told that statement over the past few months. Too many. We agreed. They would contact a surgeon and get the ball rolling.

They came back to us and said, "We have consulted three surgeons that we recommend. They don't want to do the surgery because they are worried about his heart."

I said, "Consult his heart surgeons. They can tell us if his heart will be okay."

Good idea, they did just that. Dr. Zureikat actually spoke to Dr. Walters. He assured him they had fixed Cody's heart and that he was a fighter. To go ahead with the surgery. He even gave them a doctor he would use. He told him he would even speak to him. There are so may interconnected threads here at work for our son. God's hands were all over this. The surgery was scheduled, and we were set up to meet him. No time to waste. Cody was having one of those healthy windows. They hadn't come around often. We were able to meet the doctor the evening before surgery. I was, of course, a bit anxious, having never met him. I guess that is to be expected. My anxieties were quickly quieted. He was a smiling, confident, kind man. He was seasoned and unafraid to perform surgery on our son. He explained the details and set me at ease. Of course, he did. He came recommended from Dr. Walters. Still today, I have so much gratitude for that man. All of my son's doctors really.

Surgery was successful. Thank you, God. He came through it with flying colors, you might say.

What's next? I thought. Keeping him healthy for sure. Him growing hopefully and us, at some point, taking him home. After spending months in the hospital the thought of taking him home came with so many emotions. Excitement for sure was my first thought. To have our son home, he could finally see his room that we had worked so hard on to prepare for him. However, I knew it wouldn't look like I had envisioned when preparing it. Monitors, machines, and medication would all be part of the visual now. The image of that invoked fear, caring for our son at home would be quite the task. He still had oxygen, a feeding tube, heart medicine, and let's not forget what's still looming overhead: his sweet crooked feet.

The Journey Home

Our son was improving little by little, day by day. After all he's been through, after all the pain and suffering he's endured, after all the sleepless nights, could he really come home? Could we really care for him the way he needs to be cared for? That was now the topic of conversation for sure. Our insurance company had sent a very friendly nurse of their own to meet us, to observe the situation.

I thought, *Who could blame them?* I can't even process how much this was costing them. Can you put a price on our son's life? What were they thinking? She popped in at different times of the day and stayed longer on some days. She talked with me, asking if I was okay, asking if there was anything I needed that we weren't getting. She told me what a good mom I was and was impressed at the knowledge I had of the machines and care that was needed for my son. Really, at the time, I told my husband our insurance company seems to be very caring and that I really liked the nurse they sent. She seemed to be very compassionate and kind.

I remember one day, Cody's day nurse, Stephany, talking to me pretty seriously about our insurance, about the nurse observing me.

"Observing me?"

"Yes," she told me. "She is watching you, assessing you."

"Why?" I asked her.

She said, "Be careful, don't do too much for Cody while she's here. Let us care for him when she's present."

I, of course, questioned her. You see, Cody wanted mommy to do everything—bathe him, clean his central line area, which had to be a completely sterile process. Professionals usually did this. He also wanted me to clean the area around the feeding tube, etc. If a machine was sounding with alert sounds, I had learned to quiet them, quiet him, and settle the situation. Staff in the hospital used to tell me I could be a nurse. When it came time for his breathing treatments, he wanted me to hold the treatment. They let me. He would be calmer; they knew that. His heart rate wouldn't spike or soar through the roof as it did at times. They helped me, trained me, so I could help my son. They even had a sign on his bed for other aids or nurses who weren't aware and were just trying to do their job. "Leave patient's bath for mom." His heart rate would soar if anyone else would try to bathe him. That was our time. It was special. He loved it. We both did. After the bath, I would warm lotion between my hands and give him his baby rub. That's what I called it. It was more of a massage for his little weak muscles. I would exercise his arms gently in the process. It was a form of physical therapy for him. The nurses showed me how. He wouldn't let them do that at all. He got so angry with them, no matter how gentle they tried to be with him.

His nurse, without coming right out and saying it, was worried about me knowing too much, doing too much for my son. Looking back, she knew what I didn't at the time. She knew we were going to need help at home caring for our son, and she knew how the insurance game was played. I surely did not. I did back off care a bit when the nurse from the insurance company was around. However, I feared it might be too late. I had let my guard down, chatted openly with her. I thought she was there to help us. Was I fooled! I wish the nurses had spoken up sooner. However, they were not supposed to get involved at all. Stephany tried, but just couldn't. She knew our struggle and had a good window into what the picture at home would look like with no help. How difficult that could be for us. At the time, I was so focused on that happy picture bubble in my head, the one with us at home, happy, and Cody growing and thriving. I needed that picture to get me through. I needed it to be real, to come to fruition.

A meeting was set up with Cody's doctors. They met with both my husband and me. They shared with us the next steps in Cody's care and our journey to get him home. We needed to iron out all the details, to be on the same page with one clear vision, to set us up for success the best they could. They too were trying to warn us. They told us there would be a meeting set up with us, them and our insurance company. Wait, our insurance company? My husband pretty much took over here.

"What do they have to do with Cody going home?"

The doctors explained, "They get to determine what he needs at home."

"They get to determine? They're not doctors," I told them.

Aw, the insurance game again.

They assured us to let them handle our insurance and what we need in the meeting. They had been through this many times. They warned us it can be a difficult meeting, to stay calm and let them deal with it. This didn't go over so well with my husband. During the meeting, he tried, he really did. He stayed quiet for a long time. In preparation, he thoroughly studied our insurance and knew our benefits. He was ready if the doctors were having trouble, and trouble we had. There was a lot of discussing and back and forth between the insurance company, like a bartering session was happening. They would pay for this and not that. The equipment we needed at home, they would only pay for a certain company, which only carried a certain brand of machine the doctors didn't want us to use. This meeting went on for a long time.

All the while the nurse who had been so kind sat there. She chimed in, "Mom can do that, I've seen her. They don't need any nursing help at home."

"Really? Our son needs twenty-four-hour supervision and care. He's fragile. He is on several medications, serious ones. Oxygen, a feeding tube, we needed a suction machine that is used to clear out mucus to help him breathe better if he needs it. No help at all?"

She said, looking me in the eye, "You are capable and smart. You don't need any help."

It's amazing how these once-kind-looking, helpful eyes were piercing through me. She was never there to help me. I looked at her with disgust. How can she live with herself? How can she lay her head on a pillow at night and just go to sleep? Does she have two personalities? They sure hired the right person. She knew I would drop, never getting any sleep. No one can never sleep.

After she said her piece, she tried to make herself feel better. She tried to talk with me or ask me questions.

I looked at our doctors and said, "What now?" never looking at her or answering her ever again. I was done with her. I hope she couldn't sleep that night. That maybe God could do a good work in her so she wouldn't deceive anyone else. It is so hard what we were all living through; we didn't need her making life harder.

She asked me one day in my son's room, "Did I think I would need help at home?"

I was real with her. I told her it would be impossible for me to care for him twenty-four hours a day, seven days a week, that no one could. She told me she understood. She said she wouldn't be able to either. She lied and manipulated me.

In *Proverbs 1:13*, it says, "*The integrity of the upright guides but the crookedness of the treacherous destroys them.*" In my mind, she was as crooked as a day was long. In *Luke 6:31*, it says, "*As you wish others would do to you also do to them.*" I knew if I continued to speak to her that day, I would not treat her the way God required me to. I was angry at her. In *Ecclesiastes 7:9*, it tells us, "*Not to be quick in your spirit to become angry, for anger lodges in the bosoms of fools.*" I would have looked and sounded very foolish that day if out of my mouth came what I was thinking in my mind. In *Proverbs 29:11*, it says, "*A fool gives vent to their spirit, but a wise person quietly holds it back.*"

Oh, I tell you, that was hard to do that day. It would not have helped our situation. The doctors and my husband were taking the insurance company on just fine. The meeting almost ended at a standstill.

The doctors finally told the insurance company, "We won't release him home without care. He can just live here, that will cost you a lot more money."

The room suddenly became quiet.

They said, "We are done here. Don't worry, Mom and Dad, we won't let them do this to you or to Cody."

God was in that room with us that day. He's in every detail we invite him into, and I had prayed before our meeting and was praying during it. In *Joshua 1:19*, it says, "*Be strong and courageous. Do not be frightened, do not be dismayed, for the Lord God is with you wherever you go.*" He was right there with us. It was nice to have our son's doctors fighting for us. The insurance company explained to us how much a month our son's equipment would be if we didn't use the service provider they recommended even though the doctors weren't in favor of them. This was a lot of money, and with me still unable to work, our finances were already challenged. The insurance company made concessions, and so did we. They finally agreed to pay for some nursing care, the key word being *some*, and we had no choice but to agree to use their medical supply company. Cody was doing quite well for him. He was a fragile boy and might be for a long time. This brought a lot of pressure, especially on me. I would be his caregiver most of the time as my husband had to work, and our nursing help was limited. Nothing would happen immediately. Plans had to be put into place. We had to be put through some training for the equipment, nursing staff setup, etc.

Things were set in motion now. We had just one more obstacle, Cody's club feet. The doctors had been waiting for him to improve, grow, and get a little stronger before they dealt with his feet. They knew they couldn't leave them that way. The decision was made to cast them before he goes home. Thoughts and questions started racing through my mind. How much will this hurt him? Will it agitate him? Will his heart rate go up? Anytime anyone is in pain, typically, their heart rate goes up. So far, it didn't feel like we were being set up for success here. The doctors explained, over the course of a few months, he would have several casts as to gradually turn his feet in hopes not to stress him too much. In hopes?

Our team was in place. Cody's casts were on. The day was here. Once the insurance company had determined we could go home, they wanted us gone from the hospital and now. Things in hospitals take time: discharge papers, medicines, etc. The image or picture bubble created in my mind would soon take on its own visual. We were about eight months into our hospital journey, and thoughts of going home were now reality. Our home in the country with horses in the backyard near our small barn, inside the white wooden fence my husband had worked so hard on was not the same. The barn and fence were there; they were just empty. What I haven't shared with you previously, before my pregnancy journey, my sweet Boutique, Star's mama, got very sick. I went out to the barn one day after work. She and Chantel were both in their stalls in the barn as it was really cold, windy, and snowing that day. When I opened the barn door, it was as if a heater had been turned on high in there. Boutique was in her stall soaking wet with sweat. She was clearly in a tremendous amount of pain. I called the vet right away, and he came out as soon as he could. He checked her over good. He felt like it was her stomach, maybe it's twisted. It could be a number of things. He gave her medicine in hopes to help her. We did all the things he advised. I was counting on her improving. I had already lost her son, my sweet Star. I couldn't lose her. I had to go to work. My husband stayed with her. He went to the house and called his work. He went back out to check Boutique within an hour, and she was already gone. Chantel, who was right next to her stall, was having a full-blown horse fit. She was rearing up in her stall, her feet hitting Boutique's stall. The scene was awful. There lay Boutique, dead in her stall. This wasn't the plan, God. What is happening? Boutique was gone. We had a good friend who I called for help. He had a tractor, and we were going to need one. Trying to get a deceased large horse out of a stall door was, to say the least, a big challenge. Let alone it being my sweet Boutique. It was traumatizing, to say the least. We buried her on our small farm so her body could be at home with us.

This, however, wasn't just traumatizing for us; it was traumatizing for Chantel. She was scared, spooked, and now alone. Horses, just like us, don't like to spend all their time alone, and she and Boutique were inseparable. I spent as much time with her as I could. We both needed that.

Back to going home with Cody and our empty barn. During our hospital journey, it was so sad to leave Chantel all alone without me and without Boutique month after long month. My neighbor could care for our sweet dog, Briecin, who was having her own struggle without us. There were days she didn't want to eat, as if to say, "I won't eat until you come home, Mom." But that wasn't an option for me.

Chantel needed attention, to be ridden. She needed other horses. I asked a dear friend of mine, Lynn, to come and get her and take her home to her house. That was no problem, anything she could do to help. I felt guilty because our time in the hospital was so long. I ended up selling her to a man I knew who lived near my family five hours away. He assured me he would keep her and that my family could come ride her. He had a beautiful Tennessee Walker farm. As much as it killed me inside, I knew all of my focus needed to be on Cody, and I thought this would be best for her. So now you see why the barn is empty. To come home and see it that way broke my heart in two. You see, it was collateral damage, if you will, of my new reality. It was painful for me. Life was never going to be the same. Horses were such a big connection to my dad and family memories for me. This, on top of everything else, almost broke me. I reminded myself I will see her again. She is near my family. She's okay. Unfortunately, people in this life at times are dishonest. That is hard for me to accept. Honesty doesn't cost anything. I gave the man such a great financial deal on Chantel with the promise he was keeping her and me and my family could see and ride her. He wanted to breed her. Maybe I could get a baby of hers when my life got back to normal, if it ever did. He kept her for a while, my niece rode her, told me she is doing well. Then I find out he sold her. He was offered too much money to pass it up. If I could have punched that man in the face the day I found out, I would have, several times. I know that's awful. I'm just being honest. In *Proverbs 12:22*, it says, "*Lying lips are an abomination to the Lord but those who act faithfully are in his delight.*" In *Proverbs 16:28*, it says, "*A dishonest person spreads strife and a whisper can separate close friends.*" I thought this man was helping me and I was helping him. Boy, was I wrong. It's not like I didn't know him. I grew up in the small town we had both lived in while I was growing up. *Romans 12:17–21* says, "*Repay no one evil for evil, but give thought to do what is honorable in the sight of all. If possible, so far as it depends on you, live peacefully with all. Beloved, never avenge yourself but leave it to the wrath of God."* That is hard to do, my friend. I wanted him to pay, not financially, though God knew we could use it. I wanted others to know of his deceitful ways. I wanted to tarnish his, to me, fake, shiny reputation. Let people know what he did to me, especially in my situation, which he obviously took advantage of. *Luke 16:10* says, *"One who is faithful in a very little is also faithful in much, and one who is dishonest in a very little is also dishonest in much."* Who else had he taken advantage of? My hands were full. God would need to deal with him.

The empty barn, pen, and horse stalls, so quiet and that once held such joy for me, were a clear visual of the emptiness I felt every time I looked out our back window and they weren't there. It took me back to the empty barn and pasture, to Buttercup, our pony, all those years ago.

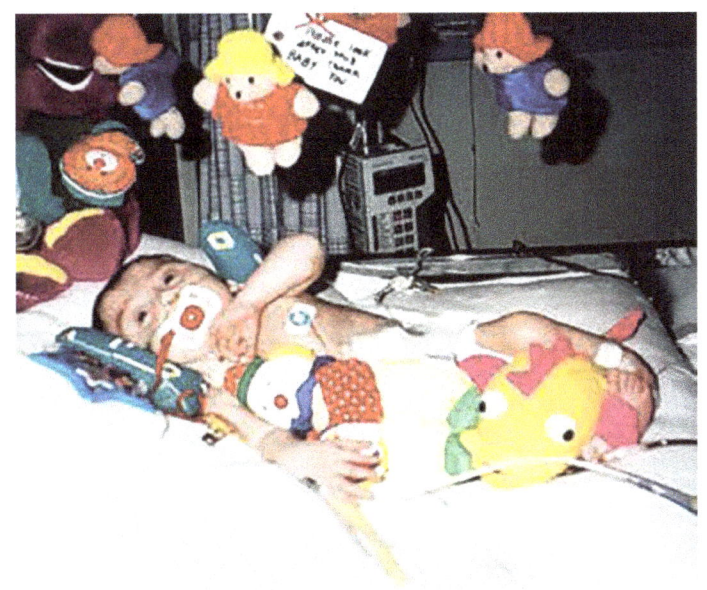

The Journey Home

Precious Time

After getting everything in place, it was late afternoon by now. The plan of success was to get us home early in the day, meet the equipment company at our house, etc. As I said earlier, this was not setting us up for success. My sister and her husband were flying in from an Alaskan trip that evening, and my husband was to pick them up. Then there was the car seat, the medicines, the lack of hospital staff. The hospital staff were trained, skilled, trusted. What would I do if things went wrong? Will the machines work the same as the ones I've been trained on? His heart medicine was in a clear liquid form that had to be drawn up with a syringe. It was a small dose and needed to be exact. A mess up in that would cause real problems. The pressure I felt was intense. I remember saying, "It's getting late. Can we wait until tomorrow?" That wasn't an option. The insurance company had already signed on the dotted line, if you will. Goodbyes were said, hugs all around.

"You've got this," I was told more than once.

Do I have this? I thought. *Are you guys sure? You have more faith in me than I do.*

I knew I was geared up for the fight. I had tried to grasp anything and everything that I could to gain all the knowledge that doctors and nurses had gone to school for years all wrapped into this very unique, difficult, stressful, puzzle if you will. All the pieces had to fit together perfectly as fragile as our son was. There could be no mistakes. How could I ever forgive myself if there were?

The car ride home went smoothly. Cody looked around with his bright-blue eyes as if to say, "Where are we going? What am I seeing?" It was all new to him. A sterile hospital room was all he ever knew. As nerve-racking as it was, we made it home. First things first, he met our boxer, Briecin. Usually overly excited to see us and jumping up and down, now she was still happy to see us, but she was extremely calm. When she met him, she gently smelled him and looked up at me as if to say, "So this is why you've been gone so long."

Cody's eyes got very big when she sniffed him, but he never cried. He just looked at her calmly as if to say, "Okay, I like you, whoever you are."

It warmed my heart and put me at ease a bit. We showed him his room with Briecin in tow, staying in step with us every moment as if she were on watch. She was going to protect him like she tried to do us.

We weren't home long, and down our long driveway the medical supply van came. Things happened so quickly. I remember telling the man who delivered the feeding pump, "This feeding pump looks different." He explained they all work the same. It was larger, and nothing looked right. I wanted him to show me how to use it. He said he just delivered them. The suction machine was larger as well, and the suction tube was bigger than we had ever used. Again, I can call the company. He is just the delivery guy. I should know all of this, he'd been told I had been trained. So you remember back when the doctors were fighting for the equipment we had been using? I now knew why. This added so much stress, you have no idea. We were given oxygen and, of course, told no smoking. That I get. No problem. We don't smoke. That's one thing we've got. The oxygen monitor was different. I could read it, so that was okay. The delivery guy gave me the company phone number and went on his way. Everything was timed out to the T. His medications, all at different times of the day, and his feedings were broken up as well. I was still nervous about the feeding machine. We were to hook it up; and it dispensed formula slowly, drops at a time, so his body could process it. That was the only way he could handle eating at all. Medicines were drawn up and given through his central line, which if you remember had to be a completely sterile process. We couldn't chance infection. His body could never take that. I had called the medical supply company earlier; and of course, because of it being late, they had a message saying that they were closed, to call back tomorrow.

This frustrated me. Deep breath, I told myself, one step at a time. You don't want Cody to feel my stress his first night at home. He needed me, and I needed that laser focus I had in the hospital. In this situation, I just wanted to hold him, rock him in the comfy blue-and-white rocker we had bought for him. I wanted to just be able to be mom. That wasn't possible. I had to be mom, caregiver, nurse, doctor, etc. It wasn't time for his evening feeding quite yet, but it was time for my husband to leave for the airport. Cody and I were snuggled in the rocking chair as he left. That was the first time things felt a little normal since the day I found out he was a boy, not a girl. I relished our time together, singing to him and rocking him, with Briecin right there beside us. I remember thanking God for these few semi-normal moments. Figuring out the feeding pump was still lingering over my head. Feeding time was quickly approaching, and I needed to figure this machine out. I tried, oh, how I tried. I got the door open and tried to connect the tube. I made several efforts but couldn't. I was really frustrated, and Cody needed to eat. I thought I will take a break, wait for my husband. We had both been trained, and he was good at remembering details, I told myself. It won't be much longer. Cody wasn't fussing at this point. He loved being home except for this stupid machine and it being too late to ask for help, which is not okay at all. I'm sure now they have an emergency number for these things. They needed one then. My husband got home with my sister and brother-in-law. They were happy to see us and Cody home. They had been with us at the hospital a lot, and they saw all our suffering firsthand. We chatted just for a short bit, to hear about their trip, when I told my husband I hadn't been able to figure out the feeding machine. Things turned serious quickly.

"Okay," he said. "He needs to eat. I can figure it out."

I felt relieved as this needed to go perfectly. He finally figured it out and got it hooked up. However, when he set it to run slow and turned it on, it immediately gave Cody a big bolus of formula. He shut it off right away. He looked at me, we both knew this was not good.

"He had the fundoplication surgery," he said. "Let's pray that stops it from getting into his lungs."

We knew it stopped it if it ran slowly, but what now? We kept him as upright as we could for a long time, hoping that would help. I began to get angry at this point. We had been set up for failure, not success. The one thing that couldn't happened did and night one no less. I've always been hard on myself. I felt like I had completely failed him. He was a helpless sick child whose parents were supposed to care for him and protect him. After all he had been through, how could this happen? We should have fought harder for the right equipment. I should have refused to come home this late. The stupid insurance company, this was really their fault. To save money, they put a price on our son. How are they allowed to do that? There was plenty of blame to go around, and I was accepting mine. *How could I let this happen?* played over and over in my mind. It was a long night to say the least.

The next day, of course, the first thing I wanted was an x-ray. We're not in the hospital. This wasn't going to be quite so easy. It was the weekend now. He went home late Friday afternoon. We would watch him closely. We had no nursing help on the weekends or his first night home. The insurance company would only pay for eight hours a day, Monday through Friday. This new nurse wouldn't know him yet anyway. Not like we did. Laser focus, keeping our eyes on him, hoping and praying for the best.

Monday morning I could call a doctor I was given, and I would ask for an x-ray. We need to be safe here. Our dog, Briecin, was on watch, vigilant, not leaving Cody no matter where he was. She sensed his need for protection. If he was in his crib, she stayed underneath it, literally it seemed, without moving a muscle. We had to force her to go outside and encourage her to eat or drink. She could feel the energy, the severity of our situation; and she, in dog language, was going to do her part. We were all doing our part, or we hoped we were, except for that bolus. We had figured out the machine by now, and to be safe, we turned it on to see how fast it was pumping before we hooked it to him. We should have done that the first time. We had never been trained to do that, but we learned a very serious lesson, not to trust that machine. At least now he was getting his nutrition.

Monday came, time to call the doctor. Cody appeared okay, restful, peaceful. I'm sure all the pokes, prods, constant checks not happening now helped. For me, I was anxious about the bolus he'd been given, and I wanted hard facts, to know beyond a shadow of a doubt that his lungs were okay. If not, we needed to get on top of this right away. Of course, because of Cody's immune system being compromised, he couldn't just go anywhere at any time. We had to be careful. As I'm writing this, we're in the middle of the COVID-19 pandemic. I almost feel like it's twenty-five years ago with my son. I was living pretty much as I am now, only he is not here. We had to be so careful, hand sanitizer with us, gloves, limit people seeing him. People wanted to see him from our church, but we couldn't take the risk. No "welcome home" party. We were given strict instructions. They really didn't even want carpet or curtains in his room. Things needed to be as sterile as possible. The carpet, we had no choice on. We told them with me not working, money was tight, and we couldn't replace it; but we took the curtains down, cleaned the blinds and the whole room the best we could. I was persistent with the doctor's office on having a chest x-ray. They wanted the 'wait and see' method. I explained what a bad idea this was. They wanted to schedule it for the next day. I was reluctant. I wanted it now, today, right away. They, of course, were booked. They didn't understand. This was my fear about coming home, becoming my reality, playing out in real time. I watched him like a hawk, never leaving his side if at all possible.

As normal, by evening, he worried me a bit. His breathing seemed a bit faster, not extreme, but even a little faster scared me almost to death. We met his nurse, finally. We chose to have our eight hours of nursing help at night. As I've said previously, nights are hard, and at some point, we needed some amount of sleep. She was very nice and tried to be very careful. She understood the situation, she said, and would alert me of any changes. I was up and down most of the night checking in, checking up on her, to be honest. I had just me her, and I wasn't about to put my son's life in her hands, not just yet. Every time I checked she was awake, alert, and doing her job. That was a small relief for me. Throughout that night, she would ask me to please sleep. I decided to share a couple hospital stories with her. It gave her a better understanding or perspective of our situation. I figured that would only be fair. She needed some background and some understanding of my hovering.

Morning couldn't come soon enough. We had a machine to give him a breathing treatment if we thought he needed it. By morning, I thought he needed it, especially before messing with him to take an x-ray. It would open up his airway a bit just in case he got upset during the x-ray. He hadn't been messed with for a few days now, and I thought and I hoped it would slow his breathing a bit, making it easier for him. It might upset him, and his heart rate could rise. Both of these were always the outcome when he became agitated. I was going to set us up for success if at all possible. I saw his night nurse off, Dad had to go to work, medications were given, formula dispensed by that wretched machine that had caused this problem. His pulse oximeter that read his pulse and oxygen level was within normal limits still at this point. That gave me some security but not completely. I had seen my son fail in the past when the machines hadn't picked it up yet. I was focused but a little angry at this point. I thought let's put the insurance provider's son in my son's situation. I guarantee something like this would never happen again. Is my son's life really not worth a few extra dollars? All we needed was the right equipment, checked, and working properly. That thought played over and over in my head. Oh, how I wished I could have given them a piece of my mind.

Off to the x-ray. I hated having him in the back seat, I couldn't see him very well. I thought, *On the way home, I would buckle him in the front. Who cares at this time in my life about the law.* Don't get me wrong, I have two family members who are active, first responders in law enforcement. I try to always obey the law. Laws are made for our own safety. Not here, not now, not with my son needing me. It was safer to have him where I could see him. The x-ray went fairly smoothly. I explained to the technician the severity of our situation and to please let me position him as much as possible. I explained that it would be better for all of us this way, trust me. No problem, they had been informed. He had been scheduled at lunchtime to avoid other patients as well. In the hospital, they had an x-ray machine they would bring to his room. How I wished this could have been done in our home. The risks were high. This picture bubble of life at home is cracking a bit. The happiness I had envisioned seemed blurry, a bit out of focus.

The ride home went well, just my little man and I. His eyes so big again, looking around but always looking back at me as if to say, "Mom, you've got this." I smiled a big smile at him, held his little hand, and began to sing one of his many songs I would sing to him. It was obvious it helped us both. Oh, how I wish I could hold his hand today, wrap my arms around him so tight, and tell him, "See, son, you made it. Everything is okay."

My whole journey with my son I told him, "You've got this. Everything is going to be okay. Don't worry, Mama is here."

I was determined my son would be okay. I would make sure of it. Unfortunately, there are so many things out of our control in this life, and I already knew that all too well.

Back at home, I tried to do all the right things, in all the right order, including a lot of praying.

I thought, *If nothing else goes wrong, maybe, just maybe, this one thing won't derail us. If everything else goes right, this one machine, one bolus of formula, can't hurt us.*

Oh, but it can. Being hard on yourself, I've learned the hard way, only leads to frustration and looking back with regret. We need to forgive ourselves and look forward, my friend, and give our regrets to God. He can release us. We can trust him. He can weave both the good and bad in our lives into a beautiful tapestry. Our very own design and journey brought to life in full color. Well, you've heard it said, there's a calm before the storm. This time these past few days was my calm, my special time holding my son at home, rocking him, and loving him. This time was mine, our gift from God. Remember here, the doctors thought he would be born blue, unresponsive. We had beaten so many odds. Have you noticed before a storm how calm it is, how quiet and still it is? Even the birds stop singing and return to their nest. You can feel a change in the air. You can see the change in the clouds as if God is giving you a warning, a stillness to pay attention. I was already on high alert. I wasn't aware I even had an overdrive, but it had kicked in for sure. With just my son, my dog, and I in the house, everything was calm, very quiet, and still. It was as if God was saying, "Pay attention here. Really soak this in. Lock it in your memory, his touch, his smell, this precious time. It could all be over soon." The x-ray and his condition could change in an instant. I had seen it many times. I could feel the change come, the storm brewing. My feelings were so mixed and conflicted. He still appeared okay, though his breathing a bit more rapid as I stated earlier. The storm that was brewing wasn't outside, it was inside our son's frail body.

That afternoon, rocking my little man is the visual, the memory, the picture bubble I treasure still today. He would just stare at me with his deep-blue eyes and once in a while make a few small cooing sounds, never fussing at all. Just mom and son enjoying each other. That's how life should be. In *Nahum 1:7*, it says, "*The Lord is good and a stronghold in the day of trouble.*" In *2 Corinthians 12:9*, God says that "*His grace is sufficient for us and his power is made perfect in our weakness.*" I wasn't sure what was next, but I knew for sure this time was priceless. I was soaking it all up, locking it up safely in my memory vault, forever.

Evening brought an uneasiness in Cody. Not really fussy, just uncomfortable. His breathing slightly faster. The call came in. The results of the x-ray were in. The voice on the other end of the line telling me there were some white hazy spots in his lungs. The radiologist said he could be getting a virus or maybe the bolus played a role. They assured me it wasn't bad enough to go to the hospital at this point.

Again, I heard, "Keep a close eye on him."

I thought, *You're kidding me, right?* I know they're just doing their job.

He became more uncomfortable the later it got. I made a call to the doctor they gave me. It could be his feet. They told us to cut his casts off. Us cut them off?

"He's not going to like this either," I told them.

They knew, but they explained it could give him a lot of relief, and they didn't want to expose him any more than he had been getting the x-ray. Point taken.

"You are right," I told them. "We will do our best."

His casts weren't as hard as a normal cast, thank goodness, or we would never have been able to take them off. Still today, we have one of his little casts tucked away with some of his memories. It took patience, a lot of patience, and persistence. However, we finally managed to get them off. My husband did the cutting, and I did the comforting. He did seem relieved and more settled at the time. That gave us a sigh of relief. I used warm water and lotion to soothe them. He loved it, so content.

Night was upon us, his nurse arrived, and I filled her in. I'm sure she could see the worry and stress all over me. I tried to hide it, but it's not like I was looking in a mirror or even cared what I looked like.

She said, "You look exhausted, have you eaten?"

I thought, *I don't know, and I don't care.*

Of course, we as a society usually say we're okay whether we are or not. I'm not sure why we do that. I changed the subject quickly.

Nights are the hardest. We have so much going on here. We can't drop the ball at all tonight. I'm sure I made her nervous. She was older, seasoned, aware; and she told me so. She assured me she was up for the challenge. I'm sure at this point you can tell she would not be doing it alone. He was fed, and meds were given. It was time for a breathing treatment in hopes he could rest. The one thing he needed most was rest. Healing can happen best when rest is had. Healing has been our nonstop goal, prayer, and ever-present hope. We needed healing. He lay there in his room with Briecin under his bed, on guard. Cody was just looking around, wide eyed, taking it all in.

I, of course, gave him his treatment, and he just remained calm, peaceful. The treatments were our thing too. Holding his hand, rubbing his sweet feet, telling him how much I loved him. He knew Mama was helping him. He was one amazing little man. He slept most of the night except he woke very early in the morning. Was he hungry? Was he in pain? Did he need a breathing treatment? Was he cold, hot, in need of his pants changed? It could be any number of things, but all of the above were handled immediately. He was more restless now, breathing faster, more shallow. I checked his pulmonary reflexes in his toes and fingers. In the hospital, we would hold down on his toenail, then release and see how quickly the color or blood returned. It returned slowly. This was not a good sign. I was using all the training I had soaked up at the hospital with all the tools I was given. My husband stayed home from work. It was all hands on deck.

I told him, "You can't go. I'm positive we're heading for the hospital."

He questioned me. He wasn't sure of that. "Let's not overreact."

I called the nursing company. They sent a nurse out right away to assess him. When she arrived, she thought he would be okay.

"Keep him warm," she said. "He's a little cool."

You've got to be kidding me. I had a stethoscope. I could hear the squeaking sound when he breathed in.

She said, "Air is still getting through."

I told her, "Okay, you can leave."

We put a warmer outfit on him to appease her so she would leave. I gave him another breathing treatment, then held him close to me. I listened closely, with everything as silent as possible. He was making a small sound when he breathed in, not a squeaking, like I could hear in the stethoscope. It was almost a laboring sound.

"That's it," I said. "I'm calling the hospital."

This became more of a challenge than I had ever expected.

They said, "You can't take him to the emergency room. That would be a bad choice with all the sick people there."

"Okay. Then I will bring him up to the floor he was on with Dr. Nolan and Dr. Zureikat and with nurses and staff who know him."

"You can't. It doesn't work that way," the girl I was speaking with argued back. "You have to be admitted by a doctor."

"Okay, tell them I need them to admit him."

"Ma'am, you don't understand."

"Oh, I understand. You don't, and you're wasting my time."

I hung up. I thought, *What do I do?* God, we need help and soon.

I told my husband, "I'm calling Dr. Walters' and Dr. Hakimi's office. They will help me."

So would have Dr. Nolan and Dr. Zureikat, if I could have gotten through to them. They performed surgery at the hospital, but they also had an office, and I knew that. I could get to them.

I explained to their staff I needed them, holding back tears. They knew what Cody had been through, what he had survived. After all, it was their hands that were holding his heart, beating for him. They knew me, and I just knew they would help. They knew God and knew we did too. *Luke 1:37* says, "*Nothing is impossible with God.*" And they had seen that firsthand with our son.

Their nurse said she would page one of them and someone would get right back to me. It wasn't long, and the phone rang. Just hearing Dr. Hakimi's voice made me succumb to the tears I had been holding back. I explained his sounds, his profusion, his coloring, and, in short, the details we were dealing with.

He calmly said, "Let me make a call. Oh, and Brenda, the sounds you are hearing are called grunting. It happens when one is being deprived of oxygen."

What? Why did no one teach me that? Why did the nurse not know that?

He said, "We don't have time to waste."

He made a call to Hurley hospital, to Dr. Nolan.

He called me right back. "Go straight to the hospital, straight to the floor Cody was on. They will admit him straight away. I made sure of that."

"Thank you so much."

He said, "You are so welcome. Get going."

He knew what was coming, the storm. His oxygen saturation or numbers were down, but only a little. They should look worse in my opinion compared to what I was seeing for sure. We hurried around as fast as we could. His color was not good. I told my husband we need to suction out his nose to see if we can help him breathe. The suction machine was so strong. It has to be for an adult, not a baby. This was a disaster. Forget it. Let's go.

By the time we got in the car and headed out the driveway, he began looking worse. We looked at each other, and my husband stepped on it. We were flying down the expressway, about 90mph, when a cop started following us, of course, with his lights on. He was just doing his job. My husband finally pulled over.

When the cop got to our window, my husband said, "Our son is in bad shape."

The cop hesitated and looked at him.

My husband said, "Sir, either move your foot, or I will have no choice but to run it over."

I was crying at this point telling him to go.

"Go," the cop said. "Go and I will give you an escort."

We tore out of there, going about as fast as our car could go. We arrived at the hospital and went flying inside and to the floor we were directed to, the one we spent a lot of time on. Running down the hall, Cody was almost blue at this point. I whipped off his blanket and shouted, "We need help now."

The nurse at the desk saw me and saw him. Everyone started running. They called for a crash cart. I wanted to collapse. Why was it so hard to get help? Why the faulty equipment? Why, God, why? They worked on him with us right there in the background. Dr. Nolan was on shift. We locked eyes.

He said, "What happened?"

I could only muster tears. So much. Where do I start? They got him to respond, medication, 100 percent oxygen, breathing treatments, suction. Almost everything I had been trying to do. I just didn't have the resources. This was killing me. On my watch, how could I ever live with this if he dies? Everyone kept telling me it's not my fault, but my son was here, in this situation that we were supposed to protect him from.

On the way to the hospital, my husband said, "I will never question you again when it comes to Cody."

I wish everyone had been that way. We wouldn't be here. I explained to Dr. Nolan, once Cody was more stable, about the equip ment, the nurse, the medical supply situation, everything, and how hard I tried and how helpless I felt. I could tell he felt bad. He had been helping us. He was in that meeting fighting for the right tools. I could tell it affected him. Even with his professional demeanor and being focused on the task at hand, as he always was, he could see how worn thin and broken I was. He was gentle, assuring me I had done all I could in the situation I was in. Antibiotics were on board. The ones he had responded to in the past. There were some that never worked for him. He reminded me how strong our son was and that he was a fighter, not to give up hope.

"He'd been through a lot worse than this. He wouldn't be left alone." It was 24/7 around-the-clock care. He would be there. Try not to worry.

I thanked him but told him that was impossible for me. I knew Cody's lungs were compromised too much. We'd been told that. I knew he was tired. This time felt different. I remember asking my husband if we had our time at home, could this be all we get? Is this all just too much for him? You see, I had never ever talked like that before. I was the one telling doctors, nurses, anyone we're not done here. He's not going anywhere. I was the one telling him not to leave us, to fight. I began using statements like, "If Cody doesn't make it…"

Nurses, doctors, my husband were all like, "Brenda, he's going to be okay. Look at all he's overcome."

There was this feeling, this voice inside me saying that this is all too much for him to keep enduring. I wasn't letting it out or thought I wasn't. Looking back, I can see I was, little by little.

He made it through the night. We were all relieved. Stephanie, his nurse, was on his day shift. Boy, was I glad to see her. I felt like I could actually breathe. And she could see that. She gave me a big hug, and that cracked the seal. I broke down and cried.

She said, "I'm here, Mama. Go take a break."

I finally did just that, but only for a short time, to gather myself. I couldn't lose it now, not now. My son needed me. All day the thoughts ran through my mind. *He's tired, Brenda. He's been through so much. He has so far to go. His feet, more heart surgery. His body can't take much more.*

The thoughts irritated me. I tried to block them out. They just kept coming back. By late afternoon, Cody had started taking a turn for the worse. I could see it plain as day. I never left his side. I kept reassuring him he was okay. I tried giving him comfort. All the while, looking at him and feeling so much compassion, it was overtaking me. Feelings of God taking his pain and suffering away filled my whole body. His breathing became so much more labored. I remember Dr. Nolan assessing him, changing his medication, doing all he could within his knowledge and power. He stepped out of the room to speak with Stephanie. They weren't about to ask me to leave. His heart rate was up, and his oxygen levels down even though he was still on 100 percent oxygen. I remember plain as day Stephanie coming back in the room and looking at me, holding Cody's other hand.

"Mama, he needs help breathing. Putting him on the ventilator is best."

"Is it?" I asked.

She looked at me so seriously. "What do you mean?"

"He's tired," I told her through my tears.

She said, "What are you saying?"

She knew this wasn't me. She had watched a few very close calls and a few miracles, times when it seemed impossible for Cody to still be here. Why should this be any different? She had seen him on and off the ventilator a few times. She'd seen him on his turning bed with barely any hope, and he had pulled through. Why would this be any different?

I looked her in the eye. "Maybe it's better for Cody to go be with Jesus."

She looked shocked. She composed herself, took a minute, and said, "Either way, the ventilator is the kindest thing to do for him right now."

I wanted assurance that it was the right thing because he hated it. He fought it so much at times they had to use a paralyzing drug to keep him from pulling the tube out. I told you he was a fighter. She told me struggling to breathe, in her opinion, was worse than the ventilator. She assured me they would use Versed so he would forget the procedure. That was the drug we fought the insurance company for. He responded well to it.

My husband was at work. I called him to come to the hospital and explained the situation. He came right away after the ventilator was placed. Cody's oxygen came up, and his heart rate slowed down. Stephanie assured me these were the signs of doing the right thing. I look back, and she probably thought I was exhausted and just wasn't thinking clearly the way I was talking. It wasn't me, not the me they had known every day for months. I now know it was God working in me and through me. I alone could never, even remotely, think of possibly saying goodbye to my son, or even thinking the thoughts he can't do this anymore. He was opening my eyes wide to his suffering. Not that I hadn't seen it every step of the way. This was different. I was fighting for me, for our family to be with Cody. I wanted what was best for all of us. Now, somehow, I clearly was seeing what was best for just him. In *Revelation 21:4*, it says, "*God will wipe away every tear from their eyes and death shall be no more. Neither shall there be mourning, crying or pain anymore.*" I knew this. My grandpa read this to us. I have it marked in his worn-out Bible. I knew Cody would live forever in heaven, pain and suffering free. I also knew that would mean us living here on earth without him. That is a picture I hadn't let myself imagine ever.

As it got later, it was time for his night-shift nurse, Sharon, to take over from Stephanie. We had been through a lot of rough nights together in the past months. Tonight appeared to be a rough one as well. She was geared up, ready, a fresh perspective, another set of eyes. She knew our son. She was technically doing everything she could. Cody's urine output, that they were now paying very close attention to, checking his diaper often, hoping to see some urine. He was looking a bit swollen, so another medication was added to try and pull some fluid off his body. I let Sharon work, chart, and check machines, not saying much. She knew the seriousness of the situation and needed to be laser focused herself. We called our parents to let them know the severity of Cody's condition. They, as well as my husband and the staff, knew this was nothing new to Cody. He would fight through this too. However, my mom and I have always been close, and she could tell by my voice I didn't sound the same.

I told her, "Mom, he's tired. He's so tired. I'm afraid he's had enough."

The silence on the phone said a lot. She lost her husband, and I lost my dad. She lost both of her parents, and I lost both of my grandparents. We both were no stranger to loss and the grief it brought with it. My father wasn't one to go to church with us if you recall, but the chaplain before he went into his coma asked my father if he wanted to be saved, to ask God into his heart. He shook his head yes. That assured me, assured us, that one day we would see him again in heaven. My grandparents were possibly the closest people to God, besides my mom, that I have ever been around. We both knew they were in heaven. If it was Cody's time, he would be there with them. There was some comfort in that for me. In *Psalm 116:1–2*, it says, "*I love the Lord God because he has heard my voice and my pleas for mercy.*" I was pleading with him all day to have mercy on our sweet little man. I wanted immediate healing. I wanted my son's body to be whole, to be healed, for him to be out of pain, to struggle to breathe no more. But I wanted him to do that here on earth, not in heaven. God can see the full tapestry, the entire picture. We cannot. We only see the here and now. We all want the healthy, perfect here and now for us, for our families, our friends, and especially for our children. In *1 John 3:1*, it says, "*See what kind of love the father has given to us that we should be called the children of God.*" Remember, God sees our tears and our pain. We are all his children. Cody was his child before he ever was mine. Only he knew what was best for him.

The scene in Cody's room was serious, constantly assisting him, trying to do all humanly possible to save our son's life. I remember Sharon having a metal tray by his bed with all of the supplies she needed so she didn't have to step away from him at all. All hands on deck now. Dr. Nolan checking in every few minutes, checking the machines, the ventilator, the medicine. Everything they were doing—all the tricks, medicines, treatments. Nothing seemed to be working. Tensions were running high. We had spoken to our parents again, telling them they should probably come, things weren't looking good. Before those calls were made, Sharon kept trying to work on our son, looking very worried. We would lock eyes, and her look and mine said it all. No words needed to be spoken. Words, however, needed to be spoken to my husband. He was so sure Cody was going to be fine, he would pull through. He didn't like the way I was talking. It made him angry. He even spoke of going home at one point to rest. It was so late, and he needed to go to work in the morning. At this point, this was all he could process. He couldn't and wouldn't process an alternative. Who could blame him? I seemed to be processing however. It was almost like an out-of-body experience. Words were coming out of my mouth calmly, despite the situation. I think I was confusing to several people that night, even myself. I had asked for God's mercy on my son and for his help to hold me up with his right hand, because, trust me, I could never do this on my own strength.

In *Romans 8:18*, God says, "*Consider that the sufferings of this present time are not worth comparing with the glory that is to be revealed to us.*" I tell you, my friend, my son, my husband, and I have done our share of suffering. I remember trying to get my husband to stay at the hospital, to call his parents again, to process the possibility that we could lose our son tonight. And if that happened, he wouldn't want to miss it. He wouldn't want to leave me alone.

Sharon was continuing to work on Cody. He wasn't putting out urine. Numbers were changing: oxygen, heart rate, etc. It all became too much for my husband. He hit the metal tray of supplies. They went flying, and he left the room. Sharon looked at me with big eyes. I told her, "I'm so sorry," and, in tears, went after my husband. We cried together, we prayed, we held each other for a bit, and then he pulled it together and made the call to his parents. I hurried back to Cody's room, and he returned shortly after. He apologized to Sharon. He's a good man, but a good man facing the possibility of losing his son.

Sharon kept moving the monitor connection. She started warming his hands in hopes it would help. She kept checking his blood profusion. Blood gasses were checked even though he was on a ventilator that was to be breathing for him. It all seemed like slow motion, yet things were definitely moving fast. There was no time to waste. Things were going downhill rapidly now. The interesting thing here was his heart. What had worried us the most was hanging strong, doing its job. It's his lungs that were struggling. I think most of us thought if we were to ever lose him, it would be to his heart. Sharon picked up the phone all the while doing all she could and called Dr. Nolan.

She said, "Please come stat."

He did just that. He said, "Okay, we're not out of options." He started telling Sharon what to do, telling us what medicine he was adding. "We're not done here," he said.

With everything in me and all the strength I could muster, I said, "*Stop. Stop.* Leave him alone."

Everyone looked at me.

"What? Mom, you told us never give up. You told Cody to always fight. You want us to stop?"

I said, "Please give us a minute." I looked at my husband.

He said, "Why?"

I told him, tears streaming down my face, "He's tired. He's so tired. He can't. He just can't." I told him, "We need to tell him together, if it's too hard, we won't beg him to stay. We will be okay if he needs to go be with Jesus. If it's all too much for him, it's okay to go."

With his mommy and daddy on both sides of his bed, by his head, touching him gently, we said, "Cody, we love you so much. You've been so strong. If it's too hard, it's okay, you can go."

Nurses and doctors will tell you at times our loved ones hang on for us. They need to know we will be okay if they go. Cody needed to know that. Mom wasn't there saying, "Cody Joseph, don't you leave me. You fight." I promise you never, ever did I think I could give my son permission to leave me. I needed him so much. I had to, he was suffering so.

Dr. Nolan and Sharon stood at his doorway, ready to act if needed. And, trust me, if Cody decided to fight, we were all ready. But if he chose to go, somehow Mama and Daddy would be okay. He needed to know that. He was hanging on for us. He fought so hard for us. There was never a question how much he loved us, knew us, and needed us as much as we loved and needed him. I tell you, I don't know how much more suffering he would have endured if we hadn't told him it was okay, that we would be okay. He was such a tough, strong little man.

Shortly after we told him, both of us holding his little hands, everything quickly changed. He was choosing to finally give in. We were losing him. I looked back at Sharon and Dr. Nolan. Sharon tearful, trying to hold it together. She had taken care of him so long, and she loved him. That was always obvious. She and Stephanie both loved him. Dr. Nolan looked at me and nodded his head as if to say, "Okay, Mom." He looked sad, a little surprised, but composed, strong, professional. We needed that that night. I wanted Dr. Zureikat's hugs, tenderness, but God knew what was going to be needed. He was ever present and wove every thread. He knew the picture before it was ever brought into focus.

Dr. Nolan and Sharon came back into the room. He explained Cody was leaving us. We knew that. He asked if we wanted to hold him. He explained once he passed and they unhooked the ventilator, he might gasp or take his last breath. My husband and I squeezed into a chair together, both holding him; rubbing his head; telling him goodbye, how much we loved him, and we're going to miss him. I knew the only way I could let him go was to hand him from our arms straight into Jesus's arms.

Dr. Nolan unhooked the ventilator, reminded us again there could be a gasp, his last breath ever taken. We both took a deep breath of our own. No one wants to hear their child gasp their last breath. They offered more than once for us to leave if we wanted. That wasn't happening. I think they knew that. They were just trying to be merciful to us, to spare us. If my son was going to take his last breath, I wasn't going to miss it. God that day was not only merciful to Cody by taking him home to heaven to live forever with him pain free, but he was merciful on us. He knew we didn't need to be left with his last gasping breath. When Dr. Nolan removed the tube, there was no sound at all. He looked surprised. He was already gone.

You know in watching Cody failing, we were all amazed his heart was the last thing to stop. It kept beating until the very end.

In writing about his death, I had to take a break. I was sobbing, so hard I couldn't write. I actually had to call my husband down from his office while working.

He said, "That's enough for today." He could see the toll just writing this was taking on me still today, twenty-five years later.

I told him I'm going to write this to share our son's story. That day on his deathbed, I told him I would. I told him people would know what a soldier he was for God. All those days and nights spent in hospital rooms, praying, on my knees on dirty hospital floors, him fighting back from the brink of death time after time. Many, many people had seen our prayers answered over and over again. They got to see God through him and us. When living through it, you don't care who is there watching. You needed, I needed, God, to let me hold him, love him for however much time I possibly could.

I told my husband, "There is no way around it, I have to go straight through it."

It's almost like living it all over again.

Our parents made it to the hospital just as he was passing. My mom remembers me telling the doctor I was staying in the room for the removal of that awful ventilator tube my son hated so much. He was gone; but so were all the machines, tubes, and medicines keeping him alive. After passing our son straight to Jesus, we held him so tight. We also let our parents hold him and say their goodbyes. The scene was a flood of tears all around. Our sweet little man was gone. I had a hard time letting go. In fact, I told my husband to go home and get Briecin. I couldn't leave here empty-handed. I needed her to literally move my feet. He held me, held us both.

He had to reason with me. "Dogs aren't allowed at the hospital, but she will be waiting for you at home."

Home, I didn't want to go there either. If Briecin wasn't there, I don't know if I could have ever gone back. My son was finally home in my care after eight long, painful months, and now he was gone. His empty room still full of faulty equipment that didn't do the job. His smells and sounds had penetrated that room. It would never

ever be the same. His rocking chair, where we had our mommy-and-son time. God, help me, this is too much. It is way too much. When I handed my son's body over to Sharon, his nurse, I wanted to die myself. I wanted to go with him. I wanted this pain to leave us both. She took him, and I held on for dear life, sobbing. She took my hand. "I got him, Mama." I had heard that so many times, but I knew I wouldn't be back. I would never have that again. Never to hold him or sing to him ever again here on earth.

We finally left him and said our last goodbye. Honestly, God had to be carrying me. I don't remember making it to the car. I know I sobbed all the way home and long into the night, all the while wrapped around Briecin, her not making one move. She knew Cody wasn't with us. She had looked by the car and in his room, under his bed. She was sad too. She mourned with me, with us. We managed to get some sleep. Not a lot but some was better than none. The weight of it all hit me like a brick with morning's light. Thank God my mom was there. Another presence to fill our quiet, empty home.

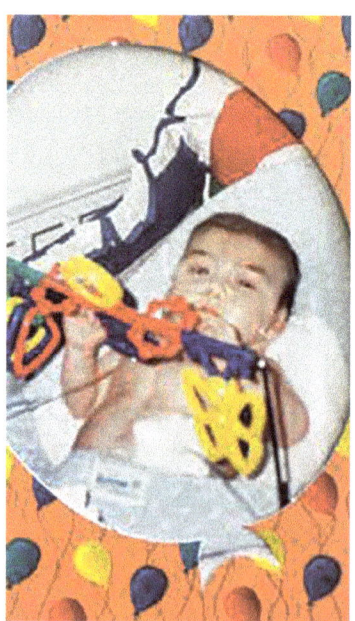

Mama's little man

Celebrating Cody's Life

Unfortunately, plans needed to be made for our son's funeral. I remember thinking, *Hasn't there been enough sadness?* It's important to us for the people we love to get to say their own goodbyes and to let them know more about his fighting spirit, about his life. There was so much more to his story than his life and his death. We mustered up the strength to meet a funeral director who had been recommended to us. We were told he had a package he had put together for babies. We were told it was reasonable and that they did a very nice job. The director was a kind, compassionate man. It takes a special person to do his job, and he was the right man for this job. He showed us the package they put together and the prices. Unfortunately, price had to be an issue. I hadn't been working for a little over a year now. That was a struggle, to say the least. The package was very nice. The casket and pillow were white and sweet. Everything was good except the brochures. I did not like them at all. They had the scripture on the front, *Psalm 23:4*. That is typical for funerals. It was, "*Though I walk through the valley of the shadow of death I will fear no evil.*" It wasn't appropriate for our son.

He said, "I'm sorry, that's what we have."

I pushed back a bit. For a baby? I think I was now making him second-guess their package at this point.

I said, "What about the scripture that says, 'Let all the little children come unto me for the kingdom of heaven belongs to them.' It's in *Matthew 19:14*."

He looked at me.

I thought, *He had to be thinking that's good, that's better.*

He said that he would look and would let us know. He would see if they had anything. Leaving felt wrong. I felt numb. Is this really happening? Are we planning our son's funeral? This was not supposed to happen. I'm sure every parent out there would think the way I was thinking. Parents aren't supposed to bury their children. After anyone dies, and I remember this well with my father, there are plans to be made, things to do, people around, food, business; but when it's all over, it's just you and your family left alone with your grief.

There were more plans to be made with our church, our pastor and his wife. What songs might we want, etc. We both knew for sure we wanted the story of his life to be told so those who didn't know him could get a window, just a peek, into his journey. My husband and I wrote together his story, through our tears. I promised him it would be told, and at least the people attending were going to hear it—if we could keep it together, through the tears. There were smiles too, believe it or not, like the time he had his oxygen tube between his toes squeezing it just like daddy or his fight when he was messed with. That one is like mommy. I have to own that one. As we wrote, the memories flowed.

Through it all, our son, Cody, was amazing and touched more lives than he would ever know. We wanted to be able to portray that. He was so much more than his multiple surgeries, his immune deficiency, or his crooked little feet. He was handsome, blue eyed, alert. He knew us. He loved music; his eyes would light up when we sang. He loved to be touched, rocked. He was a baby, sweet smelling, loving, like any other baby. We didn't want people to only see the broken parts. He was so much more. He was stronger than I've seen grown adults be and so calm, present, at ease when his parents loved on him. His baths, I will never forget his baths. Oh, how I loved being his mommy and wouldn't trade it for the world.

My husband and I wanted to speak, but we're afraid we might struggle to make it through. We decided, in our basement where it was completely quiet, to record his story. We only recorded our voices. That was hard enough. We were really glad we did. Many calls and plans were made.

It was now the day of the funeral. If you've been through this, I'm so sorry. It was hard to even get out of bed, let alone get ready to bury our son. My husband's grandparents on his mom's side, whom we were very close to, wanted to pay for his outfit. That was sweet. It was all white, like his casket. It was now just about four hours before his service when the phone rang. I'm so glad it did. You see we had forgotten about his pamphlets with so much other planning going on. It was the funeral director. He had found a card with Jesus on the front with children at his feet.

"Perfect," I told him.

"The only problem," he said, "is it's blank inside. We need what you want inside right away to be able to print them before the service."

I told him, "Okay, let me talk to my husband. Give us a few minutes."

He said, "Of course, but only a few minutes."

That's about all the time we had. I told him I understood. I hung up and told my husband. We got paper right away and went into our bedroom.

I said, "A poem would be nice."

My husband is great at writing poems, better than me, but I have written a few myself. Together, lying on our bed, we wrote a beautiful poem. It was so important; people would take them with them. It had to be perfect. My husband will still today tell you I have an issue with perfect when I'm doing things. He says that for me, the best is always the enemy of better. I know he's right. It's just one of my blind spots. Thank God, I knew he was with us. The poem flowed so easily, and we were done in minutes. We still today, twenty-five years later, have the poem, his picture and flowers that were freeze dried from his funeral in a wooden-and-glass box. The poem I still know by heart.

Although we are hurting and the tears fall like rain, our Cody's in heaven, free from all pain. He's running with Jesus, a new body he's won, we'll never forget you, our little angel, our son. So play hard, sweet baby, you've fought a good fight. We'll look forward to the day we'll again hold you tight.

A moment in our lives, a lifetime in our hearts. All our love, Mommy and Daddy.

For me, this was perfect and the visual I needed for today and for the rest of my life. We called back right away to let the director know.

He said, "Did you have this already?" He seemed surprised.

I told him no.

Listen, friend, God knew we needed the right message right then and still now today. I'm so thankful for the visual, the picture bubble, I get every time I see it. That's every day. Sometimes several times a day. We also have the only picture ever taken of him before heart surgery in clothes with his little hat on with no tubes or machines. We were able to take his oxygen nasal cannula off for the picture. I love this picture. The happy memories flood back daily of our little man sitting in the large white frame in our kitchen.

The funeral was amazing. All of our family was there to celebrate his life. That's how we wanted it. Things went fairly smoothly except the reading of his life story we had written. We had a friend from our church read it. It was difficult for sure. I was really happy we had our recordings. Of course, there wasn't a dry eye. Our pastor and longtime friend did a great job. It's tough. I thought losing my dad was tough and my grandparents, but burying a child, that will almost rip the heart right out of your chest.

When it was over, and there was just family left, I wanted pictures. Why? I don't know. The things we do when we're grieving. Those aren't happy pictures, but they were real and part of that painful day. I also wanted pictures of our son in his casket. I know, I know... it's my process. He looked like an angel lying there, so peaceful, so perfect, no machinery, no tubes, just his precious body. I knew his soul was in heaven. He was running with Jesus with his perfectly straight little feet and perfect heart. That was God's comfort to me. That was the picture bubble I needed to hang on to. I don't look at those pictures often, but when I do, it's okay. I see my little angel all dressed in white.

After the photos, there's a time when it's time to leave. Everyone was standing around visiting, my husband as well. I was standing by my son's body, unable to move, touching him. Of course, he was cold, such a different touch. His body was just that. My son was gone. In *Ecclesiastes 12:7*, it says, "*The dust returns to the earth as it was and the spirit returns to God who gave it.*" In *Luke 23:43*, it says, "*Truly I say to you, today you will be in paradise.*" Luke is speaking about us dying. If we are saved, we will be in paradise after we die. I knew my son was there, but this didn't make it easier, unfortunately, to walk away from his body. I was sobbing alone by his casket. My brother saw me and came over. He gave me away at my wedding, for my dad. He has stepped up over the years since Dad's passing and sometimes at just the right time. That day I needed him, right then and there.

He put his arm around me and said, "It's time, Brenda."

I said, of course, "I can't."

He said, "It's okay, we will do it together."

I finally was able to leave, surrounded by family. It helped that family came back to our house after.

The days after, the quiet house, me alone with my grief, without my son. The machines were all gone, my husband working, and family all gone home. A loneliness set in. No horse to ride, nowhere I could go to escape my pain. That's when I needed God most. Anger was very present for me, at the situation, at the insurance company, and especially at myself. This definitely wasn't helping. I would rock in my son's chair asking God, "Why?" I would go into his room; hold his blanket and bear; and honestly long for him, ache to hold him. I would look out at the empty barn.

One day, while looking out, a memory came flooding back to me. It's a memory of our pastor's daughter, Holly, riding my horse, me leading her with a big smile on her face. She had wanted to ride my horse before she got too sick. She was a beautiful girl. A bright light in her family's life and so many others. She had beautiful long brown hair. I will never forget. Her parents were a bit concerned. Who could blame them? Their sweet girl had a brain tumor, an untreatable, fatal brain tumor. She loved horses and thanked me many times. So did her parents.

After riding, we went in the house for a bit. She asked if she could speak to me.

"Of course," I said.

We went into a bedroom to be alone. She asked me if she could borrow a dress of mine she had seen me wear to church and she loved it.

I said, "Of course, anything."

She proceeded to tell me she was planning her funeral and she didn't want to just borrow my dress, she wanted to be buried in it. I did all I could to hold back my tears, to be strong for her.

I said, "Of course. I would be honored."

We both shed tears. I held her and loved on her the best I could. She was so thankful, and all the while I kept thinking, *I wish I could do more. I wished I could somehow change the outcome, the picture for her and her amazing parents.*

We all had a good day. A happy memory moment that day. I did, unfortunately, get to see her wear that dress the day of her funeral. The church was packed, overflowing. What a beautiful, short life lived and a beautiful family. They had seen her through to the end. All the headaches, pain, swelling, tears, and the goodbyes until they all met again one day in heaven. I felt their pain and loss then, but I now understood their pain fully. When you are alone in your grief, and trust me, grief is something we all do alone, inside ourselves. And we all do it our own way and in our own timing. In *Ecclesiastes 3:1–7*, it says,

> *There is a time for everything, a season for every activity under heaven. A time to be born and a time to die, a time to plant and a time to uproot, a time to tear down and a time to build up. A time to weep and a time to laugh, a time to mourn and a time to dance. A time to search and a time to give up. A time to keep and a time to throw away. A time to tear and a time to mend.*

I realized I couldn't stay in the home I loved so much. There was too much pain everywhere I looked: his chair in the living room, his blankets, his room, all his toys he never got to play with, his swing, his playpen. It was too much. The grief felt like it would swallow me up whole. When my husband came home that night, he could see I wasn't okay. He could see that every day.

I told him through my tears, "I can't be here. I feel like I can't breathe. Sadness is all around me."

My dreams had collapsed in that home. I couldn't find a way out. Even with God, I felt like I couldn't find a way out. Even though I knew my son was free from pain, my emotional pain was just too overwhelming, overtaking me. In *Psalm 31:9*, it says, "*Be gracious to me, O Lord, for I am in distress. My eyes are wasted from grief. My soul and my body are also.*" This scripture describes my emotions quite well.

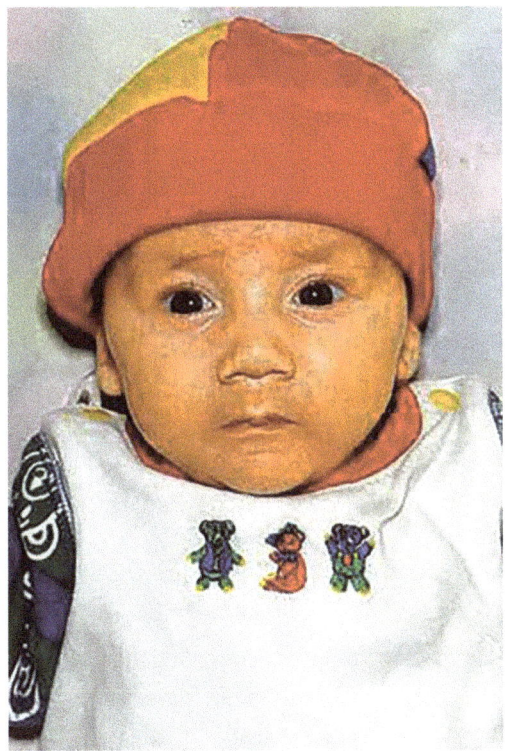

Cody Joseph Cain

Unpleasant Grief

I felt wasted in my grief, just done, a shell of what I once was. We talked, and my husband couldn't reason with me now. I wanted out, sell this place I used to love.

"I can't be here," I told him. I knew this made no sense to him. I loved our land, our home. I couldn't make sense of it myself. When people say grieving is a process, those of us that have done some serious grieving, we know that unfortunately all too well. A long, long process. I definitely can't see how anyone does it without God and the security that we will be with our loved ones again one day with no more tears or pain, only joy. In *John 16:22*, it says, "*So you have sorrow now but I will see you again, your hearts will rejoice and no one will take your joy from you.*" In *1 Corinthians 2:9*, it says, "*What no eye has seen, nor ear heard, nor your heart have imagined, what God has prepared for those who love him.*"

If you've lost loved ones and their date of death is near, I would encourage you to think about the good times you've had with them. Think about the things they loved or you loved doing with them. Once you've done that, I would also encourage celebrating their life with one or a few of their favorite things. Do them yourself. For my mother-in-law, she loved when her son, my husband, would play music and sing; but her absolute favorite thing in life was ice cream. Even until the very end, she would eat her ice cream in small bits, several times a day, as she couldn't remember she had already eaten it. That still makes me smile today. So celebrating her day of death is wonderful music and ice cream. Miss you, Mom.

Move we did. A nice couple bought our home, and we found another one. It wasn't on land, no barn, no horses. Just a house in a neighborhood where there were people close and children playing.

Life, I needed that. I missed my neighbor, our land, the tractor, and definitely our horses. I sometimes hated myself for moving, but I tell you I had to.

The last day before the move, when everything was packed up, my husband at work, I was in Cody's room lying on the floor. Taking in all the grief and sorrow. Just sobbing. What had I done? The only place he had ever been. I can't leave. I absolutely lost it. If you have loved ones grieving and they make no sense at times, can't explain their emotions, they just are what they are. I got the phone and called my husband. Through my sobbing, I told him to come home. I think I've finally lost it. He came home to me lying on our son's floor in a heap, sobbing, hitting the floor, yelling, angry, sad, grief-stricken. The poor guy. He didn't tell me what to do or to stop. He just held me for as long as it took. You can't rush grief, my friend. And you can't tell someone how to handle theirs. All you can do is love them through it, right there, right where they are. I promise you, they need you to be there, to love them, to not judge, or rush them. They can't help it. Be present in their pain and their needs whether it be food, hugs, tears, someone to yell at, a good listener, or someone to just be there. Whatever they need, just do it if at all possible. That's the best advice I can give you. Show up no matter the emotional cost. They need you even if they push you away. For me, animals have always been a big comfort. Poor Briecin, she had to live through my grief. At times I had to pull it together even just for a while so she would eat or drink. She was my shadow everywhere. Thank you, God, for dogs and especially for special ones like Briecin.

Grief, it changes you. One way or another. Some people get angry, bitter, downright ugly. Who can blame them? Some shut down completely. They have a hard time functioning at all. Some are so sad, so broken, it's hard to watch. Sometimes there are those of us who seem to want to move on, what might seem to be too quickly. They just have to. It's too much to deal with, so they distract themselves, trying to put it out of their minds or try to stay really busy. Grief, you can't run from it. It will catch up to you; and for the runners, when it catches you, it will hit you out of the blue like a Mack truck. Grief is not something you can avoid or decide you won't deal with. But I tell you, grief is something we have to meet head on—one day, one time or another. It may just be the one part of life we wish we could all skip over. I'm sorry, my friend. I've seen it over and over again. There's just no way around grief. Whether it's days or years before you are able to process it, unfortunately, we all process it. It's part of your tapestry. Part of the inner woven threads that run together that make up your journey, your life's beautiful picture. I did say beautiful. It's the part of us that makes us sympathetic to others, compassionate, caring; and our unique journey helps us to relate to others so we can help them through theirs. Believe it or not, your grief can help you, mold you, and make you better if you let it. Oh, I know, especially if you're reading this and are right in the throes of grieving at this very minute. Trust me, it can. In *Romans 8:28*, it says, "*We know that for those who love God all things can work together for good.*" Grief working for good? There's no way, at least for me, while I was in the middle of mine that I could see it working for good. Twenty-five years later, now I can see more of the tapestry, the linking threads where my grief experience has been able to help someone else; and when that happens, my friend, you know. You can see firsthand where it has been used for good. Please don't miss the strongest thread that's always running through the tapestry, holding all the frayed ends together. It is God himself. Listen, friend, if you've struggled in your life and haven't been able to see the beauty in it and all you see are dark colors, the knots, and frayed ends, remember your tapestry isn't complete. Look for the light colors. Look for the good. It's there, brightness and goodness, I promise you. It's trying to peer through the darkness surrounding you. Go to God, ask him to help you see. Seek him out. In *Colossians 2:2–3*, it says, "*I want you woven into a tapestry of love, in touch with everything there is to know of God. Then you will have minds confident and at rest, focused on God's great mysteries.*" That mystery, all the richest treasure of wisdom and knowledge, is embedded in nowhere else. There is a poem of unknown origin that Cory Ten Boom (the author of the *Hiding Place*) used in her book. It reads:

> My life is but a weaving between my Lord
> and me. I cannot choose the colors. He worketh

steadily. Often times he weaveth sorry and I, in foolish pride, forget he sees the upper and I the underside. Not until the loom is silent and the shuttles cease to fly shall God unroll the canvas and explain the reason why dark threads are as needed in the weaver's skillful hand as the threads of gold and silver in the pattern he has planned. He knows, loves, cares, nothing this truth can dim. He gives his very best to those who leave the choice with him.

Whoever wrote this poem, I'm thankful. For me, it's a beautiful representation of our journey and the tapestry of our lives. An image, a peek into the window of God and his handiwork. Have you ever really looked at a tapestry? The back shows somewhat of the image. The colors and the textures are clearly different. In the making process, the back is a mess of different-colored threads. What is seen so clearly, so beautifully on the front is not on the back. What we see in life is not the whole picture God sees. We lack the clarity, the details. God doesn't, my friend. Not only does he see the whole picture in full color, he designed it. At least for me, it's best to let him lead, to follow him. He alone knows what tomorrow brings. It brings us back to *Romans 8:28*, "*For those who love God all things can work together for good.*" When you are in the middle of your struggle, your pain, there seems to be no way to see how any of it can be used for good, let alone to be creating a beautiful tapestry. On the other side of my son's life struggle and death, I can see his beautiful life, his tapestry, all the people his life touched. Only with God and through his eyes have I been able to bring that into clear focus. I'm so thankful for that image here today. My son's body being new, whole, perfect feet, no pain. Through all we've been through, that image, our poem, has been the most treasured gift God has given me. If you are lost in your pain or grief, search out God. Search out his words. Pray. Ask for help. There is help out there, friend. If you don't have God's son, Jesus, in your heart, invite him in; and if you are grieving, grief that aches to your very bones, he already knows. He designed you, and he can turn your situation into a beautiful tapestry. He has for me, and he's still weaving today. In *Proverbs 8:17*, it says, "*I love those who love me and those who seek me diligently find me.*" Jeremiah 29:13 says, "*You will seek and find me when you seek me with all your heart.*" In *Psalm 14:2*, it says, "*The Lord looks down from heaven on the children of man to see if there are any who understand, who seek after him.*" It calms my soul to know God is looking down on me, and after all his weaving, I understand. I will leave you with this: no matter your pain, grief, your loss or devastation, no matter the form or situation, God already knows, friend. Let him help you. No one can help you like God can.

In our new home, there were so many things to do, so many distractions, that at times I could lose myself in the decorating, the situating, and the putting away. But that usually didn't last too long. I would come across a memory or a picture, and it was almost like PTSD. It would jolt me right back into my grief and my deep aching sorrow for my son. Those times were really rough and lonely.

I had a close friend ask me once, "How do you get up every day and keep going?"

I think my response shocked her. I said, "Well, for some reason, God still has me here on this earth."

When the night darkness fades and the morning's light comes, unfortunately, I have to get out of bed. I have to go to the bathroom. That one simple task forced me out of bed. The sadness came, but so did the daylight peering through the window. Briecin had to go outside as well. Alone with each other, we walked wearily through our grief. Our human body needs to drink, and going to the bathroom forced me out of bed. I'm no different than you. I'm merely human, flesh and bone. Every long day after long day, I would have stayed under my covers wrapped around Briecin, smothered under my grief. My husband knew by the look on my face when he arrived home from work each day. He also knew Briecin, along with me, was struggling. Her food bowl barely eaten. We were making it, but just making it wasn't what he or any of us needed.

One night he said, "What do you think about a puppy to play with Briecin?"

What do I think? He knew what I thought before he uttered those words. A puppy would bring much needed life into our home. It would bring messes to clean up, training for both Briecin and I. It would bring laughter and joy. We all needed that. He knew for me a puppy could be the right thing at just the right time. When he said it, he saw the light brighten in my eyes just a bit. We looked in the newspaper, and there were some boxer puppies for sale.

Yes, please. We made the call and made plans to go see them on the weekend. Finally, there was something to bring some light into our darkness. I was anxious for the weekend. Weekends were always a little better for me. My husband was home, and honestly, that made all the difference. Just being able to be together helped. I'm sure it wasn't easy for him, but he brought light home with him for both Briecin and me. He would throw the ball for her; she usually loved that. Now she would try to play along for a short time, but it wasn't the same. We had a three-person outdoor swing, and all three of us would sit there and swing. We would talk about his day, his work, people he worked with. For me, anything to take my mind off my grief if but for just a few minutes.

The weekend was here, and it was time to go see the puppies.

My husband said, "Now let's just go look. Let's see how the parents act as well. No one wants a crazy puppy."

I laughed thinking all puppies are a little crazy. He knew we weren't coming home empty-handed. It was over an hour drive. This gave us time to talk about names. I could hardly contain my excitement. Growing up for me in a house where dogs weren't allowed, I always said as a child I will have dogs in my house. They can even sleep in my bed. I grew up with animals as I talked about earlier, and we had a dog we found by the road, homeless, that we took home. However, he had to live outside. He had a small building, but I hated it. He was out there all alone. I felt so sorry for him. Still today, I do not like dogs living outside under any circumstances. My mom never had a pet in the house as a child. Her mom didn't like it, so I didn't blame her. Today, I have a small Maltese named Blizzard. He is the dog, after many, that finally won her over. It makes me smile. She loves him so much, and yes, he has slept in bed with her.

We arrived at a small place in the country. They had the puppies in the house in a makeshift playpen. That was a plus for me. They were clean and cute. The place where we bought Briecin was dirty, downright nasty. The owner didn't want to sell her. She would sell other puppies, but she wanted to keep her. She knew she was special. I locked eyes with her and had to have her. We had to pay extra. My husband wasn't thrilled with it, but for me, it had to be her. God knew when we bought her how much I was going to need her.

The puppies were all cute. The parents were calm and well-trained. That was a plus. They were all jumping, trying to get our attention, all except one. He sat there stoic, not bothered, as if to say, "What's all the fuss about?" He was chunkier than the rest. So cute and seemed chill. We had never owned a male dog. We were planning on sticking with a female. Some male dogs will mark things, and we weren't going to risk that. Well, you see, like Briecin, there was something special about him.

I told my husband, "It's him. I have to have him."

He looked at me and said, "He's a male."

I said, "I know. I can't tell you why, but it's him. I can't go home without him. I'm sorry."

He shook his head at me as if to say, "Really? I'm getting you a puppy?"

He likes dogs but is much less of an animal guy than me.

The owner said, "He loves to eat and doesn't care what the other puppies do. They climb all over him."

I said, "He's the one. We will take him."

I myself don't give our dogs a lot of space, still today. They need to be tolerant of my cuddling, my foot rubbing on them while I fall asleep. They are not just a dog; they are family. He was so cute. He snuggled up, no crying leaving the other puppies or his mama. He was content like he knew he was supposed to be with us. He was our easiest puppy still today. However, Briecin was an amazing teacher. She mothered him, got after him if he was doing something wrong. When we were relaxing and he wanted to play the up-and-down stairs game, she would follow him and make him come right back. And when she had enough, she would let him know that was it. She would block the stairs, plant her feet, and growl at him. For sure, he was easier, not just because he was laid-back but because she was the best trainer, dog, friend, comforter one could ever want. We named him Brisco. It was after a show called *The Adventures of Brisco County, Jr.* The names Briecin and Brisco had a good ring to it. God knew our house needed Brisco, and he and Briecin loved each other so much. They were inseparable. He was just what we all needed.

I remember thinking, *Oh, how I wish Cody could be here getting all the dog kisses and love they would have heaped on him.*

Brisco didn't take my grief and pain away, but he did help me to take a step toward healing. For me, my husband knew animals are a love language for me. It may sound odd to you, but I could tangibly hold Brisco, love on him and Briecin in the flesh. They were like, for me, God's love here on earth. Each day comforting me, lifting me up, bringing light into my darkness. All throughout my life there's a bright shiny thread that runs through my tapestry. That bright thread is the long line of pets I've been blessed to love and share my life with. That bright thread has certainly helped mute out the dark ones.

It was time to get Brisco his puppy vaccines. So off to the vet we go with Briecin in tow. She would make sure he wasn't afraid, give him comfort, or make him behave. I can assure you of that. Mama Briecin was on duty. He was great. He had the best and sweetest demeanor. He gave us no trouble. He didn't even make a sound getting his shots. Our vet knew us well. He was our vet with poor Boutique. He was happy how well both dogs behaved. He also knew about Cody. He asked me how I was doing. He knew my love for animals and also asked if I would be interested in working for him. I hadn't gotten past my grief let alone thought about going back to work. Working with animals did intrigue me, of course. He was hoping it would. I told him to let me think about it. I didn't want to leave a new puppy home all day. Speaking with my husband that evening, he thought it might be good for me at least two or three days a week. I agreed to a couple days a week, maybe three at times if they needed it. It was good for me, and I really liked the staff. We were all animal lovers. It made it easier.

Boxers Briecin and Brisco

Aw, Mother's Day

Time was passing, and my pain a little less, though not gone, not by a long shot. I still missed Cody. My heart still longed to be a mama. I wanted a family. I wasn't getting any younger. I was thirty when I got pregnant with Cody. Mother's Day would be in a few months, and another year would pass by without a child's cry or laughter filling our home.

One day, I was watching Regis and Kathie Lee's morning show, and they were advertising their Mother's Day show. They had a number on the screen to write in and try to get moms on the show. I thought of my mom and all she had been through. I've found, once you become a mother yourself, you can appreciate yours so much more. You know what it takes. I quickly got paper and a pen. I wrote down the information. I knew my mom was deserving, and I could take the focus off me and redirect it to her. I laid the paper on the kitchen table, and when my husband got home, I told him about it and that I was going to write in for my mom. He thought it was a great idea.

The next morning, after he was gone to work (I didn't have to work that day), I went to get the information I left on the table, and it was gone. I drove myself a little crazy for a while looking with no luck. It was time for the show to be on, so I thought, *No worries I will get the info today*. With pen and paper in hand, waiting, Regis said, "Some of you may be disappointed," and that he was sorry but yesterday was the cut off for Mother's Day information. What, are you serious?

Back to looking. I called my husband. He had no idea. What in the world? Where could it be? I found out soon where it went.

Mother's Day was approaching fast. I was definitely disappointed and not looking forward to the day. I would miss Cody more than ever, and it would be one more reminder of the family I didn't have. My husband called me. I remember it clearly. He said his work needed him to go out of town to New York City. He had a big project he was working on.

I asked, "Now?" I really didn't want to be alone on Mother's Day, or before it for that matter.

He said he had no choice. He said however, "You could go with me. Maybe we could stay the weekend and celebrate Mother's Day there."

I had never been to New York City.

He also said, "Maybe we can see a play."

We have always loved plays. My husband's parents loved plays. That was something we did together at small local venues quite often. My mom likes them too. We've gone together as well.

A play, somewhere new, a distraction for me would be a good thing, I thought. I told him, "Yes, let's do it."

Plans were made, and off to New York City we went. A car picked us up from the airport. My husband said that his work arranged it.

I remember thinking, *He must be important. He's moving up in the world.*

We talk about it at times today, and we laugh. He said he had a whole weekend planned. We arrived at the hotel. I was glad. There was so much bumper-to-bumper traffic. I wanted out of the car. I've never done well in back seats. I tend to get a little car sick, and with all the airport stops and starts, the hotel arrival was a relief. It was tall and beautiful.

I thought, *Can we afford this?*

During the check-in process, one of the clerks asked us if we would like some free tickets to see the Regis and Kathie Lee's Mother's Day show.

My husband looked at me with a big smile. He told him, "I think she would like that."

I was excited. I had never been in an audience where live taping was taking place. We got settled in our room. It was very nice with a high city view. All the lights, buildings, and activities—I was taking it all in. We decided to take a walk, check out the sights, get something to eat, and maybe check out some shops along the way.

I thought, *That's my favorite part. Maybe New York has some unique things we don't have at home. Not that I could buy, but it would be fun looking.*

We did enjoy ourselves, and we found a small bistro that had an outdoor patio. I have always loved eating outside in open air. Nighttime felt different there. No Briecin or Brisco. I had checked on them, and they were fine. Yet I felt the same bit of sadness peering through once again like every night since Cody's death. A void, an emptiness. I remember sitting up late into the night unable to sleep looking at all the city lights, wishing Cody was with me, wondering if he could see us too.

The next day was the Mother's Day show, and what sleep I could get, I knew morning's light would come, and my arms would still be empty. It was a good thing we had the morning show to go to. The morning was busy getting ready with breakfast and our journey to the show. It indeed was a good distraction just as I thought it would be.

When we got to the building, people were lined up around the corner.

I thought, *Ugh, no way. I don't want to fight that crowd. I just didn't have it in me, not on Mother's Day. It wasn't that important.*

My husband assured me, "These are people waiting for tickets. We already have ours. The tickets tell us what door to go in. Let's find that."

I said, "Okay. But if that doesn't work, I want to go."

The long walk, all the people, the deep ache in my heart. I wanted to retreat back to the hotel and go back to bed. I was tired, and it was all too much. Grief will do that. It will strip the energy right out of you. You feel a weakness like almost anything extra is too much. There is so much research out in the world today about grief. The many steps you will go through. Honestly, a lot of it you can read and maybe get some help from some advice at least. I can appreciate that. But just know your experience may be just that. No book, no exact timing or stage. Just you. Your grief. Your timing and your processing. Not many speak about how physically taxing it is on your body. Not just the emotional drain but the physical drain. For me, I have physical issues from my car accident and the arthritis I live with on a daily basis. This is different. It made me feel weak. A little bit physically sick, completely worn-out. Like I needed rest, physical rest. However, my emotional trauma was making that very difficult. Trying to put on a brave face, share smiles, and say "Happy Mother's Day" with strangers while keeping it all inside. Keeping it together was definitely taking its toll.

Grief, when it got too bad at times for me, was something I had to let out, to release like a pressure valve that would blow clean off if it wasn't released. At home, I could cry, yell, pray, loudly asking God, "Why did this happen to me?" It was Mother's Day after all. Who could blame me? We needed to find the door quickly, or move on, like now. I knew God knew my pain and was with me in my grief. In *Isaiah 45:2*, it says, "*I will go before you and make the rough places smooth; I will shatter the doors of bronze and cut through their iron bars.*" I knew not only was he with me, but he went before me. This, however, doesn't mean it isn't hard. It does, however, mean we're not alone. He's got us and will never leave us.

Aw, finally, the door. Thank you, God. My husband showed the gentleman at the door our tickets, and to my surprise, he said, "Come in. Right this way."

I thought for a minute, *That was easy.*

We were told where to go and to wait for the audience to be seated.

I thought, *Those poor people outside, they will never get in. What made us so special?*

I didn't have long to think or process all that was going on. There was so much activity all around us. It didn't take long for the doors to open up and for us to take our seats. It was first come, pick your seat. We got seated a few rows up where you could get a good view of the stage. After all, I loved the show and wanted to see everything. There were so many moving parts going on. I was entranced on the activity, not thinking again about the how or why we got in, only the excitement about being there, making a new Mother's Day memory that I could hold on to, lock away, maybe bring it up another day when the darkness breaks through. This is looking like a bright strand in my intricately woven mother's tapestry. My husband offered me gum. Later, I would find out why that was a bad idea. For me, when a lot is going on around me, I might chew a little faster or forget to keep my mouth closed, and there was a lot happening around me to say the least.

The producer, Gelman, came out to speak to the audience. He told us we would be signaled, with an applause sign, when we should clap. However, he showed us how clapping sounds louder. He had us clap loud, then he had us clap fast. I never knew clapping faster, instead of harder, equaled louder, but it did.

It was time for the show to start. Little did I know my husband had people around the world we knew glued to their TV and taping the show. Do you see now why the gum was a bad idea? People at home saw me really chewing my gum. When I watched later, I was mortified. The show had a camera on me, saying, "This Michigan mom has no ideas she's on the show today."

No kidding, you think? There I was chomping my gum, looking around next to my husband who was, you guessed it, not chewing gum. It was a wonderful day. I still today ask my husband, "Why did you give me gum?" I saw a friend from high school, and he said the minute he saw me chewing gum he knew it was me. I was heavier at the time than I'd ever been in my life. All the hospital take-out food, the stress snacking on the fly, and being pregnant had taken its toll on my body. Of course, he knew me by my gum chewing. That still makes me laugh today when I think about it. It is part of the tapestry, friend.

The sign came up. The show was starting. Let the clapping begin. There was a mother with a handicap child she had devoted her entire life to. I felt her. The powerhouse mamas that no matter what don't give up. I was her for 8.5 months. Her son was older now and harder for her to handle. Her family had written in for her. Their letter told of what an amazing mother she was. They called her down onstage. Her family had asked for a handicap van with a wheelchair lift on it. The show told her they were gifting her with one.

Wonderful, I thought. She still has her son, and this would help her so much.

Next, there was a woman who was a teacher for learning-disabled children. One of the parents wrote in telling how amazing she was with their child. They asked for a trip around Europe for her. They said she always talks about traveling, but teachers don't make much. They told all the ways she was so deserving.

All is good, I thought. These stories are uplifting. I need that.

The show went to commercial. I told my husband what a good time I was having and what a good idea this was. Coming back from commercial, the whole room was silent. They had given a hush prompt. There, over the loud speakers, was my husband's voice; and on a large screen were my son's pictures. He was reading a letter he had written from my son, as though he was writing it from heaven. The tone of the room changed. It got heavy. People tearing up. Oh yeah, of course, this was my story. My story doesn't have a happy ending. I'm sorry, folks. They waved us down onstage. All the while my husband's voice over the speaker and my son's handsome face on that large screen. Tears flooded my eyes. My sweet little man with his big blue eyes. How I missed him. I think I was in shock a bit, walking down to the stage. My husband had asked for a hot tub from Cody for his mama to ease her pain from her accident. They rolled this large Kohler bathtub onto the stage as music was playing. There was a robe and some bath products on the side of the tub. I was a bit overwhelmed and everything happened so quickly. It was over before I knew it. We still today have a copy of the show. It still makes me cry, and those we show it to tear up as well.

The show also sent us to a very nice dinner and a Broadway play. I remember at dinner Mary Lou Henner and her family sitting at the table next to us. We were told this place could take months to get into. The play was called *Les Misérables*. We went backstage and met the cast, and they gave us a signed poster with all their signatures on it. My husband still has it hanging in his office today.

It was a wonderful Mother's Day weekend. They told us we could go stay overnight at Kohler's hotel and pick our tub. Unfortunately, that never happened. They did send us a very nice bathtub. However, none of the accessories were there. When my husband asked why, he found out someone had taken them from the set. We had this very large tub that would not fit in our house. It wasn't a hot tub. I never did sit in that tub. My sister eventually put it in a house they were building, but then they sold it. For a while, I was a little sad, I never got to enjoy it. It's true what they say, it's the thought that counts. It gave me a great Mother's Day memory, and a beautiful DVD to watch over many times.

That unforgettable weekend, my first time ever in New York City, we made lasting, lifelong memories. We also ate at an amazing Italian restaurant. Italian food is my favorite for sure. We were also able to get tickets to *Beauty and the Beast* Broadway play. It was so well done. I absolutely loved it. The weekend overall was one for the record books. I made a scrapbook after we got home. I still browse through it today now and then. What happy memories it brings back.

In looking back through the book and folder of items we have mixed in with all the memories, there are a few stand-out letters we received in the mail after the show. They tell us how much our story impacted them. They speak of our faith and how it reached around the world that day on the show. One says they were at their gym and the show was on. It also says one of the doctors who treated our son was there working out. They watched the show together standing next to each other. He said the whole place was glued to the TV. That does my heart so much good. I'm not sure which doctor it was, but we loved them all. I wanted people to know Cody's story and the strength God had given us all. Now they had a peek into our amazing son and our amazing God who got us through every day, step by step, hour by hour, minute by minute. It still today seems unreal that we were on the show, let alone the countless people who heard our story. Thank you, God, for then and now.

Writing this has been a real struggle for me. I've already mentioned that. In writing, my body has been more painful than normal. I have a good friend who is a doctor. He too was in a car accident. He understands the painful aftermath. He told me when I go back through the traumatic events in my life, it doesn't just happen to my mind or my emotions, but my physical body has been along for the ride. He calls it retracing. I had to take a few days off after writing about Cody's death. I was glad it could be explained. I didn't physically feel better, but I knew it would get better soon, once I relaxed and stopped focusing on the pain. I keep the emotional pain at bay most days. I try to focus on the good and picture our sweet boy healthy, happy, and pain free. Our little man touched more lives in his short five minutes of fame than we ever could.

That year, for Father's Day, I wrote a letter to the newspaper called *The Flint Journal*. I wanted my husband to be recognized as well. He was an amazing father to Cody. The world now knew about mine and Cody's relationship. I thought it would be nice if they heard about his. My husband was playful with Cody. He had a fish stuffed toy you could put your hand inside to make it wiggle. Cody loved it. I had also told them about the show we had been on. I thought that might help. I received a phone call. They wanted to send a reporter to interview my husband. He was very surprised when I told him. In our relationship, he's usually the only one who can pull off surprises. I'm not great at it, but he sure is. We set a date and time. Unfortunately, I had to tell my husband, so even this couldn't be kept a surprise. The reporter they sent was very nice. She did a good job asking questions and trying to piece things together. It's a lot to fit into one small article.

I remember when the interview was over, she looked at us and said, "How are you doing so well?"

That's a loaded question, I thought.

We could have said many things. It was getting late. She came after my husband got home from work. He was tired, and evenings were always our time to let down, just be alone together. No one else to worry about, so it didn't surprise me when he just smiled and said, "Thank you." With my thank-you and goodbye hug she gave me (it wasn't unusual for strangers to hug me after hearing about our story), I did squeeze in. "I couldn't do any of this without God." We locked eyes for only a moment. She smiled and said, "Thank you."

I never want anyone who comes across our journey to think, *Wow, they are strong people* or *I couldn't do what they have had to do.* You could if you had to with God. Though I don't wish it on my worst enemy. Remember in the hospital I've seen people try to do it without God. It's almost like looking at a wrecking ball smashing into them, their lives, their marriage, like total destruction. It's so sad to watch. To live through it without him, no, thank you, my friend. Believe it or not, to my surprise, we received a very nice letter from the reporter telling us she recommended putting our picture and story on the front page of the journal for Father's Day. They did just that. I thought I would include the article, letter, and the frontpage picture here.

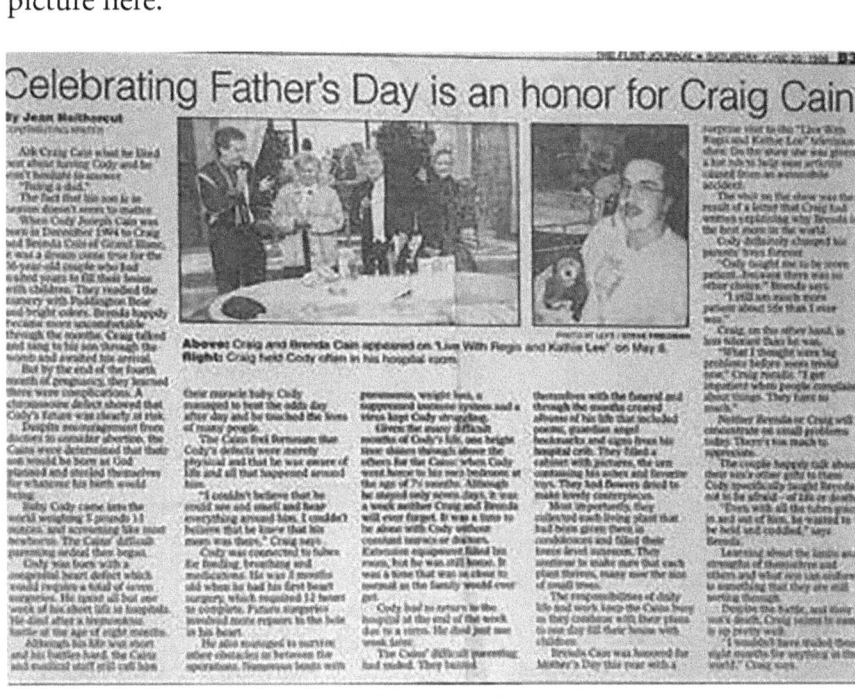

Flint Journal

Flint Journal Cover

I tell you, friend, God's handiwork was all over this. The show, this article, and the bright threads he was weaving through our dark tapestry as if to say, "I see you. I see your pain. I'm bringing light into it. It hasn't gone unnoticed, and I want others to see how you are still together, still trusting in me. To see your belief in me. To know there is a heaven and your son is there with me. You are not alone in your suffering. Good will shine through, I promise."

Mother's Day now had a bright, shiny memory for me. Now my husband had one of his own to treasure, to bring into focus on the dark days. Father's Day won't just be about his son dying; it will also be about their story living on in color for him to read, look at, and remember. I was glad she wrote about the good in their relationship. He needed that.

Through our life journey, there are hidden treasures along the way. Special moments in time like this one. There are everyday treasures like sunshine, rain, flowers, birds, friendships, family, and so many more God gives us ever day of our lives. We, at times, take them for granted. They show us God's presence, that he hasn't abandoned us. In *Colossians 2:2–3*, it says,

> *My purpose, meaning God, is that they, meaning us, will be encouraged in heart and united in love. So that they may have the full riches of complete understanding in order that they may know the mystery of God, in whom are hidden all the treasures of wisdom and knowledge.*

If today you have God in your heart, fantastic. If you don't, if you aren't sure about him, or if you question your life or your journey, for me, it hasn't just been asking him into my heart and everything's different or new at that moment or that I won't ever have any more trouble in my life, because I will and I have, it is walking with him and letting him carry me and my burdens every day. It's my daily relationship with him. It's praying, listening for his voice, spending time in his word and with his people. It's the whole journey, friend. It's not just me asking God into my heart and then going on with my life making my own decisions, not changing thoughts, behaviors, or actions. The Bible clearly tells us how we should live our lives, and I do my best to honor him every day. Remember, we're human. We don't always get it right. Neither does anyone except for God. That's what forgiveness is for. I cannot include him and do what I want if it's against his way and his instruction. If I'm letting him lead, I may not always like the outcome. Remember only he can see the full design, the whole tapestry. I cannot. This is faith, friend.

At times in my life, I think I've got a plan or the whole picture worked out in my mind. The only problem with those times is they are my plan, my design. They might not be what's best for me or for someone else. That can still be hard for me today. I have to remind myself God may have another plan.

Going back to the Regis and Kathie Lee show, I forgot to mention after the show was over, Kathie Lee asked my husband and I back to her dressing room. There she gave me a CD of hers and some pretty slippers. She talked with us about Cody for a bit. Our story really touched her. She has a son named Cody, and in tears, she told us she couldn't imagine life without her son. She asked us if we were going to try again. She encouraged us to try and told us what a blessing children are. I thanked her and assured her we knew that. And we wanted to try again. We weren't sure if we could, if there would be a problem for another child or not. That thought worried us. It hadn't been discussed much, but the worry was there behind the surface.

A while after we'd been home from New York, one evening while eating dinner I asked my husband if we should be tested. They ran a FISH test on Cody to get a clear diagnosis. A FISH test looks at the makeup of each chromosome. I wondered if they could test us to see what the chances would be of this happening again. My husband thought we could certainly do that. We both wanted children, but we just couldn't put another child through so much suffering. It wouldn't be right, and we worried we couldn't survive this happening again. We decided to contact the doctor who ran the test on Cody. We still have Cody's results today. We have ours as well.

We had the blood drawn and waited for our results, praying, semi holding our breath. Listen, neither one of us wanted to be the one missing a piece of our chromosome or to have been the one that passed this onto our son, so it was not something, for me, I wanted to know at first. I already felt so much blame for the feeding tube that I needed God to help me let go of. I sure did not need to know I was the one who had an issue that caused my son so much pain, neither did my husband. In our minds, even if it was one of us, we knew it wasn't our fault. But we're human, and that would hurt to our core for either one of us.

The results were in. They were mailed to us. The day we received them we opened them together, took a deep breath, and my husband began reading them out loud. Thank you, God, we were okay. It was unlikely to happen again. It had nothing to do with our genetic makeup. We are all designed by God, so if it had been one of us, it would have been the way God made us, and we would have to accept that. We were happy, however, that it wasn't. We began talking right away about trying again. We also discussed how long we had been trying when we finally got pregnant with Cody. We had discussed our situation with doctors already before Cody. We were both getting ready to be tested when I found out I was pregnant. We were older at this point and didn't want to wait years to have another child. We also knew in vitro fertilization was expensive. I was back to work but just part-time and not making what I was before. I was enjoying Brisco and Briecin and my job, but being a mom was at the top of the wish list. We would sleep on it, pray about it for a bit, and do a little more research. We would get some exact numbers, and then we would see if we could manage paying for it, and if this was something we really wanted to do and something God wanted for us.

After a couple weeks went by and we had gathered all of the information, we chatted. Of course, all the thoughts of collecting a sample from me and from my husband were not something we wanted to do, especially my husband. Then there were the shots for me, the checks, all on the optimal timing of course to achieve the highest chances. It was a lot without the expense. My husband hesitated, but he saw the want in my eyes and the look on my face. How could he not agree to try? I had been through so much to become Cody's mama. I deserved another chance. We both did.

The Testing

The decision was made. We would go for it. I called a local nearby lab. I tried to ask all the right questions. The girl I spoke to on the phone seemed to have all the answers to all of my questions. First, they would start with a sample from my husband. He could drop the sample off on his lunch hour one day, whatever day worked for him. Not thrilled about it, he agreed to do just that. Strict instructions were given to get the sample. Keep it warm and drop it off ASAP.

"Great," my husband said. The very next day he did just that. He kept the sample under his armpit to keep it warm and rushed to the lab. As he tells it, he walked in the door to the front desk. A very pretty young girl greeted him and asked how she could help him. He gave his name and a bit embarrassed told her he was dropping off his sample.

"Your sample?" she asked.

He explained. No one wants to explain in this situation, let alone be doing this at all.

She looked at him surprised and said, "Sir, I'm not sure who you talked to on the phone, but we don't do that here at this lab."

Needless to say, he, red faced, got out of there quickly. He was so mad. There was a field behind the clinic, and he whipped that sample into the field as hard as he could, as if to say, "I hate this—all of this." Not being able to get pregnant, losing our son, the whole awful process was wrapped up in that one throw.

He wasn't extremely happy with me when we spoke. He assumed I had misunderstood somehow. I assured him I made no mistake. I was careful to ask all the right questions. I would never want to put him through that for nothing. I called that lab the next day to clear up for them what they had done and to explain to them someone with knowledge and experience needs to answer the phone or pass the call on to a trained employee. They apologized.

I thought, *This is all too hard. Maybe we should give up.*

We needed things to go smoothly from here on out or at least for a while. We took a few days off, thinking or talking about the whole subject. We just needed some time before proceeding. This time I would be more diligent. I asked our doctor for a reference. I explained what had happened and that it couldn't happen again or I thought my husband might call it quits. His office called us back with a good referral, thank God. The calls were made, and an appointment was set. They wanted to see us both. This was not just a lab; it was an infertility doctor and lab. The whole process would take place at the same place. I was relieved and ready for some answers. We both were.

The day of the appointment came. I think we were both dreading the process. I think most couples do. The doctor and the staff were all very nice and educated. This is what they do. This and only this. A lot of information was given to us to read at our leisure. We would both be tested today, not just my husband. However, he was given a cup and pointed to a room. They told him to take his time, but they needed a sample today.

He looked at me with big eyes. "Okay," he said.

The whole process is humiliating honestly. I feel sorry for couples struggling with this. It's certainly not the picture people want to see when they think about starting a family. It's expensive, and everything has to be timed, just not natural, unfortunately. It is, however, a blessing and the way many children in this world are conceived. The appointment was over. Now we would wait for the results.

I'm trying again not to think, *Is it me? Am I the one with the issue?* This is another one of those times we needed God front and center. We certainly questioned ourselves: the cost, the process. When all is said and done, we wanted a family. If this was the path to get there, we would do what we had to. The results came back, nothing too serious. A low count for my husband, but they could work with that. They assured us. The next step was for me to take a shot every day to increase our chances, to try to produce more eggs so we had more to fertilize. I will never forget the nurse coming into the room with what appeared to be a pretty large needle.

She told my husband, "You will be the one to give your wife her daily shots."

I stopped her and said, "I don't think so."

We use to have horses, and I saw my husband try to give one of them a shot. He put the needle in so hard he almost broke the needle, and I saw how unhappy the horse was.

She explained that she would show him how today.

"Now?"

She had me bend slightly over a table so he could access my hip.

Then she told him to put it in like he is throwing a dart.

"Hold up, a dart?" I looked at him and said, "You have to live with me. I've seen you throw darts. There needs to be some finesse here. Be gentle."

By that time, I had him nervous. He actually didn't do too badly. I had to have shots for a few weeks. Appointments were scheduled. Blood tests had to be done. I remember trying to work and having to hurry to an appointment one day. When dealing with ovulation and our body's timing, we were on a specific schedule. I was rushing as I was running late for my appointment. Driving a little too fast but almost there, and I got a flat tire, ugh. At times like this in life, it can really make you question, What am I doing? Why am I putting myself through this? God, am I forcing something that is not meant to be? Tired of shots, tired of the whole process. I felt like giving up that day.

Putting it in perspective, after the tire was repaired, later that evening, I thought it was just a flat tire that happens to everyone. Tomorrow is a new day. We continued on. My work was very good. I finally had to explain the situation so they could know why I had to leave on certain days. It was now the day to inseminate me—that's what they call it. They would take eggs from me, a sample from my husband, and attempt to fertilize the eggs. I was in a separate room from my husband. They had given him his sample cup along with a pager.

He said, "What is this for?"

The nurse told him, "It is in case we need another sample. We need to make sure we have enough especially since your count was on the lower side."

"Great," he said.

They prepped me for the procedure. To the doctor's surprise, I had only produced one egg. They were hoping for more. One egg would decrease our chances. After all the shots, appointments, blood work, expense, one egg?

The doctor said, "That is all we have. We will still try to fertilize the one egg, but let's not get our hopes up."

So we are quite a pair, my husband and I. One egg and a low count. Maybe this won't happen at all again, ever. Cody was a true miracle, conceived without help against all the odds stacked against us. Our bodies are amazing, so intricate, such detail. The design truly astonishes me. With all the things that can go wrong with just the conception process. Let alone the forming, knitting together in the womb. Just imagine with me the wonders, the mysteries of all the things God can do. After all Cody and us went through, when only a hairline piece of one of his many chromosomes was missing, you and I, all of us really, are a true work of art. In *Jeremiah 31:3*, it says, "*I have loved you with an everlasting love. I have drawn you with loving kindness.*" We are all his work of art. That right there grows my faith exponentially. How can it not for all of us?

The one lonely egg in my body, the sample given by my poor husband—now we wait. The page came in.

"We're sorry, sir, we need another sample."

This was looking like things were definitely not in our favor. Another sample was given. This time they had enough. Now it was up to science and God. It was out of our hands whether or not, after all of this, we would conceive another child.

When you fall in love, get married, want to start a family, you know the dream, the plan. No one tells you how unromantic, difficult, and expensive it can be besides the roller coaster of emotions you may experience. It has always astonished me when a friend or coworker says, "I want to have a baby," and next month they are pregnant.

They have no idea what a gift it truly is. Until you go through what we have been through, you may not realize how amazing, how intricately woven everything has to be, every chromosome has to line up perfectly. Creating a child, having them come out perfect, all their toes and fingers, their perfect heart and straight feet—only God can do that. Only God can create something that unbelievable.

Time seemed to move slowly. When you are waiting for news like this, it appears to move at a snail's pace. The call finally came in. Our one egg, to our disbelief, had been fertilized. Wow, against so many odds. The appointment was set. The egg was placed inside of me exactly the way it needed to be. Lord, when will this process get easier? Go home, rest, be still for a while. That has never been easy for me. I'm more of a "let's go, move on, let's do this" kind of girl. This whole process was getting on my nerves. Yes, my husband had to give a sample, but the rest, well, that is me. Women go through so much. God certainly made us tough. It's a good thing. If having babies were up to men we might be extinct. LOL. I know my husband, especially seeing all I have been through, will say, "No, thanks." Who could blame him?

After some time, the painful process worked. We were having a baby. We got the news late in the afternoon. That evening was quieter than you would think. We should be ecstatic. Many, so many thoughts swirled in our heads. Both of us were excited, but with so much pain and sadness we had endured with Cody, letting anyone else into our news was impossible for us. What if we lose the baby? What if there's something wrong? We decided we would keep the news to ourselves for as long as we could. Hide it until we had more time and information from ultrasounds. It's hard enough to deal with all we have been through. I especially didn't have the energy or strength to share the what-ifs, the unknowns, not yet. I just can't.

As time marched on, as our little miracle grew, it was getting harder to hide it. My husband's flannel shirts began being my wardrobe. The ultrasounds looked good, very promising. With Cody, my doctor had done at least two amnios and wanted to do one now. I was very hesitant. I did not want another amnio. Everything looked good. Why? He assured me it was the right thing to do. If there were any problems we were unaware of, we would know. We would be prepared.

I argued back, "So what if there is, we are not aborting anyway. However God gives us this child we will take and love them and be grateful."

My husband had been convinced by our doctor. He was onboard. He wanted information, all the information we could get. He is definitely a person who prepares in life. He makes the checklist, crosses the *t*'s and dots the *i*'s. It has served him well in life and in business. He assured me it would be best. The doctor reminded me he had never ever lost a baby doing an amnio, that I needed not worry. Against every feeling and fiber of my being not wanting this, the date was set. I took the doctor's advice. After all, what did I know? He is the doctor. It will make my husband feel better to know. Oh, how I wish I could have listened to my body. Even the day of the appointment, I questioned the doctor, the nurse, my husband. Everyone was saying, "It's okay, don't worry." All the while, my insides were screaming, "Don't do it."

I'm blessed to live a life free from anxiety most of the time. I'm not as they say a worrywart. I was this day. I had to take my mind away during the procedure. I just couldn't settle with doing this. To me, there was no point, only risk. If we were finally going to tell people we were having a baby, this would tell us chromosomally if the baby is okay, I guess.

It's done. I was told to go home and rest. Easy for you to say, but okay. I was angry with myself and anyone in my path. I felt unheard and worried, anxiety filled. Not a good feeling. Listen, if your whole being is telling you not to do something, don't do it.

Sweet Britton

I was nearly five months along now. We had decided to name him. His name would be Britton Joseph Cain. Britton was my grandfather's middle name. The results were taking longer as they had to be very detailed with our past issues. We had decided to tell immediate family. It was hard not to share as I was showing a bit. We all waited with anticipation. Hoping and praying for good news. Everything seemed to be going smoothly. The upcoming weekend was a church softball tournament at the Covenant Hills Camp where my husband and I met. He, of course, was playing in it; and I was excited to go and to see everyone I'd been hiding from to hopefully share the good news.

Thursday was here, and no results. This had me thinking, *Maybe I won't go. I don't want people to know I'm pregnant and then something goes wrong.*

That afternoon, in the mail were the results. We opened them together. Thank God. We're in the clear. No chromosomal issues. We have a healthy baby boy. We were so excited. Several phone calls were made to family to share the good news.

What was wrong with me? I thought. Everything's okay.

The doctor and my husband got what they needed, and it's all good. I was frustrated with myself that I had been so worried and let myself be filled with so much anxiety.

I told myself, "You were foolish."

Hey, listen, I'd been through so much. I could give myself a break.

We celebrated that evening and talked about how fun it would be Saturday to tell all of our friends and how happy and surprised they would be. It was a great day. We both slept with ease that night, feeling so much relief.

Saturday came. It was a beautiful day. The sun was shining. Love, fellowship, and fun were in the air. So many hugs and happiness were shared with us. We were so happy. Light and love were everywhere. Prayers before games, good competition. I love sports. This is what happiness feels like. It had been a while since I had been truly happy. So much darkness and struggle had filled our life. This felt good. This felt right. It was a long day from morning till night.

I remember going to move a cooler, and one of the guys grabbing it telling me not to lift it. It was sweet. Now that everyone knew we were having a baby, they too wanted all to go well, for me to take no risks. You see, they knew what we had lived through at least from the outside looking in.

It was evening now, and all the games were done. It was getting dark, late, and we hadn't eaten dinner yet. Some of our friends asked us over to their camper for dinner. They were staying there. We had barbecued chicken. I was hungry, and it was so good.

After hugs and our goodbyes, we headed out of the camp for home. We hadn't even gotten out of the gate at the camp when I felt something. I told my husband to pull over. I thought I was bleeding, not heavily, but there was some blood. We looked at each other with fear. My husband said to call the doctor. So I did right away. He had given me his personal number, so I got him directly. After all we had been through, he was highly invested in us and this baby. We had gotten close.

I explained what was going on. He told me not to worry, people spot, it's okay. It didn't help me much. He could tell, so he told us to meet him at the hospital. He would do an ultrasound to ease all our minds.

We arrived at the hospital trying to stay calm telling ourselves it's been a great day. He said it would be fine. We're good. Everything happened so fast. He was right there ready to take me back as he was closer to the hospital than we were. Today, I wonder what was running through his mind. After all, he had talked us into the amnio. The doctor and I went back to the ultrasound room while my husband was filling out insurance paperwork. The doctor told me he would show me that everything is fine. Getting the monitor screen really close so I could see it, he began the ultrasound. Almost immediately he couldn't believe his eyes.

He said, "It's my fault, it's all my fault." He started to tear up, saying, "I'm so sorry."

The screen I was looking at so closely had my baby's head partially caved in on the top. Was he gone? The amnio had left a slow leak, and the fluid slowly dripped out from the hole the needle made. The needle that I didn't want killed my son. The nurse ran out to get my husband, with me crying and yelling, "No, no, no…it can't be. It just can't be."

That's it, I'm done. Just take me, God. I can't do this again. This feels like punishment. Everyone knows. My poor husband, not even done finishing insurance paperwork, finds out his son is dead. I can't face this. Nowhere to go, no way out of this suffering. Me completely broken, him in shock, anger setting in big time.

My husband asked, "Can we can be alone, please?" both of us sobbing. Nothing left. Not wanting to see or talk to anyone. They gave us some time to gather ourselves.

The nurse came in and asked if we were okay. No words were spoken at all. Silence filled the room.

She said, "I will get your doctor."

He had been outside the room, trying to gather himself. There was really nothing he could say to make it any better. He said, "You are far enough along that you will need to deliver the baby."

"What?"

He saw my face and knew. He said, "We can give you something and assist you."

I said, "Okay," all the while feeling this isn't real, and this isn't right. Someone wake me up from this nightmare. This has to be a dream. Our minds can do that when it's just too much to handle. Unfortunately, it was as real as it sounds. The next question, I guess with any sedation, Have you eaten in the past few hours?

Well, yes, we had just eaten chicken with friends and we're so happy. How did this happen?

He looked at us so sadly and said, "Unfortunately, we can't do this tonight. You will need to go home and come back in the morning. I'm so sorry."

Getting ready to leave the hospital, to actually move my feet felt impossible. In floods of tears, we went home. All the way home, we cried. I just kept saying I don't want to see anyone. I don't want to talk to anyone. No family, no friends, no one. I meant it. Not even my mom, no one. My mom and I are so close. My husband knew this is not good. We had just told everyone we were having a healthy boy. How can we go from one extreme of pure joy to the next, pure pain all in one day? No one anywhere should have to go through what we've been through. This is cruel. What have I ever done to deserve this? Sleeping was impossible, and throwing up was probable. Lying in our bed, all of my dreams shattered once again.

I was at the end of myself. I couldn't function, couldn't talk, could barely breathe from all the sobbing. As I tried to lay still, hoping I could fall asleep, to forget or to block out the pain if only for a little while, all of my senses were heightened, like I could feel every nerve in my body. Thoughts ran through my mind. Maybe the doctor was wrong. Maybe if I lay still enough I could still feel him. Maybe I could get a miracle like people talk about. Why not me? In the stillness, the utter quietness of our house, with my husband fast asleep next to me, I had to face this harsh reality. It was real and wasn't going away.

Morning was approaching much faster than I wanted. And my ever, oh so real reality that I could feel all through my body was about to get very real. I lay there in the darkness, begging the light not to come. I just wanted to keep my son with me as long as I could. Somehow hoping I could protect him, protect us, even though my mind knew he was gone. My mind and body together could not accept it. That kind of darkness, at least for me, you want to give in to it, let it take over, stay there in it, never having to face the next minute, moment, hour, breath. Any of it, all of it. Still today, all of these years later, when darkness, sadness, and pain enters my life, my whole body recognizes it immediately, all at once. My nerves are all heightened. The sheer loudness I feel throughout my body makes me very awake, aware, like I'm all at once ready for battle, ready for the attack. A fierce sense of wake up and pay attention. I'm sure now today it is a gift. An immediate gearing up to assess the situation, get all the facts, and process them quickly, to put a plan of action into play immediately. Not to overreact and, most of all, my immediate thought is God is with me. I do not have to enter the darkness, no matter the case. I have God's light inside of me, and it shines in the darkness.

The morning finally came. The sun was bright. Light flooded our house. We had a huge window in our living room. How I loved that window. It looked out over our beautiful maple tree. I sat there numb for a few minutes asking God to take this pain from me, to not make me face this day. Of course, that can't happen. I knew that. What I ask today in my difficulties as they come, and they do come, is for God to walk with me, to give me his strength to face the battle and not rely on my own. You see with Cody, as I've said, I know God. I stay close to him. This was a deepening closeness straight through my bones. In *Deuteronomy 31:8*, it says, "*The Lord goes before you. He will be with you. He will not leave you.*" Looking back, I know he was with me that day. At times like this however, it's hard to feel him through the sea of darkness. But he was there, trust me.

Heading to the hospital seemed surreal. Like you are going through the motions, but your mind can't catch up. Shortly after we arrived, the nurses got me all settled in a private room. The doctor came in and talked with us. The sadness read all over his face like an open book anyone could read. He looked like he hadn't had much sleep either. He told us he was waiting on the room to be prepared, but it wouldn't be long now, and this all would be behind us.

I remember thinking, *Are you serious? This is our child. This will never be behind us. I will personally carry this battle scar with me, on me, and inside of me forever.*

Today I get it. What else could he say? He meant the procedure would be behind us. Don't get me wrong, that procedure was the removal of my son. That was a piece of me, a part of my body and soul never to be forgotten. I suppose being him, and trying to find a way to make any of this an ounce better, it was really all he could say.

He left to prepare, saying, "I'm sorry, I'm so, so sorry." He was a good man, kind, caring, and gentle. He was hurting too. Let's face it, there was plenty of pain to go around. My poor husband had to tell any support and love from our families that we could have had to stay away. Today I would never do that. My mom and his mom especially loved God with all of their hearts and carried his light inside of them. They could have at least brought love and shared tears. When you're grieving, I mean really dark like I was, you are not always thinking clearly. For me, I was pushing away, dealing with my pain and no one else's. It's okay. It's where I was at the time, and they all understood.

Quite a bit of time had passed, and I was getting a bit anxious and irritated. Where is the doctor and why are we having to wait so long? This seems cruel. He said it wouldn't be long. We called for the nurse. Of course, she said she would find out. She was gone a long time as well. An hour and a half had passed by this time, so we called the nurse again.

She said, "There is an emergency, I'm sorry. Please bear with us."

Seriously? I have my own emergency here. There may be death to my emotional state if we don't move on here.

She understood. She was so sorry.

Quite a bit more time passed. We're at over three hours now. The tears, the sorrow were filling this room. My mental health and my husband's were at stake here. Does anyone care?

Our doctor finally came in.

My husband said, "What is going on? Why did you bring us here so early and make us wait and suffer like this? Look at her. Is there nothing you can do?"

I must have been quite a sight. He explained the surgical room he had booked was in use. That a terrible automobile accident had happened, and the room was needed. All the rooms and hands on deck were needed. Two families had collided. There were deaths that day. They were trying to save the ones they could. How awful. What unfortunate suffering was going on all around us. Could this day get any worse? Compassion, patience, pain, grief, so much all wrapped up in that moment of time. Our doctor knew it was all too much for us. My husband was fielding phone calls. Is it over? Is she okay? Are you okay? No, no, no. Am I in the twilight zone? How can this be? You may have heard someone in your life say bad things seem to happen all at once or bad things come in threes. When you are in the heat of the battle, the struggle is very real. Bad things do happen to good people, and they were happening to us that day, along with so many others. Those poor families. Their beautiful sunny day is ending in tragedy as well. Patience is something you need in a hospital. I lacked it that day. I had none left to spare.

I loudly said, "How long? How long do you expect me to lie here like this?"

The doctor and my husband knew I was done. I would never put myself first when so many need help and are suffering.

Our doctor said, while my husband is trying to calm me, "It won't be long now. The room is being cleaned."

I remember him telling my husband, "I can give her Versed so she can forget for a bit while we are preparing." He also told us that we had been through enough. He would like to put me out and take the baby rather than me delivering him. Yes, that had been the plan. Me delivering my dead child. Versed is the medicine they used on our son Cody, so we both knew it worked. Okay, that would help temporarily. Not having to deliver would help as well. He knew he would have to, as they call it, fudge the due date on the paperwork as I was far enough along to have to deliver.

The Versed worked. I woke up feeling like where am I? What happened? I now knew this really helped Cody. I have been really glad to know that personally. Then reality set in. Just about then, they came to get me, to put me out, and wheel me into surgery.

After it was over and I was awake, I remember asking my husband something like, "Is he gone? Is it over?" Not that our grief would be over, but that we could leave this awful place and go home.

He explained to me that his brother had called him and came to the hospital. He had rented us a hotel room for the night, gave us money for dinner, or whatever we needed and told him he would be staying at our house taking care of the dogs.

We had two wonderful boxers who were family. They were so stressed and worried. They had clung to me in bed all night long, almost on top of me, trying to comfort and fix what has been broken. They helped me get through that night and many, many more to come. Briecin and Brisco were both bright lights on my dark days. I thank God for their unconditional, unending presence, and love. I also thanked God for the gift of time together that night to cry, feel, hold each other with no responsibilities. No one and nothing to worry about but us.

He told my husband he didn't know what else to do. He couldn't do nothing. What he did was a lot and what we needed. Probably what the dogs needed. I need to add, he was a college student at the time and he gave us all the money he had. That's putting love into action, moving your hands and feet, doing something to help. That's God's love through loved ones helping each other. That right there is a good example of how to live our lives, sharing each other's burdens, caring, loving, giving and us receiving with a grateful heart. That's how we get through the battles of this life, survive the scars.

We did survive the grieving, the battle. We are still surviving today, never ever forgetting our son, the healthy child we never ever held. Someday in heaven when we are all together again, we will hold him and never let him go. We won't have to. We will be together for all eternity. What a day that will be. That keeps me grounded knowing I will see them again. It keeps my feet firmly planted in God. I've learned the hard way that in this life, if we let them, our battles, our wounds, our scars can become openings to the beauty God created. That beauty is within us. God calls us the wounded, the broken. He calls us to use our journey to reach out, to help others, to change the world. Even if it is one step, one person at a time. The wounds in our life, they can turn us to God. They can help us know and feel how much we need him. They can be so painful. They crack us, our souls, wide open. Those cracks, they can let God's light in so he can plant his seeds of healing and growth to help us bloom, help us to stay grounded in his word. Strong and firmly planted. That's where I am today. That's where I will stay.

In this life, there is typically no growth without change, no change without surrender, and no surrender without wounds. Take it from someone who knows. At times in our lives, our battles, our wounds, however they come, whatever they look like to you, and we all have them, at times they can be so raw, so life-altering that they literally feel like an internal earthquake. Like our whole foundation is cracking wide open. Losing another son was my internal, unimaginable, emotional earthquake. It took some serious time, serious grieving, reaching out to God, crying out to him. It's right there in all of your pain that God can begin to plant new seeds of growth, hope, and healing. Somehow for me, and hopefully for you, there is some good brokenness that comes out of every wound we have suffered. For me, I have great empathy for others. I try hard not to judge anyone and to show love wherever and whenever I can.

There is one very important thing I want to add here, so listen carefully. Be very cautious during, through and after your battle, your struggle, your opportunity for growth, not to let darkness win. You need the light. You need God's light. You need the love of others, friends, family. The love he puts in their hearts to shine on you, to lift you up, to share your pain, and to love on you. Be careful not to let weeds grow among the beautiful seeds he is sowing in you, in your heart and in others around you watching your journey from the outside looking in. They can't experience what you're experiencing, but they can walk alongside you, offer help and love. Let them, please. Don't be like I was that day. You need them, and someday in their battle, they will need you. Watch out for weeds of bitterness, anger, wrath, ungratefulness. Don't let them spring up. Trust me, they will. Try not to let them take up roots. Was there anger, "why me" days? Oh, yes. Don't let anyone fool you. When it's really tough, it's going to happen. As I have told my daughter today, be upset, be angry, break something, yell, throw yourself on the floor. Go ahead, but when you are done, get up, clean up, dust yourself off. You don't belong there. There is much life to be lived, and until God calls me home, there are many people here who need me, my love, my support port, my story, your story. They need God, his love, and our love. Tell them. Share. Love them. Heaven is the end goal, the forever destination.

No more pain or suffering or separation. Pure love and joy. Total healing, no pain ever again. Here on earth, this is our temporary, not our forever. Temporary separation from my children, my father, my grandparents. Temporary sounds good. That, with God's help and the love of family and friends, I can do that.

In my life, I was always striving, working at something, searching for purpose. I think we all are. Loving my family and friends and my pets; loving God, loving people in need—that's my purpose. Who in my life's journey needs me, my help? Who needs my story? Who needs God? Who can I take to heaven with me? What seeds can I scatter and sow? How far can the stretch, the reach of God's love, who can be helped? I've always felt I can do more. After all I've been through, there has to be more people I can help or reach. That's why I am writing this book, telling my story as hard as it is, in hopes it might help you. Sharing, helping people, even if it's just one, scattering seeds, praying over them, hoping they spring up, grow and they share God's love with others. You may have heard the saying, "Seeds of greatness." I can't tell you I've ever scattered seeds of greatness. I also can't tell you that I haven't. Only God knows how far the seeds scatter that we sow, how far they stretch out, how much light they radiate. To be frank, I don't need to know that. The seeds I sow are for God and his stretch is unlimited. If I share with one person, especially in their time of need and brokenness, if I love them right where they are, God can use them. Your love, through them, can reach many; and the seeds scatter and grow. Will there be weeds along the way? Yes. Be aware of them. Stay close to God and his words and his direction, and do not let them spring up in you. You will have down days. I do. It's okay, just don't stay there. On the down days take time, rest, read, cry, dance, sing, listen to music, fill your soul with God. When the time is right, when you feel better, scatter your seeds, my friend. Honestly, your wounds, your battle scars, they will always stay with you and be a part of who you are. Instead of hiding them, use them. I have found helping others in need has helped me fill that big gaping hole in me where my pain lives. God designed us to love others. Sharing that love helps me as much as it helps them. Take time to heal. Search out God. If you haven't, ask him into your heart. Then ask him to show you, to put into your path others in need, others to share your story with, to do life with.

I have some dear, beautiful women God has put in my life. They entered my life in a women's Bible study group in our church. You sign up online. I knew no one. We met once a week. We were split into small groups to study. I opened myself up and found lifelong friends. I shared a small piece of my story. I don't know how many people it touched, how many seeds I scattered, but I do know I love these women I met. I share life with them. We all have suffering and pain. Without sharing too much, I can tell you our journeys have all been different, unique. We may go awhile these days without talking as we are no longer in study all together. Life has taken us in different directions, but when the battle comes, we reach out. Lean on each other. That, my friend, is priceless.

With different seasons of life come different challenges. Recently, one of my friends moved back to my area after being gone for three years. It's so good to have her back. She'd been back awhile, and we hadn't talked much. Life gets in the way sometimes. I was on my back porch drinking tea and having my God time when she popped into my head. I had a dark feeling come over me.

I texted her, "You are on my mind, are you okay?"

It took her awhile to respond, so I started praying for her.

She responded, "Oh, Brenda, can you talk?"

I called her right away. I could hear it in her voice. She started sharing. Her son had just had a large mass removed from his lung. So many doctors and an 88 percent chance its cancer. I just listened.

The last thing she said is, "If it is, Brenda, I will need you. You know how to get through the really hard things. People have struggles but not like you've had."

Aw, yes, I do know how to get through the really hard stuff, don't I? I brought her comfort that day. I had survived. I could show her how to survive if need be, and she knew that. Thank God I brought her comfort. I prayed with her and reached out to our group. They prayed as well. We all geared up for battle.

Thank God, today her son is cancer free. I didn't need to walk her through the really hard stuff. She was spared. Her son was spared, and I am so thankful. Listen, she knows I'm strong, and I'm strong in my faith. I could walk with her through this. But I certainly did not want her to suffer the loss of a child as I had. Using my pain and suffering to help her or anyone takes the senseless right out of it. That's important, so important, at least for me. Helping her helps me. They go hand in hand really. My struggle was not for nothing. Eventually, your wounds will become part of who you are and not all of who you are. They will become beautiful, bold, bright, strong strings woven throughout your life that makes up the picture, the tapestry of God's love and light for all to see.

Britton Joseph Cain, I know you're in heaven with your brother and sister. Play hard, sweet baby, until we meet again.

Cancer Hits Home

Eleven years ago my husband was diagnosed with colon cancer. We had just moved back to an area we had lived in the past. It's our favorite place to be besides home in Michigan with family. We knew our past neighbors, and I was able to get my doctor back who knew me and had cared for me for many years. She said she wasn't taking new patients, but she would take me. So I asked her if she would please take my husband too. Thank God she did.

We had purchased a home on a pond that my husband and daughter weren't thrilled about at the time. They had another home in mind. It was new; this wasn't. It needed no work. This needed a lot. The lady we purchased the home from was really struggling. She was older and alone. Her kids were grown and gone. Her husband had been the Grandpa of the neighborhood and had gotten cancer. He passed away quickly, we were told. Her beautiful white boxer (you already know how much I like boxers) had lost control of his back legs and was using the hardwood floors instead of grass if you get my drift. I can't explain the feeling I got when we looked at the house. It was ugly for sure, but the pond and backyard being private, with so many trees, was beautiful. The neighbor to our right having large pine trees I could see from the kitchen window where I write today. It drew me in. However, I felt so sorry for her. I could feel her pain and her struggle in that house. It was cheaper than the other homes. We could fix it in time except for the floors. They had to be fixed right away. Its beauty I could see through the ugly. So many windows, so much light. With the price we could send our beautiful daughter to the Christian school I had sought out and had been praying about. The house had been on the market for a year. We could make it beautiful again. I knew we could. Our daughter could be in a Christian school, and we could help her sell her home. She could know a loving family would keep her home safe.

My husband went over to the house one day before we closed on the home, and she was so upset. So rattled. She had lost her driver's license. She desperately needed it. With all the stacks of newspapers, boxes, things she just couldn't let go of. Poor thing. She wasn't very friendly to us. She really didn't want to leave her home, but her kids knew it was too much for her. He offered to help her thinking this is like finding a needle in a haystack. To his surprise, it didn't take him long, and he found it. He was now her hero. I thought, *Thank you, God.* We closed on our house, and time marched on.

We moved in knowing we had a project on our hands. My husband and daughter, not thrilled, but in it with me. We enrolled our daughter in the Christian school, which, today, she is so glad she attended. I was excited as I love a project, and I loved she was in a Christian school. God's light filled that house every day. I needed that. I met one neighbor walking around the pond. She was really friendly. My nephew lived with us at the time as well. *All was well in my world*, I thought. My husband was healthy. We were young enough, in our late forties. We've got this. Now today, my daughter and husband love this house.

It wasn't long, and my husband started complaining about pain in his stomach, on the lower right side. He was supposed to travel for work. I told him he needed to go see the doctor. He called me before getting on the plane saying he really hurt.

Of course, I said, "Please don't travel."

But he said, "It's okay. I will be fine."

He was going to Reno, Nevada. He's never really had health issues except asthma, mostly when he was younger. So he figured this will pass, no worries. For me, I was worried enough for both of us. Now I know worry isn't going to change anything. I've learned that the hard way. Prayer, inviting God into the situation, will give me his strength to weather whatever storm is coming. He landed in Reno and called me right away, explaining that he was so uncomfortable and in more pain now. He said that entering the flight, he got to his window seat and had to lean on the window the whole flight while sweating and in extreme pain. By the time he got off that flight, he was exhausted. A coworker picked him up. She could tell he wasn't okay. She tried to convince him to let her take him to the hospital.

He told her, "Just get me to my hotel room. If I'm not okay, I will call you."

He didn't know her well as he had just started this job. Thus, the move and I didn't know her at all. She begrudgingly did just that.

By 2:00 a.m. he was in so much pain, he finally called her. She thought it might be his appendix. She had her appendix burst and could have died when she was young. She was ready so quickly like she was up waiting, makeup on, car out front running and ready to go. I was so thankful for her.

He called me and said that he was going to the hospital. I knew this wasn't good. I wanted to be there.

He told me, "I'm okay. I will call you as soon as I know anything."

It was a very long night. They finally admitted him. Once he got in a room, he called me. They're going to run some tests. His coworker got him some magazines and came in and out of his room a few times to check on him.

The nurses finally said, "Your wife can stay in here." They had said she could come back a few times.

He didn't feel like explaining. Finally, he said, "She is not my wife." Poor guy.

I was at home taking care of our mess of a house, our daughter, and our pets.

As the day went on, they ran some tests, blood work. He was becoming so uncomfortable, his stomach distended. He finally asked the nurse for a nasogastric tube. If you don't know what this is, it's a tube placed in your nose, put down your throat, and into your stomach. It's hooked to a suction container to draw out what's in your stomach.

"People really don't ask for this," the nurse told him.

He assured her, "Our son had one for quite a long time to keep him from refluxing into his lungs."

He knew what he was asking for. That's how bad he felt. He told me he thought his stomach would explode if he didn't. He hadn't told me this yet. As he knew it would upset me and bring back so many painful memories.

When his coworker came back to see him again and she saw the tube, she knew she had to call his wife.

She got my number and said, "I don't know you, but if this were my husband, I would be here." She told me of the tube. That in itself was like emotional whiplash.

I thanked her and assured her I would be there as soon as I could. Arrangements had to be made. What would I do? Thank God my nephew was staying with us. But my daughter, the pets, his job— we needed help. I needed to get a flight, get packed, and get there ASAP. I stopped and prayed, fighting back the fear and the tears.

Into my mind came, *Ask the sweet neighbor you met. She's right here, two houses away from you.*

I was lost for options. Okay, God, this must be from you. She had given me her number and a card with the neighbors' names and house placement on the street. She was a mama of three. She had most neighbors' keys. I called her and asked if I could come chat with her. She hugged me. She's so sweet. She told me my daughter could stay with them until my nephew got home. She could pick her up from school, take care of the pets, whatever I needed and not to worry, just go be with my husband. God knew I needed her, and so did she. It's scary to leave your child with someone you've only known a short time. Their family was so good to her. I'm so grateful for them. She put me at ease, mama to mama. I got the first flight I could, got a rental car, and got to the hospital ASAP.

When I walked through the hospital halls heading to his room, I thought, *Not this again. Dear God, I just can't.* Stopping in the hall to gather myself and pray, I asked God to help me bring his light and love into my husband's room, to help me be strong for him. I knew I had to when I walked in his room and saw him lying there with that tube in his nose. I felt weak in the knees, but I kept moving, fought back the tears, and gave him a smile and a big hug.

I told him, "I'm here now. I've got you. We will figure this out. You will be okay."

He needed comfort, and I would be that for him. God's got me, and I'm strong. He's strong. Our faith is strong. Come what may, we will do this together, and God would be with us every step. He was so glad to see me. Now it was time for me to meet nurses, his doctor, and get the details. I need details. What's the plan? What's been done so far? I'm focused, as I was with my son. I studied my husband.

We talked to the doctor, finally. That takes time in a hospital as they are busy. He came in, introduced himself to me. He had a list of things this could be. I was listening intently, writing things down. Always have something to take notes when a loved one is in the hospital, especially if they are there for a while. Doctor's names, etc. As he went down the list, on the very bottom of twenty things this could be was cancer. Okay, I thought, it is good it's on the bottom, but he doesn't have any symptoms with the rest of list. Cancer is the unknown variable. The doctor said we need a colonoscopy right away.

Okay, let's go, I thought.

Now for my husband, this was going to be a challenge—a big one. He had to drink all that yucky fluid to clean himself out. Only he had a bloated stomach. The nasogastric tube was helping, however not enough. He still had some pressure. He tried to drink; he really did. With an IV, a tube in his nose, feeling awful, trying to go to the bathroom and dragging these things along, he had had enough.

He told me, "Pour the rest down the sink. I'm not drinking it."

Well, he had to drink it, I knew that. They might not see what they needed to see. I gave him a break, rubbed his back a bit, said a prayer, and asked him to please try again. He finally got most all of it down. I felt so sorry for him.

It was time for the procedure. They whisked him away quickly. The nurse showed me to the waiting room.

The doctor said, "I will be in to speak with you as soon as the procedure is over. Don't worry."

My mind was racing, thinking of the list, if there were any symptoms he could have had that would fit. None that I could think of. It was taking longer than they said it would. Honestly, I've waited in too many hospital waiting rooms. No doctor yet. I decided to call my mom, feeling strongly cancer was the outcome.

I told her, "Mom, I think he has cancer."

The phone was quiet.

I explained he has none of the other symptoms. "I just know it, Mom."

She said she sure hoped not and she would be praying.

God was preparing me, giving me time to process. Still, no doctor. I knew, I just knew.

A nurse finally came in.

"The doctor will meet you in your husband's room and talk to you together."

Okay, I thought, *cancer it is.*

I prayed all the way back to his room for strength. When I got to his room, he was there.

He said, "What did the doctor say?"

With a hug and a smile, I said, "Nothing yet. He will be in to talk to us."

"I wonder why?" he asked, never thinking cancer.

The doctor came in quickly and out of his mouth, no finesse at all, "It's not good, you have cancer."

My husband would tell you it hits you so hard when you hear that word. Like there is so much air in the room and you can't get any of it.

"Cancer?" I said.

"Yes, colon cancer. We can do surgery here, but it has to come out right away. It is large. He will most likely lose several inches of his colon. Take some time. Let me know, but not too long."

He was in a shared room with the curtain drawn. My immediate thought was we need privacy. The doctor left the room.

For a moment, the silence was deafening. After all we have been through together, cancer. Really? We hugged, and both teared up. My husband is a strong man.

He said, "Don't worry, I will be all right."

Remember, he was on a business trip with a new job. His mind went right there.

"I have to call my boss."

I said, "Okay, I will be right back. You do that."

I went right out to the nurse and told her we needed privacy. "Can she please see if a private room is available? Right away, please."

This certainly wasn't my first or last hospital journey. She understood and said she would get on it right away. When I entered the room, my husband was finishing up with his boss. His boss told him he had a doctor in Dallas who he liked very much. You see, he had several inches of his colon removed a few years earlier due to diverticulitis. That had been one of the many options. Coincidence? No, I think not. Let's not forget, as I mentioned earlier, *Deuteronomy 31* says, "*The Lord himself goes before you and will be with you. He will never leave you or forsake you.*" He knew we would be facing this.

We talked for a bit. We knew calls had to be made. He would call his family and our daughter. He wanted to be the one to reassure her. I would call mine. Rather than talking in the same room, I stepped out. Before I could make a call, my phone rang. It was my husband's boss.

On the other end of the line came, "I know you don't know me." He introduced himself. He said, "I don't know how assertive you are, but for starters I think you need a private room."

I responded, "I know you don't know me, but I'm pretty assertive. I'm already on that. They are moving him soon."

He said, "Okay, great." He didn't want to push, but he explained of his doctor back home in Dallas. He said he could call him. He also said the owners of the company they worked for had a seat on the hospital board where the doctor worked. He said they will make a call as well.

His question was, "Do you think he can get on a plane and come home?"

I told him, "I think he can. They had cleaned out his stomach with the colonoscopy and the NG tube. If we're going, this is our window. I would talk to my husband and get back to him right away."

In speaking to my husband, he thought he could do it. We spoke to the doctor, and he said that, yes, I think he can. Everything moved very fast, it had to. The doctor in Dallas was called. Flights were booked. We had an appointment the very next morning. My husband hadn't eaten. He was cleaned out. Let's not eat until after the appointment. It was an evening flight anyway. He did well on the flight. Numb, both of us were a bit, but I was laser focused. Much to be done here. He was glad to see our daughter. My nephew and the neighbor had taken good care of her and glad to be home in our bed.

Morning couldn't come soon enough, at least for me. Let's go. Can't be late. Dallas morning traffic can be crazy. Looking back, there were so many moving parts already falling neatly into place. Oh, the intricate weaving of God. The whole picture we're unable to see at the time. We got to the office with time to spare. The doctor was right on time.

He must have thought, *Who is this guy?* He had to clear that morning's appointment. He was kind, soft-spoken, and direct. He had all my husband's tests as I had made sure of that. Notebook in hand, we both listened intently.

I thought, *Surgery?*

"Yes, the mass has to be removed. We won't know if or where it has spread to until then."

Spread?

"Or how many lymph nodes it is in. We will have a lot more information after the surgery."

"Okay, got it. Let's do the surgery. He's ready to go," I said.

He looked at me with raised eyebrows. "That will take some time. We have to schedule the room and there's my schedule to consider. There probably won't be availability for a few days at least."

I understood. My husband was quiet at this point.

"Can you just please check?" I asked him. "He's all prepped. Maybe there is an open room. Maybe a cancellation."

He looked at me again, probably now thinking, *Who is this woman?*

My husband was now tapping me on the leg.

I said, "Just check please."

The doctor said, "Okay, I can at least check."

I said, "Thank you."

He left the room.

My husband said, "Why are you pushing? We're lucky to be here."

Oh, luck had nothing to do with it, friend. I knew that. Prayer was constant for me. Family was praying, friends, strong women of faith were praying. God had everything to do with it. All the frayed strings lining up perfectly.

He came back into the room with a surprised look on his face.

He said, "To my surprise, there is a surgical room open tomorrow early morning."

I said, "If you can do it, we will take it."

Thank you, God. He said he could be there. We said we would be there.

He said, "Drink, eat very little, and nothing after midnight."

Okay, we've got it. First things first, let's get this cancer out. Then we will see the fight we are in for. The ride home was relief, nerves, and gratefulness—so many emotions. So many calls to make. Strong threads were weaving. We were gearing up for this fight. Like so many fights in the past, only now this wasn't our children, this was my husband. Giving myself the pep talk, praying for strength. I'm ready, let's go.

There was continuous prayer, the night before, the ride to the hospital and all the way through the surgery.

He came through surgery well. He was back from surgery, and we were in a room waiting for the doctor. He would have to stay in the hospital for a few days. That's to be expected. The doctor came in.

"Well, we got it. We had to remove twelve inches of your colon with it. It did get into six of your lymph nodes. Thankfully, it did not get into your liver or kidneys. We're not out of the woods yet."

Okay, processing. "What now?"

"Since it got into your lymph nodes, you will need to do chemotherapy. For now, healing from the surgery needs to happen."

We will focus on the blessings we have. The cancer is out.

While he stayed in the hospital healing, I stayed with him during the days until later in the evening. I hated to leave him at all. I remember the same awful feelings from our son. He was okay, he assured me. He knew I had responsibilities at home with our daughter, our house, and the pets. I juggled the best I could. Reassuring everyone including him and myself everything would be fine. The drives home from the hospital at night were a challenge to say the least. You see, in Texas, a lot of road construction happens at night. My hour drive could increase by a lot as the exit I was to take was closed. GPS rerouted to the next exit, only that exit was closed as well. There were times it took me 1.5 hours or longer with many different routes to get home. I would make my calls, pray, and turn on the radio. There was an evening show where they played soothing music, and there was a host named Delilah. Her voice was soothing too. She would take calls from people with various problems going on in their life.

She would say, "Delilah here, how can I help?" Just to share, at times, relieved burdens for people. To hear others had problems as well. That they weren't alone.

I never called in. My calls were directly sent to God. I was in constant communication with him and with friends and family. I will say hearing other's troubles steered me from my own. I would listen, hang on to their words, feel some of their pain. In the hospital with our son, there always seemed to be someone with a worse situation than mine at the moment. I would pray for them. This was no different. I prayed for several who called in. It was a good show, showing real empathy. It was good they had someone to talk to. We all need that in this life. We are not meant to go through it alone. Our daughter at home, she could lose her father at a young age as I did. That was so hard for me and her. I pleaded with God to not let that happen. It would just be too much for her, and I would surely split wide open. We'd been together since sixteen years old. Best friends. I told God this would surely be too much for me.

It was time to bring my husband home from the hospital. He was so ready. He said the nights were so long and waiting for me to come in the morning seemed to take forever. He couldn't wait for me to get there. I would get up early, get the pets set, my daughter to school, and drive to Dallas in morning traffic. I got there as quickly as I possibly could. I, for one, hate to be alone in the hospital. He was no different.

The doctor told us before leaving he had to have one more procedure before they started chemo. A port had to be placed under the skin in his chest. They would make a central line to his veins. That is where they would administer chemo. It is easier this way. We knew about central lines. Our son's was in his groin area. This would be easier, less pokes. Man, I wish they would have done that sooner for our son. Less pokes? Okay, that sounds good. The procedure was scheduled, no time to waste. This cancer can be making its way through my husband's body. Let's go get it. They tried to warn us what it would be like. He would have one medicine in house at the hospital and the second one would run slowly through a pump at home. My husband, still today eleven years later, says if he hears a similar sound it makes him sick to his stomach. Chemo was a long, drawn-out process. Food didn't taste good at all. I remember one night trying to make him three different meals. He was only able to barely take bites of each. It was another long, painful season for our family, especially my husband.

A nurse one day told him, "You realize you are a walking miracle, don't you?"

You see, the odds of survival from stage 3C colon cancer are about 28 percent. He was given a second chance at life when so many weren't. The chemo room at the hospital was so bleak. So many sick people with so many different cancers. And almost all ages from young to old. All fighting for their lives.

The nurses tried to keep things up beat, but there was a heavy, depressing air for sure. I'm remembering back to my husband's first day of chemo. So scary, the unknown. We were told of the risks, the pros and cons. One of them being an allergic reaction.

I perked up. *Oh no*, I thought. I was heightened, focused. The nurse said it almost never happens. Almost never is not never. Medicine in hand, she hooked him up to his port and began to run the chemo. I told her not to go too far.

She looked at me strangely and said, "I won't be far. I will be right back."

These alerts I get in my thoughts and throughout my body, I've learned to listen to them. Pay close attention to them and be ready to react.

Sure enough, my husband said, "I'm having trouble breathing."

I could see that and was already on it. The nurse came running. Other nurses helped. A large bolus of Benadryl was administered through his port.

My husband said, "I've never been drunk before. I wonder if this is what it feels like? If it is, count me out."

It made him woozy, lightheaded. Not good at all. The nurse learned a valuable lesson that day: stay with the patient when you are giving chemo for the very first time. Benadryl was added to every treatment. Thank God, his body would tolerate it. Today he says it was so awful, made him so sick. He doesn't think he could do it again. Let's hope we don't have to find out. I remind him of our dear friend we lost just a few years ago. She was a wonderful woman. We became friends with her and her husband on a three-day cruise my husband's work sent us on after the loss of our son, Cody. She had won the cruise. She was recovering from her first battle with breast cancer. She had one son. She was so worried she wouldn't be there to raise him. Both of her breasts completely removed, and chemo, which she hated as well and vowed not to do again. She was amazing. She and my husband shared a special bond as I think cancer survivors do. The rest of us just can't quite understand. We had lost our child, and her child could lose his mama. She was a fighter. She had many years. She raised her son, met his fiancé, and was there at his wedding. She even saw her first grandbaby born. One day, the phone rang. She told me the cancer was back. She found it on her chest bone.

She said, "I'm so tired. I'm still trying to work, to be normal, but it is so hard. I'm taking a chemo pill at home. I just can't do regular chemo."

This gave me a sinking feeling as I was worried it might not be strong enough. I never shared this, only supported her. This was her life and her choices. She had already been through so much. Who could blame her? A few months later cancer took her life. I'm so thankful she raised her son and met her grandbaby. She believed in God, I knew that. I know she is in heaven today with my sweet babies. She is free from pain as well.

Here's a writing I wrote one day sitting in the chemo room at the hospital with my husband. Looking back I think it describes the scene so well.

Today I am sitting in a chemotherapy room with my husband of almost twenty-five years. Here, it seems as if life stands still in a low and painful place. So much pain and suffering on the faces here. Confusion, why me, fear, anger... The feeble body shapes. The balding heads, sunken eyes, regret written all over their faces. Will I survive? Will my family have to live without me? What about my life plans? My bucket list, where do I start? Help me, let me out of here. Let this all be a dream. Please, God, if you take this awful demon out of my body I will live better. I will treat people better. I will live for you. I will be yours forever. Let me hold my baby, my child, my grandchild longer, harder, better. Let me use my talents for good. Uncover my talents I never knew I had. Make a deal with me once again. This time I will keep my promises. I will care about the homeless, the needy, the wounded. I won't be so selfish. Please, please, please save my life. I know heaven has no pain or tears, but I really like it here, and I want to cherish what I have like I should have. I will stop and smell the flowers. I will be kind to strangers. I will, I will, I will. Let me enjoy this world and share your love like I should have done every day of my life. And, God, please take care of my family. If you don't answer my prayer they will need you.

I have a hard time reading this today. It is so real, so accurate. The one thing I know in this life is do-overs don't come around often. At times, we rush through our lives busy, in a hurry. We don't take time to truly live as we should live. And when an illness or trauma stops us in our tracks, it is there we turn to God. It's there we promise to do what we should do. How about today, now, starting to live life worthy of God and all his blessings he gives us daily? Our dear friend walked worthy of God, and I will see her again someday. My husband today is still cancer free. Thank you, God. So many suffer from cancer today. I lost my uncle to cancer. My mom's only brother. My niece has had cancer. The struggle is real, my friend. Frankly, I definitely don't know how anyone walks through cancer without God. In *Romans 8:38–39*, it says,

> *For I am sure that neither death, nor life, nor angels, nor principalities, nor things present, nor things to come, nor powers, nor heights, nor depth, nor anything else in all creation will be able to separate us from the love of God.*

If you and your loved ones are with God, when or if the time comes when you are separated from them here on earth as I am (my father, children, grandparents, friends), take heart because if nothing can separate you from God, you will be together again. That keeps me going, my friend. When the battles come, and they still do in different ways and many forms, I will put on the armor of God before I go into battle. *Ephesians 6* tells us *"to put on the full armor of God. The belt of truth, the breastplate of righteousness, shoes with readiness of the gospel of peace, a shield of faith, the helmet of salvation, and the sword of the spirit."* I don't do life without my armor.

Mom's Accident

The most recent hospital battle was with my mom. My mom has fought many battles in her life: the loss of her husband, children to care for, the loss of her parents. Working hard and body parts worn right out. She was an aid at a hospital for years. The cement floors, all the walking, caring for people. It took a toll on her body. She has both knees replaced, one of them revised. Both hips have been replaced. One kept coming out of place. So much pain. She coded on the table for a bit, then that hip had to be replaced. The doctor nicked her pelvis as he had a hard time getting the hip joint out. The physical therapist pushed her way too hard. The doctor didn't give clear instructions. So many wrong moving parts. I received a call one day during my Bible study class.

On the other end of the phone, she said in a weak voice, "You won't be happy."

We had talked prior the day before about the therapist, the pelvis, and I had asked her to not let the therapist push her too hard. I was worried.

I said, "What happened?"

"My pelvis collapsed. I'm on my way to the hospital."

"Oh, Mom, I'm so sorry."

She didn't know what they would be able to do for her. She was still healing from hip surgery. She called the surgeon.

He said, "Let me make a call. I only know one man here in Florida who could put it back together, and we are friends."

If he couldn't fix it, she would be bedridden for the rest of her life. See, I told you she has been through battle. However, she was never without God, and this would be no different. The doctor was a wonderful man. He put her back together. Screws, mesh, glue, so much healing needed to happen if she was ever to heal and walk again. God blessed her. Healing happened, and she was upright walking. A miracle for sure.

Time passed, and she was doing great when she tripped on a rug and broke her shoulder. Surgery, screws, a rod in her shoulder, she healed from that as well. She has many battle scars. Her most recent battle was two years ago. Her husband didn't see a truck coming and pulled out in front of it. It hit on her side.

I felt like something wasn't right. That feeling I get, so I tried to call her.

No answer.

I called her husband.

No answer.

I had that uneasy feeling when a call came in from my sister-in-law saying my mom had been in an accident. She didn't know details. I thanked her and started calling hospitals.

The second hospital I called said, "Yes, we have her. She's in the ICU. I can transfer you back to the nurses' station."

When they answered the phone, they said, "Yes, who are you?"

I said, "I am her daughter."

They said, "Ma'am, she is in bad shape. She is yelling at us to let her die."

Dear God, how bad is this? She's eighty-five years old and has been through so much.

I said, "This isn't her. Do you have a phone you can take in her room and put on speaker?"

"Yes, of course, but I don't know if it will help." I said,

"Trust me. It will help."

They put the phone close to her. I could hear her yelling. I had to raise my voice.

"Mom, Mom, Mom."

She stopped.

"It's Brenda. I'm coming. Please let them help you. I don't want to lose you."

She said, "I can't."

I told her, "With God, you could. I would talk to the doctor, and I would pray, and I would be right there. Hang on."

She finally said, "Okay," in tears.

"Let them help you, Mom."

They told me she had been combative. I assured them this wasn't her. That she must be in too much pain, to please get her out of pain. I told them I was on my way. They were glad. They wrote on her white board, "Brenda's on her way."

Getting a flight out, getting there—it drove me a little crazy. I wanted to be there now. All of this was right in the middle of the COVID-19 pandemic. They weren't letting people in with their loved ones. I prayed the whole flight there. I got a rental car and headed straight to the hospital.

When the front desk called back and told them who I was, they said, "Send her back right away."

I thought, *Great.* And then I thought, *No fuss at all, this isn't good. What am I walking into?*

The scene was brutal. Three nurses, two doctors all trying to settle my combative mother. I walked in and told them. "I'm here." I asked them if they could give us privacy, if they could clear the room. They all looked at me in shock.

Her doctor said, "Are you sure?"

I assured him I was totally sure. If he gave me some time this would all get better.

Reluctantly, they stepped out.

I went to my mom, took her hand, squeezed it, and told her, "I'm here, just breathe."

It took her some time to settle. I assured her I wouldn't leave her and God was with us. She sobbed. I told her to let it all out. I prayed with her, sang to her softly as I did with my son. She started calming. I asked her why she wanted to die. I assured her if God still had her here, he would see her through this, and so would I.

When I finally opened the door and the doctor and her nurse came in, the scene had changed dramatically. The nurse was in awe. The doctor, not too surprised.

He said, "I tried to tell her God wouldn't give her more than she could handle."

There were things upsetting her, things not addressed in all the confusion. They listened and fixed things right away. Her pain was the huge issue. Her leg was cracked, but they thought it was stable. She also had multiple broken ribs, but they said for the most part, she is stable. I thanked them. I was asked more than once if I had experience in hospitals. Oh yes, my friend, more than I've ever cared to have. Kindness, focus, paper and pen. Stay out of their way when they need to work. Don't be a problem or I knew, especially with COVID, I wouldn't be there. Thank goodness this was Florida. I lived in Texas. Both states, in my opinion, were merciful with people whose loved ones were in the hospital. They at least gave us four hours a day.

The nurses, depending on who, would tell me to stay longer, to just try to stay in her room. We would shut the door for quiet. They knew she needed me. Some were kinder than others. One day she had a male nurse. He was not nice to her or to me. Her husband had been in earlier. He kicked him out for a procedure and then told him his time was up. I knew he and I were eventually going to have a meeting of the minds. It was tricky, especially with COVID. He had my mom worked up. This day wasn't starting well. She told me how mean he was to her. I tried to kill him with kindness and pray and only step in if I had to or I knew he would make me leave as well. If I had to leave, I would be leaving my mom with him.

As you can imagine, the day didn't go well. He attempted physical therapy saying her leg is stable. I understood movement, but they hadn't had her stand yet, and she was in a lot of pain. She tried, she really did. He raised his voice, telling her to stand. She was saying, "I can't." He got angry and let her go, and she fell back on her bed, yelling in pain. I believe that day he broke her leg all the way. He was rough doing her catheter.

He said, "You have to leave."

I said, "Okay. I will leave, but so will you. You are done here."

I assured Mom that he won't have her anymore today.

He said, "You can't do that."

I said, "Watch me." I told her in front of him I was turning him in to his boss. If that didn't work, I would go over their head. He needed training, extensive training, and I would see to it that he got it. I went to the charge nurse at the desk who knew I had been a god-send for them all. She gave Mom a different nurse. I had her call the doctor. I wanted Mom's leg checked. Her doctor wasn't on call. They ordered a blood-clot test. They were covering their butts. Oh, but I wasn't done. I turned him in to his boss, the director of nursing. They assured me he would get more training. I had names, times, dates—all the information. God doesn't expect us to be a doormat. He does expect us to control ourselves. I did that. He also expects us if something is wrong to try to make it right. I didn't try to get him fired. I just didn't want him to treat anyone else like that. The nurses told me we know how he is. They said many people have complained. That's the problem with complaining and doing nothing about it.

Mom was improving except the pain in her leg. I asked her Christian doctor if they had a pain specialist in the hospital.

He said, "We don't usually call a pain specialist to the ICU. We handle that."

I explained that my mom had a lot of nerve pain in her ankle that she also had surgery on. She had an appointment with a pain doctor to have the nerves killed.

He finally said okay.

I told him, "Maybe there is something they can do to help."

The pain doctor came, ran some tests, and said she would help if she could. She also checked the pain medicine she was on and had them change it. The doctor was open to it. He had never ever called on another doctor for pain control. He explained she was new to the hospital and they were happy to have her. He was a good man. The pain medicine was a welcome change for mom. She could rest easier thank God. We were told healing was what she needed. I complained about an x-ray for her leg.

He said, "She's more stable now, so we were moving her to a regular floor. They will take one there."

The move took place and went smoothly except the doctor on call for the last couple days of the week didn't see it necessary to get an x-ray. Why was this such a fight? The move was a blessing as they let me stay all day, from morning until night. They were busy, and I was a help to them. Help positioning Mom was a big one. Her leg still hurt so badly; she didn't want anyone to move it except me. The leg had to stay stable to heal, that's all we kept hearing. An x-ray could shed light on things, I would say. We had other issues as well. Mom's blood pressure wasn't stable. She hadn't had a bowel movement, no matter what they gave her, in almost two weeks. Lots to deal with. The blood pressure and bowel movement were top priority.

The pain doctor had come to see us finally. She asked if the medicine was helping. Thank God it was. She explained that she spoke with the pain doctor who was scheduled to do the nerve procedure (she had asked for his information earlier in the week). She was thorough explaining what was wrong with the ankle, foot, leg pain. She also explained that if Mom hadn't gotten in the accident and had the nerve surgery, she wouldn't have been able to walk on that leg ever again. All through mom's recent hospital journey you could see God's protection, his hands all over it. She told us no nerve procedure could ever be done. She needed the nerves she had. We thanked her. It was interesting a few days earlier when I asked the floor manager, who was a kind soul, to see the pain doctor (he even gave me his cell number in case I needed him, and there were a few times I did, and he came quickly).

He said, "They don't come to the floor. You have to go to them."

I said, "No, sir, she came to the ICU. We looked her up in mom's chart." (As that was the one day I forgot my notepad.)

He looked at me and said, "Huh, are you a nurse?"

I said, "No, but I'm in the details. This is my mama."

My poor mom. Extreme measures had to be taken for her to have a bowel movement. It had been two weeks now, too long. Surgery was discussed. First, they would try a last-resort medicine. They hated to use it. There could be nasty side effects on her body. Unfortunately, the next day, they had to double the dose. I remember mom saying, "Oh dear, God no." Her heart, all her organs did well with the medicine. The impaction was removed without surgery. Her blood pressure more stable now.

Weeks had passed by now, three to four, with her leg still being an issue. They had a lift to get her in and out of bed to a recliner. I would ask the doctor, "I think we need an x-ray." Each week there would be new doctors. They would do their rounds early, so I would be there early. A new set of doctors. I will try again.

The older, somewhat grumpy doctor said when he was done looking at mom's chart, "Do you need anything from me?"

I said, "Only an x-ray of her leg."

He grumped at me and left the room.

The younger doctor stayed and said, "I'm so sorry."

I said, "It's okay. I've spent a lot of time in hospitals. Some doctors are grumpy."

That afternoon, talking with mom and praying as we did every day, I left to take a small break so she could try to close her eyes. She didn't want to sleep when I was there. I saw the older doctor getting on the elevator looking tired.

I said, "Hello."

He looked at me.

I said, "Has it been a long day?"

He said, "Yes."

I said, "I'm sorry. I sure hope it gets better. I will say a prayer for you."

He grumbled, "Thank you," and got on the elevator.

We still had physical therapy looming over our heads. Mom's insurance would only pay for two rehabs, and she had been in them both. They were both really bad. One of the nurses mentioned that the hospital has a great rehab. It's on the other side of the hospital. She said, "Unfortunately, your mom's insurance won't pay for it."

I asked her to write it on mom's white board under goals. We would pray over this. I told her nothing is impossible with God. She wrote it down, and we began praying over it.

The next morning Mr. Grumpy doctor was smiling.

He said, "Is there anything you need from me today?"

"Yes," I said. "We need an x-ray on her leg."

The young doctor looked at me in shock.

He paused and said, "Okay, I hear you. We will do an x-ray."

Mom and I thanked him, and I offered them chocolate truffles and told them we hoped they had a blessed day.

The one thing I will say about doctors, nurses, and hospital staff in general is that people aren't at their best in the hospital and they are not always nice to them. Show kindness to them. Remember they are human. They have put years into training to save lives. They need grace too. I always kept good chocolate in mom's room for them, and she offered it often. With her working in a hospital, she knew how long some days could be.

The x-ray was finally taken. Now we wait. I had met with the social worker a couple of times. I told him if she can't go to Bannasch, the in-hospital rehab, I would have to take her home and do it myself.

He advised against it and told me, "I will try."

I told him, "That's all I'm asking."

The ball was rolling. A few days prior to the x-ray, we had met the doctor from Bannasch. He assessed mom. We both thought, *Great, there's a chance.* We had been praying a lot about next steps as she couldn't remain in the hospital. He was thorough in his assessment. He told us about her leg and what they could do for her. He also told her it was a two-to three-week program, and no one could be there with her. He was reassuring, upbeat, knowledgeable, and very kind.

"One more thing," he said, "if your insurance approves this program, you will have to pass an exam with the physical therapist on this floor."

After he left, we were both concerned. We asked the nurse what she would have to do. We knew her well. She had mom several times on several difficult days. She knew mom was a fighter. She explained she would have to stand, transfer on her one good leg to a chair, and use a sock aid to put on her socks. There were several steps.

Before she left the room, she said, "On the slim chance the insurance agrees, she has to pass this test or it won't matter. It's a state-of-the-art new program. It has all the bells and whistles. If someone wasn't a fighter, giving them all they had, they wouldn't accept her."

Mom passed the test. She gave it all she had. The doctor's report was in. He would accept her.

Finally, it was the evening. It had been a long day, but at least, the leg x-ray was taken. We also got the news we had prayed for: the insurance said yes to Bannasch. We were thanking God. Mom was so happy. Mom's kidneys still weren't cooperating. However, after several painful attempts of catheter removal, running water, soothing music, and prayer, the doctor in physical therapy told us not to worry, that she would be moved over there soon and they would take care of that.

It was a really good day, and we had just gotten good news, a miracle really, when we heard a knock at the door. We looked at each other. We kept her door closed a lot as to block out stress and hospital sounds. A tall man in scrubs walked in.

I looked at him and said, "Hello, I'm her daughter. Can I help you?"

He introduced himself. He said, "I'm sorry but I don't have very good news."

Big eyed, both Mom and I braced for the "What now?"

He said, "I am a surgeon here at the hospital."

"Surgery for what? She's on her way to physical therapy here in Bannasch soon."

He said, "I'm sorry but not yet." He explained, "The x-ray taken earlier in the day showed her leg isn't stable, and it's not stable going into the hip either. We will need to do surgery."

You could have pushed both Mom and me over with a feather.

He said, "This will need to be done right away."

He explained the procedure. It would be challenging. We explained her hip trouble with that hip, the revision, and her collapsed pelvis.

He said, "If we're successful, she will need recovery time and extensive physical therapy."

What does he mean if? He would get his schedule arranged, and it would take place as soon as possible, tomorrow afternoon.

When he left the room, Mom burst into tears. "I just got into Bannasch."

We held hands, talked, and prayed.

She finally said, "I guess if I have to, I have to."

I told her God doesn't make mistakes. He kept nudging me to push for the x-ray. If she had gone to therapy without it, her leg could have collapsed, and there would be no way of fixing it. There were good doctors there and so many involved, how could they not listen? How could they not do an x-ray? Friend, the one thing I know throughout all of my hospital journeys, including mine personally, is to listen to those nudges.

I made sure Mom was settled. She had accepted surgery, and we had both put it in God's hands. If this is what had to be done for healing, then this is what we would do. You see, God is the great physician. He knows what healing needs to be done. Not much sleep was had that night, at least for me. I had the nurse ask the doctor if Mom could have something to sleep. She needed to be rested before going into battle. I stayed later than usual with Mom. She needed comfort. We both did really. But Mom was facing surgery. There were concerns with her going into that kind of surgery with all she's been through and is still going through.

After making many calls and attempting to sleep, I went back to the hospital early. Mom was awake, no breakfast was had. So many mornings I had encouraged her to eat. So many hospital menus picked out to get her to this point. She remembers the sound of my shoes coming down the hall. She said she waited for that sound and couldn't wait for me to get there. She also remembers me making her drink both of her small milk cartons. LOL. I did my best to bring God's love and light into her room that day as I tried to do every day. With her door shut, we talked. We discussed the real possibility of her not making it through the surgery. She needed to do that. Well, Mom wanted to talk about it.

She said, "I will be healed one way or another."

We both shed some tears. I told her it would be good to talk to all of her kids. We, her kids, had already discussed that all of our conversations would be strong and positive for her. We have a strong family. She did just that. She spoke to my sisters and brother. They all kept their emotions in check and were strong for her. She needed that. It was a pick-me-up before surgery for sure.

As the surgery time was approaching, the room felt heavier. Mom was reminiscing. She was remembering a time when she was with her mother and she was crying. She asked Mom if she thought her father was watching down on her and could see her lonely and crying. Mom, of course, told her no. There is no pain or sadness in heaven. Sitting by her on the couch, she told Mom her favorite song was the "Longer I Serve Him the Sweeter He Grows." It's a Christian song. Together in tears they sang that song. I had been playing Christian songs on my phone in between our talks. Together, before she went into surgery, in my mom's sweet, shaky voice, a little tearful, we sang that song. I knew it would be a treasured memory especially if God took her home to heaven that day. We made a video for my siblings as well. Her telling them how much she loved them. Telling them either way she would be okay. I sent her off to surgery with a prayer, hug, and a smile. The beautiful thing, the gift God gave us both, was the young man who transported Mom (me walking with them as far as I could) asked if we minded him sharing a couple scriptures from the Bible with us. He said he had been practicing some in hopes of sharing and helping patients. God, you are so good, reminding us you were there and you weren't about to leave us now.

After hours went by, the doctor asked to speak to us, her husband and me.

He said, "I don't even want to know who had been in there before, but what a mess they made." He said he had to use a cadaver bone as the femur bone in her leg, as the leg was in pieces. He said, "I did my best. I straightened her leg. Unfortunately, this leg will be shorter than the other one. I'm sorry about that."

I thanked him.

He looked tired and challenged.

Yes, Mom came through the surgery. Now it was time to heal. There was still pain, but Mom said, "It is better now." It is surgical pain, which she was no stranger to. As soon as she was stable and her pain under control, I went straight back to fighting for Bannasch. She still needed rehab, only it would look different now. The doctor would have to see her again. She would have to pass the test again.

She did just that. Her leg was actually fixed now. She had her fighting spirit back. She knew surgery was God's protection over her.

Mom got into Bannasch. She was lonely but worked hard. We could talk on the phone. I sent clothes, snacks, and asked loved ones to send her cards for encouragement. The social worker and doctors made it clear they would not send her home unless she had help. I assured them I wouldn't leave her. They said I would have to sign a paper saying so. So many plans to be made: hospital bed, nursing to check on her twice a week, etc. An advocate from her doctor's office to help coordinate. Her doctor was so good. And, of course, physical therapy at home. I had to take her blood pressure three times a day, log it, log her pain levels, etc. She wasn't on heart medicine before the accident but was on three different ones now. I would also have to come into Bannasch to be trained. They said you will need help. Her husband is older, and they wouldn't count him even though he was still strong and could help some. I asked my husband to fly in and to come help me. I needed help with the house and the hospital bed. They wanted him there before she came home. He was great. He came, got trained at Bannasch with me and added much needed humor as always. It was good for me as well to see him. It had been almost eight weeks now.

Mom's journey has continued for two years. So many moving parts all intricately woven. I stayed with her, and then my sister came. She wasn't able to be without me yet. That would take some serious time. My sister took notes and did all the things. I showed her the physical therapy we were doing as I was the therapist now. Insurance will only pay for so long. We decided my sister would fly back to Michigan with Mom if I could get her in and out of a car, using a walker and a therapy belt. We would get her a wheelchair, but she would have to transfer to the airplane seat and go to the bathroom if needed. I worked on all of that. My husband flew down again. I needed his help, his strength. My sister-in-law was a nurse, and she was there taking care of her mom, my mother-in-law.

Our parents were in the same Christian park only a few hundred yards from each other. My sweet mother-in-law was wonderful. She was a teacher, great mother, grandmother, and a Christian woman.

She suffered in her later years of life with Parkinson's and dementia. I was happy to be so close so we could help one another. God knew we would both need each other especially at that time in our lives.

Mom accomplished all we needed her to. Plans were made. Mom was ready. My sister flew in, and I flew back home to Texas to gather my things and to head to our cabin on the lake for Mom to stay with me there. She loves the lake as much as I do. Arrangements had to be made there as well. I made a call to my brother, measured Mom's wheelchair to make sure she could get into the bathroom and bedroom. He had to take the bedroom door off and build a ramp to get her into the cabin. So many challenges ahead of us. It was comforting to get her there. I would have three of my siblings there if and when I needed them. And she could at least be with three more of her children. My other sister lives in Wisconsin. She eventually made changes to her home. Her family built a ramp. She bought a lift chair. All of us would try to do our best to care for Mom. We drove Mom to her. Showed her all the medicines, therapy, etc. She had worked in hospitals herself. She has this. I wasn't worried. Mom stayed with her for a while. They had precious time together. I had been at this for months in the trenches. To be honest, I could use a bit of rest. Mom did great. We all had priceless family time. Cards, movies, family dinners, such a blessing and a gift. So many gifts that will be treasured forever.

That summer, I was able to find a doctor not far from us who was able to build up Mom's shoe. Finally, she could walk without a three-inch difference. He was amazing. She is doing well today, walking with a walker, using a wheelchair when needed. But the big miracle is she was put back together and can walk at all. There is so much more to the story. So many bright spots and so many dark, rough, tough strands of threads running not only through her tapestry, but all of our tapestries making up this beautiful journey we call life.

The tapestry is still in the making for all of us who remain here on earth. God only gives us one day at a time because that's all we can handle. Interestingly enough, my father-in-law was in a golf car accident. His leg was sticking out and got caught on another golfcart.

The scene was awful. So much blood with the bottom half of his leg ripped open to the bone.

Here's a strong thread, my friend. He went to the same hospital as my mom. My husband flew down. He had the same surgeon as my mom. He had a long hospital stay and needed rehab like my mom. I told my husband and sister-in-law that he needed Bannasch. I told them they would have to fight for it, and we would all pray. I gave them all he would have to do and that he had to give it all he had. He was denied twice. I said to try again as the third time is a charm. He got in and is walking today. That is no coincidence. That is the power of God.

Later, a family friend took a fall. He was hospitalized at the same hospital. He was weak and needed therapy as well. Our friend, his daughter that we have known for years, came down and visited us at my in-laws' house. She too was tired. Her father is a very large man. Her sister and both of their husbands were there trying to help the hospital lift him. They had tried multiple rehabs. They wouldn't take him due to his size. They didn't know what they would do. I looked at them and said Bannasch. They can do it all. It has to be Bannasch. I explained the fight, the details. They were happy and ready to fight. So was he. He, too, finally went to Bannisch, and he, too, is walking today. Oh, the mighty weave, the strong strands God can weave if we all help each other.

Brenda and Mom

Family

After all these Years

I sit here today at my kitchen table all these years later. A different table, a different view, a different season in life than when I started writing this book. So fragile and broken it was almost impossible to write. I still carry the scars, the cracked parts. I can, however, look back on my life and see the beauty between the broken.

My husband and I, against so many odds, are still together. We were blessed with a beautiful daughter who is twenty-two today and in her senior year of college. I did get to be a mom. I'm so very grateful to God for that.

I have told many people throughout my life, over different seasons, being a mom is the best and hardest thing I have ever done. Let me explain here. I love my daughter with all my heart. As she grew up we have had so many adventures. Too many to count really. To mention a few here, I think back on our morning and evening swims in our Texas pool. She loved the pool and would swim her little heart out. After our morning swim it was lunch, nap time, and mommy work time. She sure wasn't afraid of the water. She would put on plays for me and then would jump off our hot tub into the large pool to end them. She was, of course, wearing her pink camo floaty suit for safety and the biggest smile our little girl could wear. No fear, that little one.

A different scene, a different day, though very similar except for one thing. This was the hard part. She was wearing a pink waterproof cast on her arm. She had fallen out of a shopping cart trying to grab something she wanted to show me. You heard me right. It all happened so fast. One minute she was sitting down, the next she was on the floor crying. She was so worried about not being able to swim.

Swim she did. And the plays and jumping continued. She is a tough one. As parents we all do our best to keep our kids safe.

We had a beautiful bedroom for our sweet girl full of toys. We made sure not to buy any toys we deemed unsafe. My husband tells a story of his childhood. One Christmas he begged his parents for a toy that was called *Incredible Edibles*. Now that was a toy that I'm not sure should have been called a toy. It was more of a hot plate with molds on it. It came with a liquid that you poured into the molds. You would plug it in and it would harden the liquid. One time, he put a toothpick in the center of the mold and the gelled liquid stuck to the toothpick. He shook it and the gelled liquid hit him square in the chest. He tells of running through the house screaming, "Mom, help me!" She helped him alright. She did the only thing she could do as it was burning him. She ripped it off his chest as quickly as she could, taking his skin with it. That was one story that was traumatizing for him as a kid. He swears today that if he didn't have hair on his chest the critter outline would still be there. OUCH!

One evening we did our routine like we did every other night. Snacks, bath, brush teeth, *Bear and the Big Blue House* show and then off to bed but not before saying our prayers. It was a normal evening like most evenings until about 1:00am when a loud breathing sound, almost like a barking sound, came over the monitor we had in her room. Safety first. I was so happy we had a monitor. My husband and I both heard it. We rushed upstairs to her room thinking, *What's in her room?* Fear will grab you quickly when it's your child. We both realized very quickly the sound was coming from her. We did our best to stay calm. My husband whisked her up quickly and we rushed her to the hospital emergency room. Not knowing what's wrong with your child, that's hard. Thank God the doctor came into the room quickly. He knew right away what it was. He said she has the croup. What's that? We had no idea. For those of you who don't know what the croup is, it's an upper respiratory infection that can come on very quickly. I guess so. She was fine when she went to bed. The doctor said it restricts the airway and makes a barking sound. It sure does. They treated her and she was so brave. I was happy the croup never visited us again.

Rewinding here just a little. When we made our move to Texas, we moved into a neighborhood with no kids. This was hard for her and me. I wanted her to have kids to play with. No mommy and me groups there. As much as I loved our alone time I knew she needed to get used to playing with other kids. So at about the age of 3 1/2 she went to the daycare our neighbors owned. They were good God fearing people. The husband had been a preacher. I knew she was in good hands. The first day came and she didn't want me to leave her any more than I wanted to. I cried all the way home. She did well but we both decided three days a week was enough and she was the early one out on most days. She missed me and I missed her.

Fast forwarding a little further was public school, kindergarten. That was an adjustment for sure. There is making friends, mean kids, and it's all day long. By the end of the day she was ready to come home. Then came the first ever sleepover at a friend's house. It was okay but that didn't happen often per her request. She liked being home. She and I stayed very close as my husband traveled and worked so much.

I decided to give up my job and only work part time and mostly at home doing accounts receivable. Eventually, I gave that up too. Trust me, staying at home work was no joke. Putting my family first was important to me. My daughter was happy with that. I could help out at school. I was room mom and brought her favorite snacks. I had snacks ready to go when I packed her up and she was happy with that as well. Her broken arm, preschool, the croup are just a few of the hard times. But there are so many best times that are all mixed in.

One year my husband bought me a silver scooter. We both loved it. Every night after bath time, in her pj's, we would go for a ride. We would look at all the lights on the landscaping and the houses. We would ride down to the pond to see her favorite white duck. We would walk to the pond during the day and she would feed him by hand so, of course, we had to say goodnight to him. Oh how she loved the pond and the ducks. That year for Christmas we bought her a silver scooter of her very own. She rode it all over the house. We still have that scooter today. Some memories are too hard to part with.

As I look back, another best memory was our big tube, Mabel, that we would pull the kids on with our boat. How she loved Mabel. We had so many boat rides from our cabin but none more memorable than riding Mabel to town with my niece to get ice cream. We loved our walks as well. We would walk from our cabin to the end of our road where the water would open right up. There was a large rock where we would have a picnic on. We would talk about what adventure we wanted to have next. Hunting for rocks was always fun as well. She has always loved rocks and always will I believe.

Our cabin is located on Lake Huron in the upper peninsula of Michigan. We have lots of frogs at our cabin. She learned to 'ribit' just like them. She and my niece would build houses to keep them in after they caught them. Of course, after they went to bed, mom would let them go. In the morning, they were so confused as to how they got out and they would try harder the next day. It sounds mean but think of the poor frogs. What we don't do as parents.

Throughout her life we built her three different play houses. She loved them all. The last one built here at our cabin. We had it redone to be part adult and part kid. This way she can enjoy it as an adult and, if she has children, they can enjoy it too. Some of her special toys are in there—her doll house, her tea set, her retro green oven that has two light bulbs that can really cook. Some of her books are on the upper shelves. There hangs a light in the ceiling that is made of wooden beads and there is an electric fireplace as well. I love to go in there and remember all of our good times. I am still adding things to this playhouse. Her old one had what they call a dumb waiter to lift things up and down. It also had a boat steering wheel on the rail of the deck overlooking the lake. We can't forget the periscope or the flower boxes to plant. Of course there were dry erase boards on the walls. Today, there is a dry erase board and a chalk board. I think one of her favorite things was her firefly jar. She loved to chase and collect fireflies and watch them glow at night. Of course, mom let them go after bed. That's part of the fun chasing and catching them. My how the years fly by.

The teenage years came and not needing mom so much came with them. This was hard for me. Fast forwarding came learning to drive and then driving herself to school. That meant, for me, no more Starbucks in the afternoon after school, sitting in the car and talking about her day. It also meant no more rides to school, her eating breakfast and me drinking my coffee. The first day she drove herself to school, I stayed home and grieved a little all by myself. I knew things would never ever be the same again. I thought, *This is how my mother felt.* That was hard. Oh, to go back in time for just one more day or to freeze time as I say all the time. Life flies by so quickly.

Of course, after that came graduation from high school and then came college 4 hours away from home. We have so many memories. I'd like to share one more if you will bear with me. With my husband's different jobs over the years, we have lived in many different places and parts of the country. I have met many people from so many different backgrounds.

One stint was in Virginia, near Washington, D.C. We lived in a town home, an attached town home. They were Italian style. They set the town homes in rows of four. I remember clearly my daughter's first day of school there. We had to walk to the end of the street where she would get on the bus. Both of us were ready to go, ready to meet our neighbors and their children. Ready to embrace our new experience. We got to the end of the street where all of the children and parents gathered. I noticed they were all standing away from one another, not speaking to each other, like they were all in separate groups and wanted it that way. Trying to make things easier for my daughter, I introduced us and tried to make conversation. One group at a time. The children were friendly to her. I was relieved. I thought maybe when they get on the bus the kids will talk. People came from different directions, not just our row. After the kids got on the bus, everyone went home without speaking.

I thought, *What is this? This is not what I was hoping for.*

Every day we would go to the bus stop and I would, as I say, kill people with kindness. I would smile, ask questions about their day, their life. I would be so sweet, they would have to answer me. I was determined these people would all get to know one another before I leave here. My row was especially difficult. It appeared not only did they not speak to each other, they did not like each other. As time went on, I learned the family right next to us were Muslim. Next to them were Mormon, and next to them were Catholic. When your belief system is completely different, and you have children you're trying to raise up in your beliefs, you want separation. Living where our houses touched, there was not a lot of that. God stretched me there. He grew me and my faith. He helped me love on people no matter the situation. Love on people I did. We all became friends. Some not as close as others, but smiles and hellos at the bus stop and conversations were had.

I have to admit it wasn't my favorite place to live—the traffic, the helicopters circling. I came from a small community in northern Michigan. After about year two, some gang activity had entered our area. The school got locked down. We were told to keep a close eye on our children. My daughter got roughed up on the bus for sticking up for one of our neighbor's children. Needless to say, I wanted to go home where kids can catch fireflies and frogs by the lake. This wasn't for me.

My daughter and I went home for a visit. I told my husband we will stay with my sister. She had a young daughter too, one year older than mine. After one day of being home, I felt peace, calmness, nature, and safety.

My husband had to work, so he was still there. But it was summer, and he said, "Stay a bit, take the time you need."

I had gotten quiet at home, a little sad, not myself. He had hoped this would bring me back to my talkative, outgoing self.

Day two, I said to my sister, "I wonder if there is anything for sale on the island."

With excitement, she said, "What?"

We wanted our two girls that loved being together so much to be able to grow up together.

I said, "Let's see."

She said, "What will your husband say if there is something for sale?"

I said, "We will find out."

He had gotten a substantial raise when we moved there, so off we went with the girls driving around when we came across this small house with a two-car garage for sale.

I told my sister, "Let's stop. I can't see the lake. Pull down in the driveway," as it went downhill.

She said, "Should we do that?"

Being my bold self and feeling drawn, I said, "Just go."

There was an older gentleman outside.

I got out and said, "I'm sorry, I'm here from out of town, and I saw your sign."

He said, "No problem, are you looking to buy?"

I said, "If the place and the price is right, yes, sir, I am." My husband having no clue I'm even looking. I said, "If you don't mind me asking, where is the water?"

He smiled and said, "Follow me."

Just a few steps around the corner to my right, there it was. The most beautiful view of the lake and so close with a large crib dock. A crib dock is made of large telephone poles made into a square, then filled with rocks so the ice doesn't move it. The poles driven into the ground by large equipment brought in by a floating barge. One side of the dock was dredged. That was great, as the water over the years would ebb and flow, at times being really low where you needed to stay right in the dredge to get a boat out, and other times so high it didn't matter at all.

Both the dock and the dredge were a big plus for me. I could imagine our daughter playing in the water, catching frogs and fireflies, being a kid. Growing up like I did. Well, except for the water. As a kid, I was only on the water a couple of times with friends. But I had always wanted to be. I wanted that for my daughter so much, and I missed my family. Being in Virginia made me truly homesick. I had three sisters and a brother there plus all of my nieces and nephews.

The owner asked, "Do you like what you see?"

Not trying to seem too anxious, I said, "Aw, the lake, yes, that's what I'm looking for."

He said, "Would you like to see inside?"

"Sure, if that is okay."

Inside we went. It was dark-wood paneling. The outside had white siding with a roof, so it looked like an ordinary small house. Inside, it was dark, tight with a large wooden cabinet and counter in the kitchen; a small window into a small living room with a large window overlooking the lake.

He said, "It was a single wide trailer. And we added a living room, a bedroom, sided it and put a roof on."

Okay, again not what I expected. Three bedrooms, one being tight where only a twin bed could fit. Furniture would all stay, beds and all. Okay, that helps. The inside was ugly; the outside, with the lake, God's masterpiece.

My sister said, "That's ugly."

I said, "I don't care. I don't plan on spending much time in there. There's nothing paint can't fix."

"Okay," she said.

There were two big maple trees. And birch and pine trees gave privacy up by the road. I liked that. I thanked them and said I would be in touch. I told my sister I'm going to buy this place and spend my summers here. I'm coming home. I took the realtor's information from the sign. I called him and got the price. It seemed reasonable. I get it, the house isn't super. I didn't care.

"This could be doable," I told my sister.

Right away, with my daughter and niece excited, I called my husband, talking fast like my usual self. Bursting with excitement I told him, "I'm buying a cabin on the lake." I prefer cabin rather than little house or lake house like most people say. I like cabin. It was small, cozy, and had a small burning stove in the living room. Cabin it is.

He said, "What, hang on, we've never talked about buying a place there."

I rattled on and on about all the joy it would bring. How it was only a seven-hour drive, the view, family. I had to have it. I wasn't taking no for an answer.

He finally said, "Can I at least drive up this weekend and see it?"

"Yes, that would be great, but I don't want to lose it."

He said, "If it's meant to be and we can afford it, you won't lose it."

I settled down. He had heard me. I'm buying this. I've moved all over, and I don't like it there. I'm going home for the summer, period. I can be a tiny bit strong willed. LOL.

Okay, he made plans to come see it. In shock and pointing out the flaws and the ugly, I assured him I could make it cute. He looked at the smile on his two girls' faces, looked at the view, ran the numbers, and the rest is history.

We have owned our little cabin, our piece of heaven's view, for fourteen years now. Oh, how we have treasured our precious summers and all our treasured family times. So many memories made. So much paint. LOL. Candy-apple red kitchen cabinets, light-yellow walls, white, light blue… We still have the olive-green sink and bath tub in the bathroom. I painted olive green-and-white wide up-and-down striped walls to make it cute. And a large blue-and-green whale hangs on the wall. It's all in the eye of the beholder. The tiny trailer window in the kitchen is big now and has a wooden ledge to set family pictures on. The tiny bedroom became a laundry room with the large cabinet counter that was in the kitchen taking up space in there to fold clothes on and for storage. We also added another toilet. We have a large extended family and certainly needed more than one. The ugly little house has become our cute little treasured cabin. We've had some struggles over the years as we all do in one way or another. The job in Virginia didn't pan out so well. The housing market crashed. We lost so much money on our home. We had to live in that little cabin for a year, in the harsh winter, down the hill, with three dogs and four birds. Wonderful memories were made. I have pictures of my daughter building a snowman on the dock with the dogs right there. Another season God brought us through. My husband's job, would we be able to keep our little cabin? As I look back, I wouldn't trade the journey for anything. That year my husband helped my daughter build a sled for Snowfest. We cleared snow on the shore of the lake, and the girls and their dads ice skated on the lake. Many snowmen were built. Sledding down the hill over and over. A simple Christmas with a small humble tree. Cards and games were played, and movies by the little stove were watched.

The memories made that year, though trouble loomed over our heads, were some of our best ever; and even though I didn't like where we lived in Virginia, I met and made friends with my neighbors, shared God's love with their children, worked with a boy named Johnny who one of my neighbors' adopted from Africa. He had been left on the edge of the jungle to die as he had many health problems. I had told my neighbor of my son Cody's story and all the medical equipment I learned to use. She had to use a suction machine on him and was nervous. She was scared she had taken on too much. Our daughters were friends, best friends. I agreed to help her with Johnny. I enjoyed my time with them. Johnny is no longer with her today. We had many long chats while I was helping out. We talked about how he would need a wheelchair, how would they lift him as he grew, if he grew. I told her all we can do is love him, care for him while he is here with us. God is in the details. He knows what Johnny needs and how long he will be here on earth with us. I had told the doctors all those years earlier with my son that he was here until God took him home to heaven. Johnny's physical condition was different, but the situation was the same. Love them, care for them, and thank God for every day, every moment with them. Johnny and Cody are both whole today in heaven, free from all pain and suffering.

That's a beautiful thing, friend. A bright, beautiful thread in the tapestry of our life, both of our lives, intertwined if only for a moment in time. We can help one another, share our journeys, our love. We can leave our mark, God's imprint on this world. Our tiny cabin that we share openly with family and friends, I pray all who enter feel loved, cared about, and blessed as we do. I promised God all those years ago that if I could have it, I would share it always. Without the move to Virginia, and my inner struggle, we would never have the cabin. Some struggles are rewarding, and this one was for me. It's the reward that keeps giving year after year, and I hope it keeps blessing others as much as it does me.

Our Muslim neighbors in Virginia were a welcome, wonderful addition to my life at the time. So were the Mormon family. I learned so much about their culture, their religion and faith. I learned the Mormon faith, at least theirs, did not want them to stop having children. They had two beautiful daughters. The wife, so sweet and kind, had a hard time with her last pregnancy. She could have died. She wasn't raised in the faith. She was raised Christian and didn't want to sacrifice herself for more children. We had many talks. I agreed. She wanted to be grateful for what she had. She felt pressure from the church where men and women worshipped separately. She felt pressure from family, friends, and her husband. I felt for her, prayed for her and with her. I don't know today if she had more children. I wish I could see her. I loved her and her beautiful children. I assured her God knew her journey. It was her body, and I would take the doctor's advice. I told her it's between you and God. Children are wonderful gifts. I get it, so is our life.

One day, visiting with my Muslim neighbor, which I spent quite a bit of time with, I loved her too and was good to her children (she had four, three girls and a boy), I asked her if I could take them trick or treating for Halloween. I took all the kids in our row, me and two other moms. She said she would have to ask her husband. The girls wanted to go so badly. He could see their excitement.

"They have no costumes," he said.

I said, "No problem, I will help them dress up like I did when I was a kid. Dad's clothes, whatever we could create."

He said, "Okay."

The girls had so much fun. I will never forget that, and my daughter loved it. I would give his wife clothes or the kids things. I would cook and give them goodies. He always smiled and waved at me, never speaking much.

One day his wife invited me over for tea and a visit. She was excited. They were going on a trip. Just the two of them. They worked hard, both of them, and their old van broke down often, so this was a very big deal. She told me just the husbands and wives are going, her brother and sister-in-law.

She seemed troubled. I asked her what was wrong. She teared up. What would she wear? Their wives always look so nice, and their wives didn't have to keep their head covered on vacation. She wished she didn't have to either. Anytime I saw her, her head was always covered. You could see no hair and barely see her face.

She said, "I want to feel beautiful like them. I don't want to cover up."

I said, "Okay. The kids are at school. I will help you."

I gave her clothes to wear. I let her try on lots until she found things that fit or she looked good in. Skirts and tops were special since she always wore one-piece oversized dresses. Then I helped her with her hair and makeup, jewelry, etc. She was so beautiful. I hadn't ever seen her like this. I was a bit nervous. I didn't know if her husband would be happy with me or her for that matter. We decided she would make a nice dinner, and when he got home greet him that way. Element of surprise. Let him see his beautiful wife, and they could talk.

"He is a quiet, kind man," she said.

I told her, "Let him see you, the real you, in all your beauty and share your feelings with him."

The girls were so excited. They couldn't believe how beautiful their mom was. They kept staring and smiling.

They asked, "Why?"

She explained, "I don't mind covering up. It's our way, but sometimes, I just want to be seen."

They told her that they hoped he would let her do that as he had let them dress up and trick or treat. That he did. He came home that night, she said, shocked, surprised, and in awe of his beautiful wife. He told her he was sorry that he had forgotten how beautiful she was. When they met she wasn't covered. He teared up and told her he would be honored to take her on vacation uncovered for all to see his beautiful wife who had been so loyal and faithful, such a good mother and hard worker. She deserved this.

She told me all about it the next day, of course. That night I was outside with my daughter. He walked over and thanked me. He told me I was a princess in his eyes and that would never change. He thanked me for all of my kindness to his wife and children. If their van broke down, I would give them a ride, he mentioned it. He hadn't missed anything. I told him I was happy to do it, and

I was glad we were speaking. He told me he would like to have us over for dinner sometime. I said great. We both told each other if we needed anything to just ask. He walked away shaking his head, smiling, saying, "You are a princess, that's all I can say." I laughed, saying, "Thank you," as I knew that meant a lot to him, thinking, *I am no princess.*

We had dinner at their house, and he shared his faith with me, his beliefs. I learned so much. He wanted to assure me his beliefs, his bible, his Koran, was not violent and never should be. I assured him mine wasn't either. I wish I could see them again too.

Little did I know with the move to Virginia, the challenges I would face, the people I would meet, the things I would learn or the longing for home I would feel, especially that little cabin that I would have and hold so dear today. A lot of colors in my tapestry from the 3.5 years we lived there. Some dark and some very bright threads.

The vacation they went on was wonderful. They took many pictures, smiles all around. When they came home, she washed, folded, and packed up the clothes I had given her to wear. She brought them over with all the pictures. We visited and had tea. Before she left all covered up again, she thanked me again and started to head out the door. I felt like she was saying when we talked, "It was wonderful, but I won't get that again." I gave her back the clothes and makeup. I told her they were perfect for her next trip and she must keep them. With a big hug, she gladly accepted. I wonder if she still has them today. Looking back over my life, there has been some very difficult dark seasons, but there has been some bright, beautiful ones too.

Husband and Daughter at Cabin

Pets Today

Brenda and Her Husband

Cabin From Lake View

Cabin From Road

Daughter {left} with niece, older years

Daughter {right} with niece, younger years

Daughter with Snowman at Cabin

Peace

The Final Peace

In this life, we're all searching for purpose. We all want to be something, someone amazing, to change the world, to dream big. You can do it if you only work harder, get better grades, do all the right things, then you will have it all. Listen, friend, we only have it all when we have God. That eternal place he has prepared for us with no pain, no suffering, no anguish with streets of gold. Colors so bright we can't imagine. Living forever with our loved ones. Doesn't that sound amazing? That's where I want to be.

Listen, no job, no husband or wife, no child, no perfect house, or perfect family can give you what God can. Through all of my suffering, God has taught me first, I can't go through it without him. Second, he has me. His ways are higher than mine. And third, but not last, he wants to use my circumstances to help others, to benefit his kingdom of heaven, to share in others' pain, to share my story—the good, the bad and the ugly, coming out on the other side using God's strength in my weakness to make me stronger. There is power in the name of Jesus, my friend. Don't miss this. No matter your path or what you accomplish in this life, there is no better feeling than being used for God's purpose. Helping others to really know him.

I once had a man named Lavelle in my counseling office at the food bank where I gave some of my time. He was very large in stature. He wore many chains and had spent some time in prison. He had just gotten out and needed some help. He was not proud of it. God gave me the best gift that day. I got to hold his very large hands and pray with him. As the tears rolled down both of our faces, I got to share Jesus's love and forgiveness, his grace and mercies. He told me his grandparents raised him, and he knew better. They took him to church and loved on him. You know, Christ's love was showered on that man that day.

Today, right now, if you are feeling guilty, wrong, unforgivable, sad, or downright worthless, it's okay. God's grace and forgiveness are enough for you, too. Repent, ask for forgiveness. Ask for healing. Turn away from the wrong and do it no more. Ask Jesus to come into your heart. If you do that, friend, all is forgiven. If you haven't asked Jesus into your heart please do. He's been waiting for you.

You know that day in a little food bank in Grand Prairie, Texas, I thought God was using me, but he was using Lavelle too. The last thing he said to me was, "You know, God paints us a new picture every day. When we wake up, all we have to do is see it."

His grandparents would tell him that. So sweet. Now that was a blessing for me that day, and I will never forget it. A dear friend put it on a plaque for me that sits in my kitchen today. It's a wonderful reminder of God's amazing paintbrush, all for us to see and enjoy. Don't miss the beauty around you, my friend. The smells, sounds, the wonderful tasting food, beauty truly is in the eye of the beholder. I have a quote that I cling to. It has pulled me out of some very dark days. So I will leave you with it.

> Today is an incredible, unrepeatable gift from God.
> Let's embrace the journey no matter the treacherous path.

Whatever the outcome, be present. Let God guide you. Stay close to him always.

We all have our own journey in this life. With God, I hope, you can embrace yours. The good, the bad, the ugly, and the beautiful—it's all about the journey to our final destination, heaven. Never forget *1 James 2:4*, which says,

> *Count it all joy my brothers and sisters when you meet trials of various kinds for you know the testing of your faith produces steadfastness. Let it*

have its full effect so that you may be perfect and complete, lacking in nothing.

Going forward in your life, remember *Hebrews 12:2*, which says,

> *Let us fix our eyes on Jesus, God's son. For the joy set before him he endured the cross, its scorning and shame, and is in heaven at the right hand of the throne of God.*

He endured that to save us from our sins.
Godspeed, my friend, I hope to see you there.

Biblical Toolbox

Scriptures Referenced in This Book

Let the Journey Begin

2 Corinthians 5:17—Anyone who belongs to Christ has become a new person. The old life is gone and a new life has begun.

Ricky: Faithful and Strong

Psalm 105:4—Look to the Lord our God and his strength, seek his face always.

Proverbs 3:5–6—Lean on, trust in and be confident in the Lord God with all your heart and mind and do not rely on your own insight or understanding. In all your ways know, recognize and acknowledge him and he will direct and make straight and plain your paths.

Good News

2 Corinthians 12:9—My grace is sufficient for you, for my power is made perfect in your weakness.

2 Corinthians 4:7—We are like jars of clay, we crack under pressure, we experience brokenness and sometimes we fail completely.

Isaiah 40:29—God gives strength to the weary and increases power in the weak. Even the young grow weary, stumble and fall. But those who hope in the Lord will receive renewed strength. They will soar on wings like eagles. They will run and not grow weary, they will walk and not be faint.

Luke 12:7—Even the very hairs of your head are numbered.

2 Corinthians 4:18—So we fix our eyes not on what is seen but what is unseen for what is seen is temporary but what is unseen is eternal.

Philippians 4:13—I can do all things through Christ who strengthens me.

Sweet Little William

2 Corinthians—Our suffering is temporary and is producing for us an eternal glory that is far greater than we can imagine.

Home Will Never Be the Same

Colossians 2:7—Let your roots grow deep down into him. Let your lives be built on him. Then your faith will grow strong in the truth you were taught and you will overflow with thankfulness.

The Accident

Ephesians 4:31–32—Let all bitterness, wrath, anger, clamor or slander be put away from you. Along with all malice, be kind to one another, forgiving one another as Christ forgave you.

My Sweet Star

Ephesians 4:32—Be kind to one another, tender hearted, forgiving one another as God forgives you.

Matthew 6:15—If we do not forgive others neither will our father in heaven forgive us.

Luke 6:37—Do not judge or condemn other people.

Colossians 3:13—Bear with one another, if one as a complaint against another overlook the offense. Forgive as the Lord God forgives you.

Ah, Pregnancy

1 James 1:2–8—Count it all joy when fiery trials come, knowing that the testing of our faith will make us complete, lacking nothing so we can truly know God.

The Bubble Busted

Isaiah 40:29—The Lord gives power to the faint and to those who have no might he increases their strength.

The Waiting

Psalm 46:1–3—God is our refuge and strength, a very present help in trouble. Therefore, we will not fear, though the earth be removed and though the mountains be carried into the sea, though the waters roar and the mountains shake, there your hand will guide me still.

Worst Best Day of My Life

Matthew 6:34—Therefore, do not worry about tomorrow, tomorrow will worry about itself. Each day has enough trouble of its own.

Heart Surgery

Psalm 139:13–16—God you created my innermost being, you knit me together in my mother's womb. I am fearfully and wonderfully made. My frame was not hidden from you. I was woven together. Your eyes saw my unformed body. All the days ordained for me were written in your book before I ever came to be.

John 1:5—Light shines in the darkness and the darkness has not overcome it.

A Healthy Window

Isaiah 55:9—As the heavens are higher than the earth, my ways are higher than your ways and my thoughts higher than your thoughts, sayeth the Lord.

Lamentations—The steadfast love of God never ceases, his mercies never come to an end.

Proverbs 19:11—Good sense makes one slow to anger, and it's in their glory to overlook an offense.

Hebrews 12:14—Strive for peace with everyone.

Matthew 7:12—Whatever you wish others would do to you, also do to them.

Philippians 2:3—Do nothing from rivalry or conceit but in humility. Count others more significant than yourselves.

Romans 14:13—Let us not pass judgment on one another but rather decide never to put a stumbling block or hindrance in the way of another.

1 Thessalonians 5:11—Encourage one another and build one another up.

Colossians 4:6—Let your speech always be gracious, seasoned with salt, so that you may know how you ought to answer each person.

Proverbs 16:24—Gracious words are like a honeycomb, sweetness to the soul and health to the body.

Proverbs 15:4—A gentle tongue is a tree of life.

Proverbs 18:21—Life and death are in the power of the tongue.

Hope Enters In

Psalm 71:5—For you, God, are my hope and my trust.

Hebrews 6:19—We have this as a sure and steadfast anchor of the soul. A hope that enters into the inner place behind the curtain.

Psalm 119:114—You, God, are my hiding place and my shield. I hope in your word.

2 Corinthians 1:3–4—Blessed be the God our father. The father of mercies and the God of all comfort, who comforts us in our affliction so that we may be able to comfort others in their affliction with the comfort we receive ourselves.

Isaiah 41:10—Fear not for I am with you. I am your God. I will strengthen you. I will uphold you with my righteous right hand.

Psalm 34:18—God is near to the broken hearted and saves the crushed in spirit

Habakkuk 3:17–19—Though the fig tree does not bud and there are no grapes on the vine, though the olive crop fails and the fields produce no food. Though there are no sheep in the pen and no cattle in the stalls I will still rejoice in the Lord. He is my strength. He makes my feet like the feet of a deer. He enables me to go on heights.

Psalm 28:6—Praise be to God, he has heard my desires for his mercy. The Lord God is my strength and shield. My heart trusts him and he helps me.

Transition to Hurley

Psalm 19:1–2—The heavens declare the glory of God and the skies proclaim the work of his hands. Day after day they pour forth speech and night after night they display knowledge.

Hebrews 11:1—Faith is the assurance of things we hope for, the proof of things we do not see and the conviction of their reality. Faith perceives real facts that are not revealed to the sense.

Job 37:16—Do you know how the clouds hang poised, perfectly balanced? Oh the wonder of God who has perfect knowledge.

Job 38:12—Oh God, you have commanded the morning since your days began and caused the dawn to know its place.

No Wiggle Room

Psalm 56:8—Oh God, you have seen me tossing and turning through the night. You have collected all of my tears and preserved them in your bottle. You have recorded every one in your book.

The Journey Home

Proverbs 1:13—The integrity of the upright guides but the crookedness of the treacherous destroys them.

Luke 6:31—As you wish others would do to you also do to them.

Ecclesiastes 7:9—Do not be quick in your spirit to become angry, for anger lodges in the bosoms of fools.

Proverbs 29:11—A fool gives vent to their spirit, but a wise person quietly holds it back.

Joshua 1:19—Be strong and courageous. Do not be frightened, do not be dismayed, for the Lord God is with you wherever you go.

Proverbs 12:22—Lying lips are an abomination to the Lord but those who act faithfully are in his delight.

Proverbs 16:28—A dishonest person spreads strife and a whisper can separate close friends.

Romans 12:17–21—Repay no one evil for evil, but give thought to do what is honorable in the sight of all. If possible, so far as it depends on you, live peacefully with all. Beloved, never avenge yourself but leave it to the wrath of God.

Luke 16:10—One who is faithful in a very little is also faithful in much, and one who is dishonest in a very little is also dishonest in much.

Precious Time

Nahum 1:7—The Lord is good and a stronghold in the day of trouble.

2 Corinthians 12:9—His grace is sufficient for us and his power is made perfect in our weakness.

Luke 1:37—Nothing is impossible with God.

Revelation 21:4—God will wipe away every tear from their eyes and death shall be no more. Neither shall there be mourning, crying or pain anymore.

Psalm 116:1–2—I love the Lord God because he has heard my voice and my pleas for mercy.

1 John 3:1—See what kind of love the father has given to us that we should be called the children of God.

Romans 8:18—Consider that the sufferings of this present time are not worth comparing with the glory that is to be revealed to us.

Celebrating Cody's Life

Ecclesiastes 12:7—The dust returns to the earth as it was and the spirit returns to God who gave it.

Luke 23:43–47—There is a time for everything, a season for every activity under heaven. A time to be born and a time to die, a time to plant and a time to uproot, a time to tear down and a time to build up. A time to weep and a time to laugh, a time to mourn and a time to dance. A time to search and a time to give up. A time to keep and a time to throw away. A time to tear and a time to mend.

Psalm 31:9—Be gracious to me, O Lord, for I am in distress. My eyes are wasted from grief. My soul and my body are also.

Unpleasant Grief

John 16:22—So you have sorrow now but I will see you again, your hearts will rejoice and no one will take your joy from you.

1 Corinthians 2:9—What no eye has seen, nor ear heard, nor your heart have imagined, what God has prepared for those who love him.

Romans 8:28—We know that for those who love God all things can work together for good.

Colossians 2:2–3—I want you woven into a tapestry of love, in touch with everything there is to know of God. Then you will have minds confident and at rest, focused on God's great mysteries.

Romans 8:28—For those who love God all things can work together for good.

Proverbs 8:17—I love those who love me and those who seek me diligently find me.

Jeremiah 29:13—You will seek and find me when you seek me with all your heart.

Psalm 14:2—The Lord looks down from heaven on the children of man to see if there are any who understand, who seek after him.

Aw, Mother's Day

Isaiah 45:2—I will go before you and make the rough places smooth; I will shatter the doors of bronze and cut through their iron bars.

Colossians 2:2–3—My purpose, meaning God, is that they, meaning us, will be encouraged in heart and united in love. So that they may have the full riches of complete understanding in order that they may know the mystery of God, in whom are hidden all the treasures of wisdom and knowledge.

The Testing

Jeremiah 31:3—I have loved you with an everlasting love. I have drawn you with loving kindness.

Sweet Britton

Deuteronomy 31:8—The Lord goes before you. He will be with you. He will not leave you.

Cancer Hits Home

Romans 8:38–39—For I am sure that neither death, nor life, nor angels, nor principalities, nor things present, nor things to come, nor powers, nor heights, nor depth, nor anything else in all creation will be able to separate us from the love of God.

Ephesians 6—Put on the full armor of God. The belt of truth, the breastplate of righteousness, shoes with readiness of the gospel of peace, a shield of faith, the helmet of salvation, and the sword of the spirit.

The Final Peace

1 James 2:4—Count it all joy my brothers and sisters when you meet trials of various kinds for you know the testing of your faith produces steadfastness. Let it have its full effect so that you may be perfect and complete, lacking in nothing.

Hebrews 12:2—Let us fix our eyes on Jesus, God's son. For the joy set before him he endured the cross, its scorning and shame, and is in heaven at the right hand of the throne of God.

About the Author

Brenda was raised in a small town in Northern Michigan and grew up in a loving Christian family. She resides in Texas today with her husband, daughter, and several pets (she is definitely an animal lover). Brenda's friends describe her as down-to-earth and accepting of others while always keeping it real. Throughout her life, she has led many Bible studies and counseled several women of faith, family, friends, homeless, and people straight out of prison. She is an advocate for those who can't advocate for themselves. She is a prayer warrior and walks closely with God daily. Brenda never meets a stranger and walks boldly in her faith.

Piece by Peace with Christ

www.ingramcontent.com/pod-product-compliance
Lightning Source LLC
Chambersburg PA
CBHW051138120626
46547CB00012B/850